Southern Africa:
The People's Voices

Perspectives on Democracy

Edited by Padraig O'Malley

National Democratic Institute for International Affairs
School of Government, University of the Western Cape
1999

Published by the National Democratic Institute for International Affairs, 25 Wellington Road, Parktown, 2193, South Africa, and the School of Government, University of the Western Cape, Private Bag X17, Bellville, 7535.

Under a grant from the National Endowment for Democracy (NED) with contributory funding from the United States Agency for International Development (USAID).

First published in 1999

ISBN: 0-620-24215-9

Edited by Padraig O'Malley
Cover design by Page Arts, Cape Town
Typeset in Times New Roman
Printed in the Republic of South Africa by Creda Communications
Print Consultants: Mega Print, Cape Town

Southern Africa:

The People's Voices

Acknowledgements

This publication represents the work of hundreds of people who realized the value of incorporating the views of ordinary citizens in the building of democratic institutions in southern Africa. Their enterprising endeavors to seek out the opinions of people have taken them to villages, refugee camps, farms, informal settlements, urban townships and affluent suburbs. They dedicated themselves to recording and reporting with meticulous detail the nuances of people's aspirations and anxieties as experienced in sometimes rather tumultuous political transitions.

The authors of the articles, herein presented, were involved in the analysis and presentation of the original survey work. NDI appreciates their willingness to revisit the material and present this work for the edification of those whom are observing and commenting on the development of democracy in the region.

Particular appreciation is extended to the National Endowment for Democracy (NED) in the United States which provided NDI with a grant to publish this book and organize a conference of political leaders from countries in the region where elections are schedule to take place in 1999 and 2000. The support of the NED was augmented by grants from the United States Agency for International Development (USAID) that underwrote the actual focus group studies in several countries. NDI's President Ken Wollack rendered the leadership which placed the Institute in a position to meaningfully contribute to the democratic transitions that are occurring throughout the region. In addition, the University of the Western Cape (UWC) in South Africa and the University of Massachusetts/Boston (UMB) in the United States are accredited for the institutional support for those who worked on this publication.

The accomplishment of this publication rests with the dedication of four people. In accepting the invitation of NDI and UWC to edit this publication, Padraig O'Malley exceeded expectations in the fulfillment of his mandate. His tirelessness pursuit of authors for contributions to this publication, made this book a reality. Leanne Bell, NDI's regional Program Coordinator, kept the entire project together and moving forward, always in good humour and with unending patience. Keith Jennings, NDI's Director of Citizen Participation, provided editorial comments on a majority of the manuscripts. Last, but most importantly, NDI appreciates deeply the copious and unerring editing of Gerry Morse who has made this publication literate and understandable.

Preface

"Our continent has just invented another," wrote Montaigne about the discovery of the New World. At the time, of course, to *invent* was a synonym for to *discover*. The need to reinvent history has both accompanied and characterised literature of most of the great 'thresholds of change', those periods in which, in Santayana's words, "mankind starts dreaming in a different key".

– André Brink
Reinventing a Continent

Southern Africa: The People's Voices represents a cross-section of people's opinions and attitudes on transitional democracy in southern Africa. This book is primarily based on an analysis of public opinion surveys conducted by the National Democratic Institute for International Affairs (NDI)[1] between 1992 and 1999.

Several country-specific focus group surveys were the principal method of research for articles in this publication. A focus group survey is an extended discussion between members of the public about specific issues. The group usually has a moderator who introduces the topics in a specific way and guides the discussion. The data collection process differs substantially from survey methods, in that, unlike quantitative survey research, where questions are issue specific and concise, focus group questions are open-ended and respondents are encouraged to open up and state their opinions frankly. Moreover, focus groups have the advantage of eliciting complex responses from participants and are often used to help define major issues that can later be more accurately measured through the use of questionnaires and interviews[2].

One limitation of focus groups is that, by their nature, they produce data that can be subjective and difficult to interpret accurately as a representative measurement. To compensate we have, when available, supplemented the focus groups studies with conventional polling data drawn from different sources.

The subtext to this book of essays on democratic perspectives in southern Africa is a conference held in Johannesburg, South Africa from March 26 to 28, 1999 which brought together over forty parliamentarians – and their inevitable entourages of "technical" assistants – from nine southern African countries.

From the proceedings of that conference we have called the following quotes because they reflect not only wisdom, but wit, not only the reality which is the burden of those who have to consolidate democracy in southern Africa, but the poignancy beneath the humour, the passion behind the rhetoric, the hope beyond the suffering, the insights that belie lives of having so much to do to preserve what has been achieved that there is often no time to think and reflect on the uncertain future.

We do not attribute authorship of each quote to individuals because to do so would denigrate the contributions of all those who we have omitted to include – equally wise, equally mixing the gallows' humour of survival with the guillotine of oblivion. In the anonymity of all, we hope all realise their togetherness at that memorable conference and acknowledge the uniqueness of each other's contributions.

If beauty is in the eye of the beholder, perceptions are in the eye of the seeker.

A sampling of their observations on the future of democracy in southern Africa should serve as a brake on our propensity to become harsh in our judgements and judgemental in our harshness when we consider the mammoth obstacles of countries in transition to democracy in southern Africa which they have to address – and resolve.

> A wise man once said that once turning the despair and pessimism which presently affects wide circles of people inside and outside Africa into hope and optimism for the future will only be possible if the actors involved in African development are ready to question the premises on which they have based their outlook, their strategies or actions to date. No-one escapes this challenge. There are no short cuts to progress.

> Reality calls upon the world to accept this fact. Namibia's political history has not known democracy and none of the country's proposed mentors and midwives attempted to show that by example. Attempts at democratisation must depart from this recognition and therefore be predicated on the reality that the independence of Namibia was a product of efforts by Namibians themselves based on their own methods. The movement towards democracy therefore may have to develop along this path at a pace perhaps slower than expectations and this will call for patience on the part of Namibia's well-wishers and supporters to exercise some understanding as to why this may be progressing slower.

A statement made by Vezeru Kandetu, not just on behalf of Namibia but on behalf of all the countries in southern Africa.

> There is a need for a stronger opposition.

This position was endorsed by all participants.

> After eight years Namibians recognised the country's political institutions as

their own. Whether or not they agreed with all aspects of the political system Namibians from across the political, racial spectrum and gender divide expressed a strong sense of ownership of the country's political institutions. But we are disturbed by the decline in voter participation in recent elections is a phenomenon that deserves serious attention. People vote for change and they become disillusioned if they do not experience change in their communities. Second, respondents across every country complain about the insufficient contacts between parliamentarians and the electorate and the lack of information about the workings of parliament.

Most people in most post-colonial countries believe that their countries are better place to live in than they were ten years before independence. Participants point to the difference between the former and the current political dispensations. All agree much is still needed to be done and government and broad society need to guard against complacency. Participants felt that despite the changes brought about by independence and democracy much still needed to be done and government and broad society needed to guard against complacency. The degree of satisfaction that people expressed varied considerably. The younger participants were far more critical than their much older compatriots".

The impetus for change therefore will come from young people – the 'non-struggle' generation and given population growth rates, it won't be that long – perhaps a generation or so, before the 'non-struggle' generation outnumber the 'struggle' generation.

In some countries there seem to be limited aspirations among opposition parties, because time had moved on, that they would one day govern the country and the opposition parties seem complacent on being in the opposition.

In short, opposition parties no longer consider themselves to be alternative governments and have therefore lost sight of what opposition parties are.

In South Africa, euphoria has not quite gone. People had expected this democracy for many, many years and they are prepared to let their euphoria linger for quite a while. Yet we also see a state of waiting, expecting more, seeing very little, in many cases very little around them, but knowing there has to be more to democracy than what they are seeing at that stage between elections. We see expectations but also uncertainty. We, however, do not only see uncertainty. In this period between the elections we see a serious growing assertiveness amongst the electorate demanding more, growing into the culture of democracy and democratic participation and actually learning how to use their rights and how to use their rights to try to put pressure on politicians.

The development of democracy in Africa, in the formerly colonised world, has to be appraised in the context of the long view. While global accords reached in international fora such as the League of Nations and its successor the United Nations may have been pronounced with honourable motives in favour of guiding those nations that were hitherto not able to navigate their course, the fact is that these noble intentions did not work and in the end the secondary nations had to struggle their way to freedom and self-determination albeit with international solidarity and material support.

So we see hope and suffering. We also see a preoccupation with unemployment, with jobs, despite democracy how people's lives often have not changed in very tangible ways. Hope is a golden thread running throughout these discussions. Many people vote because they have hope. Others vote even despite the fact that they do not have hope any more, have given up on the politicians saying, 'They will lie to us again, but vote? We will vote,. There are also a number of participants in these focus groups who emphasise and express alienation, disengagement because of disappointments and therefore intend abstaining come the 1999 elections.

Delivery is like the rain, it always first rains somewhere else but eventually it will come this way as well.

Voters believe in competition. They think it's good and they want parties to compete because they see better performance resulting from that. Very often their commitment to multiparty democracy does not seem to go very deep. Multiparty democracy, serious competition is fine but at this stage for the majority of the electorate it's better to be done by other people. Other parties can do it, "Don't yet", in the words of many of these people in focus groups, "ask us to vote for other parties".

The post-independence political developments in Botswana, by way of context, the post-independence political developments are characterised or have been characterised by a dominant ruling party and a weak and fragmented opposition. That is the defining feature of post-independence politics in Botswana, a dominant ruling party, weak and fragmented opposition. In the last few years we have witnessed a radical change in the political landscape subsequent to a series of electoral reforms that were introduced ... that underline the ... commitment to democratic values. After the 1994 elections the voting age was reduced from 21 to 18 and an Independent Electoral Commission was established. Since 1965 up to 1994 there was never an Independent Electoral Commission to run the conduct of the elections in Botswana and opposition parties considered that a very contentious point and actually charged on occasions that the elections were being rigged. There has not been any evidence on the ground from the field work that indeed the ruling party rigged the elections but there were perceptions that the elections were not free and fair.

The evidence from the field suggests as follows, that the general crises are as follows, that there appears to be general ignorance or apathy among the voters about political events, a low level of political participation in the country and in fact it is also clear that most of the electorate do not have an understanding of the role of the opposition for instance in a multiparty parliamentary system.

From our discussions here it would appear that people in South Africa believe that politicians will lie again but nonetheless they will vote. In Malawi, I think, the feeling is that they will lie again and therefore why vote. So the question is, can you assist us before 1999? We want everyone to vote. We take issue with the premises that we are lying. We think we are saying the truth but can they at least vote for us.

What could we perhaps do in terms of voter apathy for political parties to be in a better position to combat that? And secondly, this perhaps goes directly to the views or perceptions as alluded to by the presenter from Botswana and that is that politicians in general tend to be very economic with the practical realities, that is the truth. Now that perception perhaps needs assistance from the academicians, the society at large, to be undone because I think rightly or wrongly that could equally go as the truth for many involvements in our society. No single person can stand up and say that he is strictly speaking the truth at all times in the field of his involvement or that he is only speaking untruths at all times. Wherever human beings are involved, sometimes they are bound to the situations that you might necessarily be tempted to say things that you normally would not say. So for the general perception to be continued, and that is also equally true in the area that I come from, Namibia, the politicians are being seen as not telling the truth but those are one of the perceptions that perhaps contribute to the fact that voter apathy is enjoying the levels of stayaways, for lack of a better word, that we are experiencing in our part of the world. What can be done to do away with these kinds of perceptions?

The thesis is that lower turnouts are due in part to the fact that people think politicians are not telling the truth. But the author also makes the point that it is not only politicians that are economical with the truth – perhaps the people themselves harbour a corresponding propensity to be economical with the truth, no doubt because anything that has to do with economy at the expense of extravagance elicits a certain innate empathy.

In South Africa and a number of other countries in the region too, there is a serious amount of apathy and confusion. In South Africa the two are very much linked especially when we get to first time voters, the young voters who are confused about politics, who do not have the long term party loyalties, histories to build on to guide them in their electoral decisions so they very often feel confused. They say they don't really need voter education, they basically know how to vote, but they don't know what's happening in party politics with political parties. And there voters without a serious background of traditional participation can become disempowered, can become apathetic as a defence mechanism. We also know in the broader context of elections apathy very often results from people's perceptions that it does not matter whether they vote or not, that maybe elections have been rigged, that there is corruption and where they sense that their own vote will not make a difference. There we find typically apathy.

In summary, all countries are satisfied with transitions to democracy. The lack of oppression is better than the fist of oppression. Memories of colonisation continue to weigh heavily. Indeed, South Africa's Truth and Reconciliation Commission has triggered a world-wide "do you remember what damage you did to me" syndrome. The holocaust is alive and well, the Irish famine of the 19th century has spurred an Irish renaissance, the Aborigines are asking for their due. The Yugoslavs slaughter each other in the name of past grievances. Minority/majority damage and the need for forgiveness or the acknowledgement of wrong-doing has become one of the paradigm shifts of the last years in this century.

What does it mean? The Age of Acknowledgement. Beyond acknowledgement lies the thorn of reparation. The West "raped" Africa; therefore, besides the act of the need for acknowledgement is the need for the West to put a face on that acknowledgement i.e.. reparation. In the case of Africa, this means at a minimum the forgiveness of debt at a maximum it means sustainable developmental aid.

Notes

1   The National Democratic Institute for International Affairs (NDI) is an international non-government organization headquartered in Washington DC. It supports democratic development worldwide - election processes, parliamentary governance, and sustainable civil society organization. The Institute has programs in seven southern African countries and a regional office in Johannesburg.

2   See Appendix A for a description of the regional survey research conducted in southern Africa from 1992 to 1998.

Southern Africa:

Regional Overview

Padraig O'Malley

"Perhaps in future there will be some African history to teach but at present there is none. There is only the history of Europeans in Africa. The rest is darkness and darkness is no subject of history".

– Hugh Trevor Roper
Regius Professor of Modern History
Oxford University, 1963

Without Darkness, there is no Light. And history is made of Light and Darkness. Light and Darkness are the Siamese twins of the existential, partly visible, mostly invisible, only existing in contrast to each other; contrasts we create in our own lack of understanding, contrasts invariably and inevitably irreconcilable yet in the essence of their being reconcilable.

There are many ways of looking at the changes taking place in southern Africa. Each way will yield a different set of conclusions, because each begins from a different set of starting points.

What is perceived by some as a learning curve is labeled mismanagement by others. The constant emphasis on consultation is dismissed as indecisiveness by some, as a necessary component of nation-building by others. What is harshly condemned as corruption by some is excused as almost an obligatory sense of duty by others.

Traditions clash; values differ; notions of civil society vary; deference to authority is rejected by some and overemphasized by others. In fact, there is not one southern Africa but several, each with its unique characteristics, each with its unique responses to the tumultuous transitions that are sweeping, Phoenix-like, across its vast, heterogeneous terrain, laying the foundations for the southern Africa of the new millennium – a southern Africa that does not lend itself to easy definition.

Padraig O'Malley is a Senior Fellow at the McCormack Institute of Public Affairs, University of Massachusetts Boston, US and editor of the New England Journal of Public Policy. He is particularly noted for his writing on democratic transitions and divided societies, specifically on Northern Ireland and South Africa.

Moreover, it yet remains to be seen whether in many countries the process of transition is a revolution in the broadest sense of the term, or whether it will degenerate into one more ill-fated attempt to hoist a form of governance, which the West call the best – to paraphrase Winston Churchill's famous epigram: democracy may have its imperfections, but where does there exist a system of governance that has fewer imperfections? – on to the backs of people who have little understanding of what democracy means, and little capacity to master the next-to-insurmountable obstacles they face, some inherited from the wretched past, some self-inflicted delusions about the boundaries of democracy itself; almost all antithetical to synchronizing the relationships among diverse cultures, a prerequisite of democratic development, not only in the developing world, but increasingly in the developed, despite the latter's vehement denial of new growing pains.

Democracy, we like to think, is about values and standards. But we rarely ask: Whose values? Whose standards?

In his article, *The Winds of Change*, Vezeru Kandetu says that "history has not known democracy [in many developing countries] and that no countries' proposed mentors and midwives have attempted to show that by example".

> And whatever attempts at democratisation in Africa must depart from this recognition and must therefore be predicated on the reality that the independence of countries in Africa was a product of Africans themselves based on their own methods. The movement towards democracy therefore has to develop along the path which is perhaps at a pace slower than Western expectations, and this will call for patience on the part of all of Africa's well-wishers and supporters. They will have to exercise some understanding as to why democratisation may be progressing slower than they wished.

The West is silent to the listening.

In fact, few countries in the West, despite their affirmations to the contrary, know how to learn or how to reach out to other cultures, especially those that appear to threaten them. At the same time, however, they like to see themselves as responsible citizens, who give, at the very least, lip-service, even in the absence of belief, to the need to rectify the socio-economic imbalances of the past, provided, that is, that this will mean no change in their own socio-economic status, no pain, something more in the way of an "unbundling" of excess largesse, rather than a sharing among equals.

But they are incapable of knowing where to start or what to do, or even how to begin to learn what to do. To reach out to other cultures would require them to acknowledge, in some way, their implicit collusion in the darkness of the past.

They will not confront the dark, or their collective responsibility for the actions of past colonial eras that made the racial superiority of whites the *raison d'être* of their existence. And if errors were made, they were, of course, errors of ignorance, not of malice. To this day, in what they regard as a gesture of profound magnanimity, western democracies will contend that their own individual brands of colonialism were the product of the best of intentions, of their sense of obligation to "free" blacks.

What, one might reasonably ask, is the test of success in the new political theater? Is it the degree to which the state devolves powers? Or some vague notion of a monarchy's special position in a new dispensation? Or some fine balance between a unitary state and a federal system in which residual powers would be "left" to the center rather than the converse, in which residual powers would be devolved from the center to the peripheral provinces?

These may sound like arcane considerations, more abstractions than the stuff of day-to-day living, but it is out of such subtle distinctions that countries live or die. Blood merely cleanses the argument.

Revolutions are rarely about unemployment or lack of housing or the poor delivery of services. We simply use such pointers to try and understand revolution, to place it in a context that we can assimilate, to make comprehensible what is often incomprehensible, and, therefore, threatening to our neat understanding of how things work and change.

One can see this propensity at work during the current "world" crisis. Globalization is here to stay, Thabo Mbeki informs the citizenry. The crisis much of Africa faces is not of its own making; rather it is a case of Africa being caught in the fallout following the collapse of the Asian markets. "The stark reality," Mbeki told the Non-Aligned Movement (NAM) summit, "is that the power to influence markets lies exclusively in the hands of those who dominate those markets, which we, even collectively, do not."[1]

The "Asian Tigers," which before their ignominious implosions were the International Monetary Fund's (IMF's) models of probity to be emulated by all emerging markets, were now harshly condemned for the laxity of their banking systems, and a new phrase – "crony capitalism"– was coined to describe their disgrace. They were put in quarantine for the contagion they could spread. But the contagion did spread, and hence Africa's dilemmas.

Perhaps the beginnings of Africa coming to its senses came in Washington DC at the annual meetings of the IMF and the World Bank. The glitterati of the financial world gathered to discuss what was now being routinely described as the worst financial crisis to engulf the world economy in 50 years. What lent *gravitas* to the occasion was the fact that the crisis they had gathered to discuss was never supposed to happen. Hadn't the integration of global capital markets, the sophistication of the instruments that allowed for risk diversification management, disclosure requirements, financial regulation and supervision, the omnipresence of rating agencies, the plethora of complex risk models, real-time transactions and instanta-neous communications protected the kind of collapse that was gathering speed as they pondered the question: What had gone wrong?

Great minds knitted their brows and looked for fairy-tale remedies. But there were none. Symposiums, workshops, plenary sessions, one-on-ones, the mighty and the not-so mighty clustered together applying their collective wisdom to unravelling the monetary mess that was causing financial gyrations in world markets and threatening economic chaos. It was if the free market had gotten away from them, had discovered that its power was unbounded, that the unfettered movement of rapacious capital, as it zigzagged from market to market and from markets to havens of shelter, could devour whole economies, and yet find its appetite still insatiable, searching in apoplectic fits and starts for the carcasses of other bankrupt countries.

The South Africa delegation, *Business Day* informed its readers, were quietly celebrating amid the frenzy of concern that consumed the bearers of ill-tidings. Moody's Investor Service had revised South Africa's rating from negative to stable – the patient could leave intensive care. But the patient had nowhere to go.[2] When the South African delegation gathered to brief the world's financiers about South Africa's stalwart efforts to stave off collapse, it found that few had come to listen, disregarded, considered an irrelevancy although the Johannesburg Stock Exchange (JSE) in terms of market capitalization was the 12th largest in the world. "I have been here three days," Cyril Ramaphosa complained when he addressed one of the keynote assemblies, "and I haven't heard the word 'Africa' mentioned once. Does Africa count? Is Africa on the agenda?"[3] To which the smooth-talking Michel Camdessus, president of the IMF, urbanely replied that Africa was lucky; it not being on the agenda signified that it was not in trouble. Which was, in a rather condescending fashion, reiterating Ramaphosa's point in the more gentle but inscrutable language of the international financial community: Africa didn't count. If all the markets in Africa went into free-fall, it wouldn't make the damnedest bit of difference to the markets in London, New York, Hong Kong or Tokyo. Africa simply wasn't on the financial map, and South Africa was simply a rather anti-quated engine that drove something that didn't count; a shark in its own sea; a minnow in the larger ocean.

"The world must stop ignoring Africa," said Finance Minister Trevor Manuel. But he was not overly hopeful that his demand would be met. "We are facing ongoing battles [at the IMF and World Bank meetings], and the biggest battle is to indicate that there is a world beyond the G7, and it is largely a world of poverty. It's a very hard battle against Afro-pessimism. The world is centred on the north-ern hemisphere, which does have large problems. We have to scream even louder for people to understand that there are millions living in Africa."[4]

The flow of funds to the continent, he noted, was getting progressively worse. " There isn't much foreign direct investment, there has been decreasing aid from donors; there's no change from the World Bank, and HIPC (the Heavily-Indebted Poor Countries Relief Program) is too slow."[5]

Since 1990, more than half of the 48 sub-Saharan countries have demanded an end to one-party rule.[6] These "uprisings" gave rise to the dawn of a new political era in Africa, bringing with it multiparty systems of government through democratic elections. The number of democratic elections held on the continent during the early 1990s was three times higher than the number held in the entire 1980s.[7] Before 1989, most of the sub-Saharan countries were under the leadership of either a one party, military or dictatorial state.

In most sub-Saharan countries, the dawning of a multiparty era saw one-party states giving way to multiparty systems of government, while autocratic leaders were ousted from office and replaced by democratically elected officials. By 1994, a large number of the sub-Saharan countries had either undergone some democratic process or were at an advanced stage in the democratic process.[8] This was a historical period for the African continent, a period of hope for representative, transparent, accountable and participatory democracy, the rule of law and respect for human rights.[9]

Indeed Mr O.K. Dingake speaking about Botswana, ranked by the United Nations as one of the more developed countries in southern Africa, had this to say:

> Botswana is unique and among the few countries in southern Africa that have operated a presidential Westminster form of government, a constitution embodying universal suffrage, a multi-party parliamentary system, regular elections, separation of powers and the rule of law. But observers complain that the law is too lax when it comes to regulating formation of political parties. I also want to highlight the post-colonial developments, the post-independence political developments in Botswana by way of context to say that the post-independence political developments in Botswana are characterised or have been characterised by a dominant ruling party and a weak and fragmented opposition. That is the defining feature of the post-independence politics in Botswana, a dominant ruling party, weak and fragmented opposition.[10]

This was a recurrent theme throughout the conference "Southern Africa Elections Summit" held in Johannesburg, South Africa, hosted by the National Democratic Institute for International Affairs (NDI) and the School of Government, University of the Western Cape.[11]

All participants were facing transition from one-party states to one-party dominant democracies. All transitions deeply affect the manner in which the way individual countries democratize.

No approach is unique, and less, still no approach is perfect. Perhaps our search for perfection in how we govern ourselves hurts us. Of its nature democracy is perhaps ill-equipped to deal with some of the most pressing problems facing developing countries.

And perhaps in this regard there is no better example than the way in which we treat/regard/make opinions about/have strong attitudes about/have convictions about AIDS.

However, the new political dispensation came with its own set of new challenges. While some countries that participated in the democratic elections, such as Mali, South Africa and several others, continue to work towards consolidating their new democracies, other countries such as Sierra Leone and the Central African Republic have experienced remarkable reversals. In Nigeria, Lesotho and Gambia, the democratic process has been derailed by military coups – although both Nigeria and Lesotho are on their way to "recovery."[12]

Countries holding democratic elections for a second time like Zambia have experienced record levels of voter apathy followed by a strong protest against the election results.[13] Low voter turn out during parliamentary by-elections in countries such as Malawi is so common that it is almost expected and quite often the outcome of the election ends up being contested in the courts.[14]

On the other hand, most sub-Saharan countries that embraced the new political order have yielded meager returns in terms of economic and political development during the few years that this new apparatus has been in existence. The economic situation in most countries has either been stagnant or regressing while polarization among political parties has become the order of the day; health prospects have worsened, while infrastructure and social institutions are on the brink of collapse.[15]

These developments have led to a debate within some sectors of African society on whether democracy can work in Africa, while others are calling for democracy to be re-defined or at least be "africanized."[16] The interesting part of the debate is that there are no significant ideological differences on either side of the fence when it comes to the consideration of common democratic principles such as freedom and fundamental human rights, the rule of law, constitutional checks on elected officials, efficiency and transparent governments.[17] The issues that underline the debate are in most cases economic concerns that people expected the new political dispensation would address.[18]

Nine elections will take place in southern Africa in the next twelve months; elections that will determine whether the fragile roots of democracy that have been nurtured in the region will continue to blossom or wither on the vine.

During the last several years, the NDI has carried out a number of focus groups in these countries, partly to monitor the evolution of democratic governance; partly to assess the changing moods and attitudes of the people as transitions to democracy has occurred; partly to assess the degree to which governance capacity is being complemented by administrative capacity; and partly to examine the relationship, if any, between democratic institution building and sustainable economic and political development.

The project was undertaken to help policy makers gain a better understanding of the needs and expectations of the people who are part of their democratic transformations, to identify the impediments to both more cathartic transformations and to development itself.

In most respects the results duplicate themselves, indicating perhaps that peoples' wants and needs are universal, and not specific to particular regions and countries. There are of course many variations as the idiosyncrasies of diverse cultures are taken into account, but the variations pale in comparison to the widespread commonalities the countries have experienced in their tough and often grim journeys towards a better life for all their people.

A focus group study is a research method whereby representative groups are given the opportunity to thoroughly talk through issues and question under the direction of a trained facilitator. It is a good indicator of perceptions and attitudes that are hard to gauge with other research techniques.

It is important to bear in mind that social policy research is only as good as the data it draws on, the quality and experience that the researchers bring to their work, and that even the best of work refers to feelings and attitudes that exist at a point in time, and that extrapolation of findings without strict adherence to these considerations is foolhardy at best and erroneous at worst. With these caveats in mind, we will wander into the mysterious world of transitions, often unfathomable in their own genesis, and never predictable in their outcomes.

There is a certain discernible pattern to transitions to democracy in the sub-Sahara region.

A one-party state, a dictatorship, an authoritarian regime is either overthrown or ousted from power. The people demand democracy – a multiparty political system. Political parties are organized, voter education programs organized; nongovernmental organisations (NGOs), both foreign and domestic, play leading roles in this regard; electoral commissions are established; party rallies are held; and the electorate enthusiastically goes to the polls in the belief that they are ushering in a new tomorrow. Usually, one party dominates the election, but smaller parties are also elected to the new Assemblies; new constitutions are drawn up guaranteeing rights and liberties for all. The new Assemblies get down to business – in many cases a one-party state has been replaced with a one party dominant state – and in short order things begin to change – but not in the manner that people thought.

- Initially people associate democracy with "freedom;" "an end to oppression;" "being able to say what one likes;" "not being afraid of saying or doing the wrong thing;" "meeting their expectations of a better life;" "of a better future for their children;" "of a better tomorrow;" "of being able to participate in their own governance;" "of their communities being involved in decision making;" "of ending poverty". And most of all with hope – hope that their lives will improve, that things will get better.

- Within a short period of time disillusionment sets in. Expectations are not met. Expectations that were raised by the political parties during electoral campaigns or unrealistic expectations the people themselves held that the politicians in their quest for votes did nothing to dampen. Delivery is sporadic at best. Rather than standards of living increasing, people find they often decrease. The poor remain poor; the homeless homeless; the unemployed unemployed. Promises made by politicians are not kept. People become cynical about the political process. They rarely see their elected representatives. Government remains distant. But the people's hope remains. Hence, initially, although most will express their disappointment, they still believe things will get better. Hope remains strong, and few want a return to the repression of the past, during which they had also been promised much and received little.

- Their belief in democracy remains strong, although their belief in government becomes disaffected. To paraphrase Foster Mijiga in his essay *Transition to Democracy: The Case of Malawi,* "Government as a vehicle in Malawi has not been driving very well since independence in 1964. So far Malawians have identified the drivers of this vehicle, not the vehicle itself to be the major problem and hence the need to replace them. Democracy as a means of survival and a solution of social and economic problems has thus far proved to be unsustainable, leading to an increased desire to replace drivers of this government machinery."

- Hope is in many respects all they have to cling to. Without it life would become intolerable. In many countries, the countervailing opposition is coming from civil society. In Zimbabwe, Masipula Sithole informs us in *Zimbabwe's Electoral Experience: Toward Election 2000 and Beyond* that "civil society formations have coalesced into the National Constitutional Assembly (NCA) demanding a new constitution for Zimbabwe. Top on the NCA's agenda is the rehauling of Zimbabwe's Electoral Act. The demands are that there be a permanent Independent Electoral Commission to oversee and administer the conduct of all elections: local, parliamentary, presidential, and the by-elections that may arise. Under mounting pressure, the ruling party and government have taken a separate initiative to reform the country's constitution and have agreed to the idea of a referendum on a new constitution before Election 2000".

Thus, on the surface, Zimbabwe might seem to be moving in the opposite direction from the rest of the southern African countries, but there are underlying forces at play that are moving it in the democratic direction of the rest of southern Africa, despite the personal attitudes of her leaders. Civil society, which is growing from strength to strength by the day, is that force. Thus, Zimbabwe might conduct its next general and presidential elections on an "even playing field;" not only that, but with a viable new political party.

Looking at the elections scheduled to take place between now and the year 2000, four external constraints will determine southern Africa's future.

War: The State of the Continent and the Impact on South Africa

In March 1998, *Time* magazine boldly entitled its cover story "Africa Rising." It proclaimed with the kind of grand benediction magazines of its ilk and influence inspire that "after decades of famine and war, life is finally looking up for many Africans".[19] The years ushering in the millennium were to be Africa's years, when its promise, for so long captive to the "aberrations of a host of African tyrants, endless coups, looting of national coffers for the enrichment of the few at the expense of the untold suffering of the millions, internecine strife, corruption and nepotism,"[20] would finally come to fruition and transmogrify its immense potential into concrete achievement.

Within months of President Clinton's visit, the political landscape of Africa had changed utterly. The continent was once again wallowing in the kind of conflict that has bedevilled it for decades. In the past year, one of four countries in Africa were engaged in conflicts,[21] as were eight of the fourteen southern African Development Community (SADC) members.[22] Half the world-wide deaths from conflict occurred in Africa:[23] the continent was embroiled in old conflicts, once thought settled, and new conflicts, once thought implausible. Warfare ranged from Angola and Sudan to Ethiopia and the Congo. From Lome to Luanda, from Kinshasa to Kigali, war had broken out. The Democratic Republic of the Congo (DRC) had collapsed under the new dictatorship of Laurent Kabila. In addition, Lesotho, Angola, Rwanda, Uganda, Ethiopia, Eritrea, Burundi, and Sudan were in various states of implosion; Zimbabwe, Angola, Namibia, Chad and Sudan had dispatched troops to assist Kabila from being deposed; Uganda and Rwanda backed the Tutsi-led rebellion against Kabila; Nigeria headed the Economic Community of West African States Monitoring Group (ECOMOG) forces in Sierra Leone, Sierra Leone and Guinea Bissau tethered on the brink of collapse; Congo-Brazaville smouldered with discontent, while Liberia, and Somali could hardly be called havens of stability. In Algeria war raged without restraint, savagery sanctified in the name of religion. Sudan's long civil war was no more amenable to settlement, despite the fact that its major casualties were the emaciated children used by combatants on both sides as human bargaining chips. What had once been unthinkable – southern secession – would have a direct impact on Egypt's access to the Nile, and thus Egypt was being ineluctably drawn into the outer perimeters of the conflict, not engaged, but not as disengaged as it heretofore had been. In Sierra Leone rebels merrily mutilated civilians, and fought ECOMOG forces which were under the direction of Nigeria. Nigeria, having dispatched of Gen. Abacha was once again promising an end to military rule and an eventual return to democracy.

"The wind blowing from Europe has begun to sweep Africa," the late Francois Mitterand grandly gushed in 1990.[24] But the wind dropped to a sparse-like breeze, and finally to a whisper, breathing the awful calm of the suffocation of life.

Pillage, rape, murder, wholesale carnage, massacres of women and children, slaughter of the innocent, genocide, obliteration of villages and towns, destruction of infrastructure built at great, and invariably foreign-donor cost in the hope of opening the way to development, famine, and unending stream of refugees seeking safe haven in countries increasingly hostile to their presence and increasingly unable to meet their needs – of the 22.4 million people displaced world-wide, 7.4 million were in Africa – were the foundations on which the new Africa of the 21st century would be built – the legacy of Africa of the 20th century.[25]

"What will it take for Africa to reject military solutions to political challenges," asked Kofi Annan, Secretary General of the United Nations (UN) during the Security Council's second ministerial meeting on Africa in September. "When will the realization [dawn] that no one – not a single one – of these conflicts can end in the absence of compromise, tolerance, and the peaceful resolution of disputes." With armaments exporters, including South Africa's, queuing up in increasing numbers to ply their trade in the newest, most sophisticated, and deadliest of weaponry, the answer to Annan's question is as simplistically rhetorical as the question itself.

Months later, Annan again addressed the question when he addressed the second Tokyo Conference on African Development: "Chronically insecure neighborhoods," he said, "are not ones that attract investment."

The conference sounded a warning note that like the cry of "Wolf!" will be ignored until its reality impinges on the well-being of the developed countries: "Poverty in Africa has become even more serious," it concluded, and, "if the present situation continues, the growing disparity [between the rich and poor] will become a major cause of worldwide social disorder." To halve the number of people living in poverty in Africa by the year 2015 – a goal the conferees set themselves – African countries will have to achieve a real annual growth in GDP of more than five per cent.

In his analysis of the African condition at a conference on the African Renaissance, Eskom chairman Reuel Khosa was far less restrained. "Africa," he charged, "is a pathologically diseased, drug-addicted, malnourished patient." "Nothing," he warned delegates, "will be sufficient to rehabilitate Africa unless it unconditionally acknowledges its problems, develops a sufficient understanding of its problems, and expresses a desire and unwavering will to solve them." In the absence of such a rigorous process of self-examination, the unquestioned belief that the proliferation of institutional structures would in itself be sufficient to rehabilitate the continent was wishful thinking. Most of Africa's problems, he stressed, were of Africa's own making. "It does not benefit us to externalize the causes of our problems. We are a sick continent and we are largely to blame for it."[26] War, famine, incompetence, corruption, crime, and a generally declining quality of life were the prevailing conditions in Africa.

Africa's politics, Khosa said, were permeated by group rights, rather than individual rights, which resulted in ethnic or ideological schisms. Africa also suffered a victim mentality and its concept of wealth was closer to a feudal economy than it was to an industrial economy. A stage had been reached where black in general and African in particular were synonymous with failure and inferiority: "We have learnt and our children continue to learn, that there is nothing to admire or emulate in Africa."[27]

Not many were listening.

In the mid-1990s, Thabo Mbeki, then Deputy President of South Africa, spoke eloquently of an African "renaissance," of the need for Africa itself to weed out and dispense with its home-grown tyrants, for a post-colonial order free of dictatorship, corruption, nepotism, and dispute resolution through armed conflict. US President Bill Clinton, in one of his more hyper cheer-leading moments, fêted the democraticization of Africa as he jet-hopped from Cape Town to Kampala, from Dar-es-Salaam to Dakar during his "historic" trip to Africa in April 1998. Peace and prosperity, he prophetically intoned, were at hand; the canons of democracy were replacing the cannons of artillery.

The events of 1998 in the Great Lakes region and elsewhere in Southern and Central Africa were a salutary reminder of how fragile emerging democracies in the continent were; how tentative and unpredictable transitions to the rule of law were, how politics were driven by domestic considerations of national self-interest rather than by the amorphous altruism of global alignments.

In the Congo it appears that nothing can hold the country together, and that whatever the outcome, the DRC looks set to break up, partitioned from north to south along ethnic and battle lines.[28]

In Africa, in order for emerging democracies to survive, they have to face the acid test of being able to stand on their own without the artificial props well-meaning and sometimes self-serving benefactors erect to hold them up; they must be capable of withstanding the cycles of violence that periodically sweep the continent and develop the internal resilience that allows them to weather the vagaries of a capricious world where national self-interest in the context of a global market is the commanding imperative. "Previous attempts to resolve

African conflicts," wrote Mondli Makhanya in the *Star,* "have foolishly assumed a certain level of maturity of leadership. But the fact we have to face is that Africa's political elite is composed mainly of power-mongering kleptomaniacs who couldn't give a damn about the well-being of their populations." Permanent solutions to Africa's problems, he concluded, "will require greater intervention in the affairs of sovereign nations than the international community thus far has been willing to undertake."[29]

For the most part, the outside world ignored the Great Lakes conflict, adhering to the dubious, if not entirely fictitious, position that since the Africans were responsible for the mess, it should be left to Africans to clean it up. Moreover, African wars were not seen as "war" in the western sense but more of a perpetuation of pre-modern tribal conflicts now fought with post-modern weaponry. Africans, prevailing beliefs concurred, had a less than special regard for human life, a penchant for massacring each other at the most trivial of slights, an innate inability to govern except in the most tyrannical or at best dictatorial ways, a passivity that encouraged a pathological obsequiousness in the face of the despotic, an abhorrence of the work ethic, a distaste for social discipline, and an intolerance of political difference. In short, Africa was a continent on the periphery of the global stage, too unstable to be taken seriously, too impoverished to be worth the investment that might realize its promise, and if not quite beyond redemption, at least beyond caring about

If one could draw any conclusions from the convulsions of the inter-regional conflict, the most pertinent would be that calls for elections in countries that are patently not ready for them can hamper rather than hasten the advent of democracy. A second conclusion might well be that attempts to "impose" supposedly "free and fair" elections" in countries in which the concept of elections has no meaning, in which democracy itself is alien, in which there are no institutions of civil society, or no civil society to speak of, to develop a culture conducive to the principles of democracy and its emphasis on the primacy of human rights – although the abuse of human rights is not uncommon in many countries that believe they are democracies – in which poverty is endemic, illiteracy pervasive, and norms of individual rights theoretical abstractions suggest an ingenuousness that pampers first-world elitism, encourages delusion, and most probably impairs the cause of democracy itself.

Disease: **The Spread of AIDS in Sub-Sahara Africa**

In the countries, that is, for the most part southern Africa, AIDS is impeding, perhaps destroying the process of democratization and has made a pretense of the notion of sustainable development.

Or perhaps – we daren't ask ourselves this – democratization is impeding the control of the disease in these countries. The fact is we simply don't know. And our pretensions to the contrary are an impediment to finding solutions to a plague that we refuse to call a plague because the idea of plague conjures up images of disease and death we no longer wish to think of in our "cleansed world." Better not to hear than to be bothered. Being bothered, after all requires questioning of values. And as the millennium dawns, we increasingly seek to avoid the question of values. Celebrity events, yes; reflective events, no.

Unless we begin to acknowledge that epidemics such as AIDS or any other disease for that matter are not bound by national boundaries, we will seek to understand the nature of our own evolution in parochial terms, i.e. concepts of sovereignty fought over for hundreds of years have evaporated, and the more we cling to their tenets the more ethereal they become. The net result of the debates and wars that have ensued is that 50 million people in Europe in this century died for ideas of nationalism that are now outmoded, outdated and in many instances a threat to our further "development". Europe, of course, with the blind hubris of its own pretence to a divine past, shrugs its internecine wars off with supercilious disdain.

Considering itself the "cradle of civilisation," it has managed to excuse itself from anything that would interfere with its self-definition. We all know civilized people don't kill civilized people – especially if we are white. Whites after all only fight wars for noble causes. And the rest of humanity God knows for what.

We must either understand the uniqueness of our interconnections at all levels of being or we will suffocate ourselves in our lack of understanding.

One form of death is perhaps as good as another.

Southern Africa: The People's Voices is about putting all the wild cards on the table. If you choose to pick one you are a player on a global table. If you do not pick up one, you will be eliminated in the pre-game play. In short, you have no choice.

This book draws heavily on the contributions by experts in the southern Africa region on HIV. If we do not listen to these voices we are slowly condemning ourselves to a world of stillness.

The relentless spread of AIDS throughout the sub-Saharan region is threatening the existence of the continent and its people. The problem is almost unimaginable in scale, beyond relief in the suffering it has wrought, and, apparently of little concern to the rest of the world – one more African problem among the innumerable Africa problems that appear to grow exponentially and prove immune to inoculation against resolution. The fact that in some countries in the region up to 32 per cent of the populations are HIV positive evokes little emotion and no response.

A full-blown AIDS epidemic is beginning to wreak havoc in South Africa, which, according to the most recent United Nations report, enjoyed the egregious distinction of having the fastest growing number of people with AIDS in the world, and the second highest number of HIV-infected people in Africa.[27]

A survey carried out by the Department of Health found that there had been a *fourteenfold* increase in HIV prevalence in South Africa in six years. One in 10 adults is living with AIDS.[31]

Indeed, the gravity of the crisis and the devastating impact it will have on society can be gleaned from the frightening fact that unless the spread of the virus is brought under some measure of control in sub-Saharan Africa, and resources are allocated to the control of the disease and campaigns to increase public awareness of it at all strata of society, it could see the region implode, ravaged by the disease to a point where the social and economic viability of southern Africa itself becomes a question, not of concern but of fact.

According to AIDS experts, combating tuberculosis (TB) is probably the most cost-effective way to prolong the lives of HIV-infected Africans. TB is a major public health problem in its own right. It is also the dominant opportunistic infection affecting people with AIDS and the leading cause of death among HIV-positive people in sub-Saharan Africa. TB also often sets in during the early stages of HIV infection and hastens dramatically the onset of full-blown AIDS.

Without intervention, southern Africa's HIV epidemic will run a predictable course, cutting 10 to 15 years off life expectancy compared to 15 years ago. Rates of active TB will soar as a result of the exponential growth of HIV infection.

Not that the catastrophe in the making is South Africa's alone. According to the UN world population survey for 1998, AIDS has achieved pandemic proportions in 34 countries, 29 of which are sub-Saharan countries, where at least one in four people is HIV infected.

The UN reports that "of the 30 million persons in the world currently infected by HIV, 26 million, or 86 per cent, reside in these 34 countries. In addition, 91 per cent of all AIDS in the world have occurred in these 34 countries."[32]

In Botswana life expectancy has dropped from 61 years in 1993 to 47 in 1998, and is expected to drop to 41 between 2000 and 2005. In Zimbabwe, one of every five adults is infected. The high mortality rate has significantly cut the country's population and its growth, from 3.3 per cent a year between 1980 and 1985 to 1.4 per cent in 1998, and a projection of 1.1 per cent beginning in 2000. Had it not been for the virus, Zimbabwe's population would be growing at a projected rate of 2.4 per cent. Current projections suggest that both Botswana and Zimbabwe will loose up to one-fifth of their populations within the next decade.[33]

In Botswana, the projected population growth rate would have been 2.4 per cent. With AIDS it will be 1.1 per cent.

For Namibia, the population growth rate is 1.1 per cent instead of 2.4 per cent. For Malawi 1.7 per cent instead of 2.7 per cent, and for Zambia, 2.1 per cent instead of 3.3 per cent.

And looking at death rates: Without AIDS, there would have been 7.8 deaths per 1,000 people in South Africa. Instead ,it is 12.3 per cent. In Zimbabwe, the rate without AIDS would have 6.2 deaths per 1,000 people. Instead, it is 20.1.

And as the virus spreads, the demographic composition of these countries is rapidly changing, with unforeseen and hence non-provided for consequences at all levels of society. Sustainable development in these circumstances is simply a misnomer. The unwillingness of international or national development agencies to admit to this – not that there is any malign intention behind their failure to do so, only bureaucratic compartmentalization – or for development agencies to work hand-in-hand with health agencies in highly coordinated joint ventures means that continuing to direct resources into programs and projects that do not take into account the inevitable impact of AIDS on the projected outcomes is little short of being willfully irresponsible or woefully inept.

Adding to the tissue of problems is the fact that national governments in these countries usually understate the level of HIV infection due to unreliable and inaccurate reporting of the disease, an unwillingness to do because it may interfere with tourism, the fear of being labeled a pariah nation, or because of national pride, wanting at all costs to avoid the stigma of being rubber-stamped as AIDS-infested, a country to be avoided as if it were plague-ridden, which in a sense it is.

The developed countries must also acknowledge their share of the blame for the virus's deadly march through the continent, especially in the poorer countries. Once the disease did not progressively decimate their populations, confining itself to the gay and drug-addicted segments of the community, and with medical protocols emerging that added years to the incubation of HIV and the onset of full-blown AIDS, and between the onset of full-blown AIDS and death, and perhaps most important, when the strains of the virus that developed in the West turned out to have very low rates of heterosexual transmission, the West, having put its own house in some kind of order, shelved the issue and aid to developing countries in dire need of it.

As in most things, when a disaster only impinges in a marginal way on the West, or having impinged is brought under an acceptable level of control, it ceases to command "flavor of the month" status, is expunged from the collective mind, and to that extent ceases to exist, except in some dim subliminal awareness, although wreaking its ravages on the destitute nations to whose existence they were blind.[34]

Globalization: **The Global Economy and Africa; Southern Africa and the Global Economy**

The debacle in the Congo and the unravelling of Central and southern Africa coincided with the unravelling of the global economy. First, collapse of financial markets in Japan engulfed all of emerging Asia, and the economies once heralded as the "Asian Tigers" – the economies the rest of the developing world were told to emulate – South Korea, Thailand, Malaysia and Indonesia followed suit in domino-like fashion. The anachronisms of "crony" capitalism were suddenly discovered, although they had been there to see all along, vision blurred not by myopia but by rapacious greed spurred by what seemed to be the endless prospects of quick profits and fast bucks. South Africa, the most sophisticated emerging market in Africa, priding itself on a first-world stock exchange and financial service institutions it believed could hold their own with the best, was sucked into the raging vortex.

When Russia found itself in the position of more or less having to declare itself bankrupt, its coffers empty, banks penurious, foreign reserves a pittance, and political uncertainty aggravating the financial crisis and finally overtaking it with the implosion of the country's weak political infrastructure, global economic meltdown became the catch-phrase for global recession. Always vulnerable to market forces and the shenanigans of wily speculators, South Africa's struggle to reintegrate itself into the world economy with the demise of apartheid, collided with global capital run amok: under pressure, the rand depreciated in value several times, leap-frogging the six rand to the dollar benchmark, almost halving its value in six years. In one week, the JSE lost 17 per cent of its value. The price of gold fell to its lowest level in 19 years.[35] Growth projections for 1997 were in the region of 0.5 per cent. Some 40 per cent of world GDP was in recession, with more to follow.[36]

Africa in general, with its debt-burden, non-existent reserves of hard currencies, and its fledgling emerging markets in particular, was vulnerable to the reverberations of what seemed to be an impending economic meltdown. South Africa had already contracted the "contagion" disease, although not yet terminally infected. Nevertheless, the disease had taken its toll. At the beginning of October, industrial shares had fallen 45 per cent in five months (from April to September 1998), the rand 45 per cent since the beginning of the year, and interest rates 45 per cent since June.[37] The exodus of foreign capital continued with a doggedness that resisted every effort to curtail it – the dumping of bonds wiped out all the net foreign investment in the market, and by September, net disinvestment had reached $1 billion,[38] causing a shortage of liquidity in the financial markets. Business confidence, not unexpectedly, fell, but the drop to a twelve-year low indicated a level of uncertainty not even surpassed during the most tense days leading up to the elections in 1994 when for one brief moment it seemed that the negotiated settlement would fall apart and the country would be engulfed in a vortex of violence.[39]

"Global capitalism is under siege," *Newsweek* intoned. "The idea was to open markets to trade and foreign investment. Last week [the first week of September] markets were being shut. Malaysia imposed exchange controls, preventing investors from reclaiming funds. Earlier Russia had defaulted on some foreign debt and stopped converting roubles into hard currency. And then there's Hong Kong's stock-market intervention. Although it doesn't evict foreign capital, the abrupt change of rules could frighten away investors."

Weeks later, there were few investors, and all were frightened.

What went wrong?

The orthodox explanation:

> On one level (writes *Newsweek),* the answer is simple. Countries became overdependent on foreign capital, which, having entered in huge amounts, is trying to leave the same way. In 1996, South Korea received $42 billion of inflows: a year later, outflows totalled $21 billion. What initially triggered the reversal was the recognition that much foreign money had been squandered through "crony capitalism" or misguided industrial policies. Asia was dotted with empty office buildings and surplus factories. Overseas banks refused to renew their loans; mutual fund investors sold shares and converted their funds back into dollars.
>
> But now the fear of capital flight is feeding on itself – and spreading to Latin America. If people fear the Mexican peso will be devalued, they may convert pesos into dollars. The frightened include locals, not just foreign investors. But countries need hard currencies to pay for their imports; and they can't afford a depositor run on their banks. High interest rates are one way to halt the process by rewarding people for keeping their funds in local currencies. Hong Kong's short-term interest rates have risen to about 15 per cent, Mexico's to 36 per cent. The trouble, of course, is that punitive interest rates also crush local economies.
>
> If a few economies face the squeeze, it's their problem; if many economies do, it's everyone's problem. This is happening. The threat of capital flight has shoved so many countries toward austerity that it induced a worldwide slump. And, again the process feeds on itself. Feeble economic growth has depressed the prices of raw-material exports. Between June 1997 and August 1998, oil prices dropped about 30 per cent (affecting Russia, Mexico, and Venezuela, among others); coffee prices fell 43 per cent (affecting Brazil and Columbia); and gold prices sank 17 per cent (Russia, South Africa). Earning less abroad, these economies must slow their economies to cut imports. This depresses U.S. exports and the profits of multinational companies operating in these countries.
>
> Thus, does the Third World's distress threaten the First World's stock markets and prosperity. *But global capitalism's failure demands a deeper explanation. After all, capitalism, is supposed to excel at allocating investment funds efficiently. In this case, it didn't. The deeper explanation is that market capitalism is not just an economic system. It is also a set of cultural values that emphasizes the virtue of competition, the legitimacy of profit, and the value of freedom. These values are not universally shared. Other countries have organized economic systems around different values and politics.* [My italics.]
>
> *As a result, spreading capitalism is not simply an exercise in economic engineering. It is an assault on other nations' culture and politics that almost guarantees a collision. Even when some countries adopt some of the trappings of capitalism, they do not embrace the basic values that make the system work. This is what happened. Led by the U.S., global agencies (the*

World Trade Organization, the IMF) sought to persuade poorer countries to become more open to trade and global capital. These countries tried to maximize the benefits of the process while minimizing changes to their politics and commerce. [My italics.]

Mutual deception flourished. Countries like Korea and Russia pretended that they had. American, European, and Japanese bankers, executives and government officials pretended the claims were true – or might become true. Loans were made on the basis of incomplete or faulty statements. Or they were made on the faith that, if a loan went sour, someone (the government, the IMF) would cover the losses.

Global capitalism has become a dangerous hybrid. On the one hand, investors committed huge sums and expected high returns. On the other, the money often went – through bank loans, bond issues and stock offerings – to borrowers who were not operating according to the strict rules of efficiency or profit and loss. "Crony" capitalism often meant corruption: contracts won with bribes; favoritism for the well-connected. In 1997, a group called Transparency International ranked corruption in 52 countries as judged by global executives and country specialists. Not surprisingly, Russia ranked fourth, Indonesia seventh and Thailand 14th.

But capital flowed freely, and self-deception prevailed. Banks collected interest on loans. "Emerging market" mutual funds rose, because local stocks were buoyed by new investment money. While everyone enjoyed profits, there was a suspension of belief. Now comes the reckoning. Capital flight has forced most developing countries to conserve scarce foreign exchange.

Countries cannot expand their economies unless they replenish their foreign exchange reserves of hard currencies.[40]

And the conclusion?

Even if the worst doesn't occur, the world will never be the same. Global capitalism won't regain its aura of infallibility. There was nothing wrong with the theory. Free trade and the free movement of capital, would, in a world where everyone worshipped efficiency and profits, enrich all nations. The trouble, however, is that we do not live in such a world.[41]

Nor, it would appear do we live in the world created by the IMF where structural adjustment programs were the panacea for every economic woe. The IMF, rather than seeing the conditions it attached to loans as being overly stringent, unconcerned with even basic social safety nets, and unduly punitive to the one segment of society least responsible for the mess a particular country may have gotten itself into, chose instead to see its sometimes arbitrary deficit to GDP ratios as instruments of judicious financial prudence. Short-term pain for long-term gain, only sometimes the short term became a moving chimera – almost always within reach, but never reached.

In terms of policy, the organization, once the oracle before which African countries in particular, bowed in trepidation was becoming the focus for some severe criticism. To prescribe tight monetary policy for any one country which leads to higher interest rates, cuts in government expenditure and a reduction in consumer demand might be the correct "treatment" for the ailing patient, but when every patient swallows the same economic medicine at the same time, the result is a collective collapse: deflation angina, and unless an antidote is quickly found a world-wide slowdown further hardens the global economy's arteries and recession precedes the funeral procession to the graveyard for dead economies.

Moreover, there is an increasingly invoked view that an IMF bale-out does little for the poor and the underclasses in the stricken country, but is of most assistance to the First World creditor banks and currency speculators whose self-serving actions are often responsible for the country's dire predicament in the first place. According to this analysis, as long as first-world banks and investors can count on an IMF bale-out to countries that go into an economic free-fall, they have a safety parachute that enables them to make risky loans and investments without having to worry about the consequences of their financial transactions going wrong, and the countries who can rely on the IMF as the lender of last resort have little incentive to reform their often crony-oriented banking systems and address the corruption that corrodes their economies

But globalization is coming in for the kind of scrutiny heretofore the glamour associated with it precluded. The herd discovered that unfettered capitalism is not the panacea for the world's economic ills; indeed that it has a penchant to punish the weak and reward the strong; that rather than eliminating imbalances and inequities among nations, it tends to do the opposite, increasing income differentials rather than diminishing them. No one takes issue with the fact that globalism is with us to stay; what is, however, less clear is how to regulate, in an information- saturated age guided by electronic radar that decodes stress calls as automatic instructions to exploit rather than to assist, financial flows that do not find their way into wealth-creating activities but into profit-taking opportunities, the system becomes dysfunctional.

In the longer course of events, if southern Africa continues to depend upon inflows of short-term capital, which has no commitment other than to take advantage of whatever quick-profit opportunities the markets offer and is footloose to trawl international markets in search of such opportunities, then the country is placing itself in a permanent state of vulnerability and indecent exposure to uncertainty, and guarantees that the conditions for sustainable growth will always wither on the vine of voracious capitalism.

Like it or not, the key to growth lies in dealing with the *structural* impediments to growth. It must generate domestic savings, i.e. curb consumption that is debt-financed to finance long-term fixed capital investment. With a savings ratio well below the level for countries at comparable levels of development, southern Africa seems to believe that it can attract the foreign capital to compensate for its own spendthrift ways. In other words, development will be painless.

A feature of the global economy as we enter the final years of a century not particularly distinguished for its regard for human life, is that technology has in fact made human labor replaceable as a factor of production in ever-increasing areas of economic activity. One third of the eligible workforce in the world is either unemployed or under-employed,[42] that is, there are one billion people spread across the globe who cannot provide the wherewithal for their own survival or the survival of their families. Nor will they ever be in a position to do so. Economic growth is increasingly of the non job-creating kind. The problem the world faces as it straddles the cusp of the 21st century is what to do with people.

While southern Africa pays the usual lip-service to there being a global economy, which has in a manner usurped some of the functions of sovereign nation-states, it does so with what would be categorized as a bi-polar disposition in psychiatric parlance. Perhaps this is an inevitable consequence of many countries in the region coming into being as a sovereign nation with a constitution that must certainly rank among the best in terms of the protections it guarantees its citizens, just at a time when long-held notions of sovereignty and national independence were being increasingly called into question as the process of globalization gathered momentum after the collapse of communism and trade liberalization became the fashion of the times. Caught between trying to exercise the muscles of their newly-found independence, yet having to submit to the rigorous regimen of global dictates, southern Africa countries have often veered between the two, trying to adhere to both while sacrificing to neither.

Debt: **The Catch 22**

Nor were the devastation of endemic wars the only travails convoluting an ailing Africa. In the face of overwhelming poverty, exacerbated by AIDS, dysfunctional education, the virtual non-existence of electricity, sanitation, and clean water, rudimentary and unhygienic health care, recurrent famines, the continent owed some $227 billion to international creditors, which amounted to about $600 for each person on the continent. Of the 41 most heavily indebted low-income countries in the world, no fewer than 31 are in Africa.

In 1996, the World Bank and the IMF announced a plan to reduce the debt burdens of the world's poorest countries. Two years later, a confidential report to the World Bank's executive board said that "considerable progress had been made."[43] One shudders to think what the World Bank might construe as lack of progress. Some 40 countries, again, mostly in Africa, were sufficiently poor and indebted to qualify for assistance under the 1996 debt-relief plan. Of those, 10 have had their cases reviewed, and six, three of which were African – Burkina

Faso, Côte d'Ivoire, and Mozambique – been promised help.

Only one – Uganda – has had any debt forgiven. And only a handful more will qualify for aid before the end of the century, despite the Bank having agreed to relax its restrictions at the 8 September meeting to enable countries which had put economic reform programs in place by 2000 to become eligible for assistance, thus opening the door for wartorn countries such as the DRC, Angola and Sudan. However, even with the relaxed restrictions in place, and assuming that all debt-relief conditions are met – a big assumption – only a handful of countries will receive any relief by the end of the century.[44]

One reason is that debt relief raises the cost to creditor governments, and about half is owed to rich-country governments which also pick up much of the outstanding debts of multilateral institutions that lack the resources to do so themselves. The cost to creditor countries would become much greater if the pool of countries eligible for benefits is further increased.

Moreover, with large and economically important areas slowly succumbing to the impact of the global financial crisis, the effects of which may take two years to work its way through the global market, developed countries have become more circumspect. Adding to the caution and uncertainty is the huge cost of financing the bail-out of Brazil, continuing economic and political instability – which can only worsen – and the looming crisis in China. A devaluation of the Chinese yuan or the Hong Kong dollar would devastate Asian markets, crushing their efforts to pick themselves up following the East Asian debacle, send the usual "shock waves" through the developed world, harden predictions of a global recession to the point where the near-certainty attached to the predictions creates situations in which the predictions become inevitable certainties, and lead to a global crisis of liquidity. In these circumstances, or in even less consequential ones, as the bite of economic slowdown begins to clench its teeth on the West's economies, developed countries will do what is best for themselves – the resuscitation of foreign markets to absorb their exports and cushion unemployment will be the first order of business, and hence an even more ambitious emphasis on pulling Asia in particular, and the more important emerging markets in the Americas, out of their quagmires.

Unfortunately, the less developed emerging markets or the undeveloped markets of the rest of the world, the world of the chronically poor and for the most part forgotten, will not be part of recovery programs, because not having had much to begin with, there is little to recover, and there is no comparison between the short-term return on $1 billion spent on debt-relief or $1 billion spent on bailing out the markets that count.

This leaves southern Africa in a no-man's land. An emerging market, yes; but one that has not lived up to its potential and shows little signs of doing so, especially as it has to contend with recession in an election year where the election results will be more pivotal than earlier elections since they will point to the direction of southern Africa's future well into the 21st century.

In an essay for the African Renaissance Conference entitled *How Africa was Brought Low,* Dr Peter Ewang writes:

> Bilateral and multilateral organizations have made certain policy interventions as a direct precondition for loan effectiveness. However, these activities ignore the fact that in African countries the constraints for development are not caused solely by economic factors but by institutional weakness, low level social awareness, education and healthcare.
>
> Most of the time the constraints have been ignored. Nowadays decisions are dominated by or influenced by international organizations with very limited technical and socio-cultural expertise and insight concerning African countries. Development is something that means something distinctly different to those being developed and those doing the developing. The economic structure of African countries has been developed not to feed their own people but to meet the import needs of development that have made Africa a sight of recurring famine, unpayable debts, and in need of a renaissance.
>
> There is ample evidence that international development programmes have failed in most of the African countries. Since 1980 Africa has received billions of dollars as aid through development programmes yet Africa today produces less food and has more hungry people. It is no coincidence that over the past decades, some of the largest recipients of the USA and the former Soviet Union's aid in Sub-Sahara Africa, particularly Sudan, Ethiopia, Mozambique, Somalia, and Angola, have been nations where war, famine and hunger are most common.
>
> At best the aid programmes of the past were not effective, at worst they have been part of the problem. Development has often helped destroy people's ability to feed themselves. Offers of food pour in but obtaining financial resources for rehabilitation is usually difficult. Dumping food as relief has not solved the developmental problems of Africa. Food aid extended by developed countries, following devastating famines caused by civil strife and natural calamities, has adversely affected the capacity of the continent to deal with its problems. Generally food aid programmes have introduced a harmful spirit of submissiveness and dependency into these poor societies and inefficiency and corruption into governments of most of these countries.
>
> The hunger and debt caused by the huge debts are difficult to accept. Governments in Sub-Sahara Africa have been pressured by the IMF and the World Bank into implementing structural adjustment programmes in order to acquire loans for development. These countries are made to pay their debts by surrendering the bulk of their export earnings, leasing out valuable resources at throwaway prices to earn extra income and sacrificing social and environmental considerations to earn enough to pay their debts.
>
> Many countries in Sub-Sahara Africa owe more money today than what they did 10 or 20 years ago. In fact, in 1992 African external debt had reached $290 billion, about 2.4 times greater than in 1980. In the Sub-Saharan African countries alone the debt increased from $6 billion in 1970

to $243 billion in 1994. The big question is why the big institutions (the
World Bank, IMF, and others) let this unbearable debt accrue?[45]

That such an essay should be one of the showcase features introducing the
conference is cause for reflection. The insinuation is that developed countries not
only plundered Africa in the past, but continue to do so in the guise of development programs, which although ostensibly tailored to the needs of the country in
question are in effect instruments of measured interference, designed to service the
needs of the developed countries. Even humanitarian aid – food to alleviate famine
– is viewed in a sinister light. For every dollar given in aid, there is a condition, an
unspoken agenda to mould the economies of the poorer countries according to the
dictates and, needless to say, advantage of the donor country.

The essay is an expression of anger at developed countries; at their hubris, their
"we-know-it-all" attitude; their condescension inherited from the lingering sense
of conquest and the unstated but silently-held conviction that things were better in
"their" day. Indeed, even today, and perhaps to a greater degree in the post-Cold
War era, former colonial powers vie with each other for "parental" control over
what used to be "their" Africa, and when the children are naughty, they are not
above sending in their troops to sort things out, all under the pretense of having to
"protect" their citizens who are still residents of whatever godforsaken piece of
earth is being scorched in the interests of some tinpot dictator or the would-be usurper
of his much-coveted position. It is a manifestation of deep resentment of the
developed countries' self-perceived sense of going out of the way to help, at the
altruism they smother themselves in, when the help really only makes recipients
more roiled that they have to turn to their former "masters" or clones of their erst-
while masters for help in the first place; bitterness that the help encourages a culture of helplessness, thus fostering the dependency the help is supposed to eradicate.

It is noteworthy, too, for what it fails to say. That every other country in large
swaths of the continent is embroiled in civil conflict or party to the civil conflicts
of others; that famine is often self-induced; that food relief is used as a weapon to
leverage concessions from the enemy; that food is often withheld from the starving
and mysteriously finding its way into the hands of the warmongers; that corruption
is pervasive.

Given that many of Africa's conflicts have their roots in borders arbitrarily
drawn by conquering powers with little regard to natural alignments, ethnic demar-
cations, or history, and that fears of domination by one ethnic group – often justified – are never far from the surface, that natural disasters have taken an inordinate
toll, that the 12 million refugees who are permanently homeless – and countryless
– have nowhere to go and create a permanent source of instability in the region,
and that indebtedness cripples the prospects for development, one can easily
empathize with the rage of Africa.

But the failure of Ewang to acknowledge that Africans may have anything to do
with the plight they are in, that the actions of their elites or of those who stoked

ethnic antagonisms and fanned the flames of hatred for personal ambition, of those who looted their countries of their wealth on a scale almost unimaginable, who have exploited their own people to a degree that not even the colonial imperialists of the past could match, to fail to hold Africa accountable for many of the ills that beset it, is to sink into the self-pity that is the hallmark of the submissiveness and dependency he goes to such great lengths to warn against. Commenting on the renaissance conference, Thabo Kobokoane observed that "the conflicts plaguing Africa did not dominate the proceedings."

> Surely discussion on these wars and rebellions should have been at the centre of any debate about a reawakening Africa? After all, it is the continent's all-too-familiar problems that fly in the face of a so-called renaissance; a massive stumbling block to those who will eventually oversee its regeneration.

Yet to the bulk of African Renaissance delegates, the festering conflicts did not appear important. An equally pressing question that needed addressing concerned the nature of Africa's governments. How will the African renaissance "movement," an essentially private-driven initiative, relate to those states that have no tolerance of civil society?[46]

And thus southern Africa as we enter this pivotal election year.

Notes

1. *Star,* 1 September 1998.
2. *Business Day,* 5 October 1998.
3. Cyril Ramaphosa addresssing IMF on 3 October 1998.
4. *Star Business Report,* 6 October 1998.
5. *ibid.*
6. Professor Larry Diamond, 1997 Democracy Forum Report; Bratton Michael (1994) "International versus Domestic Pressures for Democratisation in Africa" MSU Working Papers on Political Reform in Africa. No. 12, 15 November.
7. 1997 Democracy Forum Report: Africa, Wave of Elections – Wave of Democracy.
8. Bureau of Intelligence Research, US Department of State (1994) "Assessing African Democratization".
9. The data cited was gathered by Foster Majiga for use in his article "Malawi's Transition to Democracy" featured in this publication.
10. Presentation by O.K. Dingake, University of Botswana and University of Cape Town, School of Law, at the Southern African Elections Summit. See following note.
11. Southern African Elections Summit held in Johannesburg from 26–28 March, 1999.
12. Institute for Democracy and Electoral Assistance: 1997 Democracy Forum Report.
13. Professor Chisepo J.J. Mphaisha: Retreat from Democracy in Post One-Party State Zambia.
14. Khotakota South By-Election, 25 September 1995; Blantyre City Central By-Election, 17 May 1997; Mwanza North By-Election, 23 December 1997.
15. Claude Ake, Democracy and Development, Chapter 1.
16. Clark, John F. (1994) The Constraints on Democracy in Sub-Saharan Africa; International Republican Institute (1995) African Democracy Network, Conference Report, 8–10 March, Mombasa, Kenya.

17. Clark, John F (1994) The Constraints on Democracy in Sub-Saharan Africa.
18. National Democratic Institute for International Affairs (NDI) focus group report (1994) "Dziko ndi Anthu".
19. *Time,* 30 March 1998.
20. Jon Qwelane, *Saturday Star,* 22 August 1998.
21. Data cited in a report to the Security Council by British Foreign Secretary Robin Cook on 24 September 1998. *Citizen,* 26 September 1998.
22. The Southern African Development Community (SADC) was founded in Lusaka in 1980 to foster regional and political cooperation in southern Africa. It has 14 member countries: South Africa (which was admitted after South Africa's 1994 elections which resulted in the election of an ANC-led government of national unity), Zambia, Tanzania, Zimbabwe, Malawi, Namibia, Lesotho, Angola, Botswana, Mozambique, Mauritius, the Seychelles, Swaziland and the DRC. Zimbabwe was the dominant power but that changed with South Africa's admission. The DRC is SADC's newest member. Among those involved in SADC-related conflicts: Zimbabwe, Namibia, Angola, Uganda, Lesotho, South Africa, Botswana, and Congo.
23. See footnote 3.
24. *Business Day,* 18 August 1998.
25. Figures on population displacements cited by Sadako Ogata, UN High Commissioner for Refugees at the second Tokyo International Conference on African Development 1998. See *Boston Globe,* 22 October 1998.
26. African Renaissance Conference, 28–29 September 1998, Fourways, Johannesburg. Proceedings reported in *Business Day,* 29 September 1998.
27. *ibid.*
28. "The country dubbed the New Congo looks a lot like post War Germany, split in several zones, run by foreign allied powers," Uganda's *Monitor* newspaper declared.
29. Mondli Makhanya, *Star,* 28 August 1998.
30. UN data referred to by Minister of Welfare Geraldine Fraser-Moleketi speaking at the Partnership Against AIDS Conference in Pretoria on 11 September 1998. See the *Citizen,* 12 September 1998.
31. Report in *Business Day,* 28 August 1998.
32. UN population survey 1998.
33. *New York Times,* 28 October 1998, citing Lester Brown, president of World Watch Institute.
34. *New York Times,* 28 October 1998.
35. *Star Business Report,* 31 August 1998.
36. Cees Bruggemans, "Spreading global contagion need not mean Armageddon," *Sunday Independent Business,* 13 September 1998.
37. *ibid.*
38. *Business Day,* 16 September 1998.
39. *Business Day,* 8 September 1998.
40. *Newsweek,* 14 September 1998.
41. *ibid.*
42. *Financial Mail,* 2 October 1998.
43. *Economist,* 12 September 1998. The report was reviewed by the board on 8 September 1998 .
44. *ibid.*
45. *African Renaissance Conference,* 28–29 September 1998, Johannesburg.
46. Thabo Kobokoane, "It's time for Africa to take a long, hard look at itself," *Sunday Times,* 4 October 1998.

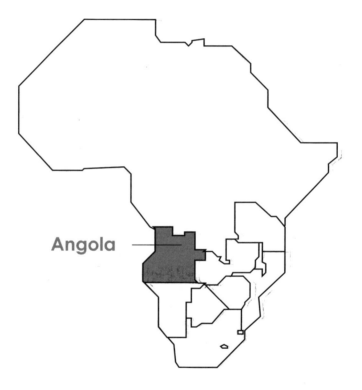

Angola

Citizen Views of Peace Building and Political Transition in Angola, 1997

Carrie Manning

> In politics, there is no such thing as reconciliation.
>
> — Focus group participant in Luanda

> Regrettably, since my last report, there has been no improvement in the already deplorable situation in Angola. The country continues to drift towards full fledged hostilities, despite the renewed efforts of the international community to avoid a precipitous turn of events.
>
> — Report of the Secretary-General on the
> United Nations Observer Mission in Angola,
> *6 August, 1998, Prologue*

During four years of relative peace, the longest period Angola has enjoyed since its independence, formal progress was made in building democratic institutions: the 1992 Constitution, a pluralist National Assembly, an independent judiciary, free media, and new civil society organizations.

Since mid-1998, however, Angola has been sliding back into full-scale civil war, rendering these developments moot, at least for the time being. During the last year, the worsening military situation has served as an excuse for the systematic undermining of what formal democratic institutions exist. The government of President Jose Eduardo dos Santos has restructured the cabinet to place more power in the president's hands, one Luanda-based faction of the National Union for the Total Independence of Angola (UNITA) has sought to use extra-constitutional manoeuvers to remove its rival faction from Parliament, and journalists from independent print and broadcast media have been arrested. Thousands have been

Carrie Manning is Assistant Professor of Comparative Politics, Georgia State University. She researches comparative processes of state building and democratic transition, particularly in post-conflict settings.

killed and more than 700,000 people have been rendered homeless by fighting between the two principal members of the Government of National Unity and Reconciliation.

In this bleak environment, there seems little hope of sustaining the gains made toward establishing workable democratic institutions since the Lusaka Protocol was signed in 1994, and it is clear that the skepticism of the ordinary Angolans surveyed in 1997 toward political leaders' commitment to peace and democratic politics was well-founded.

This is, however, the third iteration of civil war for Angola. An optimist, even a very sober one, could find evidence to support the claim that Angola's successive descents into civil war have rarely succeeded in obliterating all the progress made during previous periods of peace. For example, despite the extremely intense and bitter nature of the resumption of civil war after multiparty elections in 1992, when the Lusaka Protocol was signed in 1994 it honored the remaining provisions of the previous peace agreement. The UNITA deputies elected in 1992 were finally seated in 1997, and UNITA has been a vocal and trenchant participant in the National Assembly. The Ministry of Justice proceeded with plans for the training of its local-level magistrates and prosecutors in an attempt to ensure that rule of law prevailed over retribution at the community level.

Of course, at the same time, civilian defense forces employed by provincial governments were being used in some places to intimidate demobilized soldiers returning to their home villages, while UNITA made liberal use of intimidation tactics in some of the areas it controlled. But even the spotty and limited progress toward establishing rule of law and formal democratic institutions in the1994–1998 period offers a faint glimmer of hope for the next period of peace in Angola. The political institutions created over the past four years continue to limp along. Social and political leaders interested in improving governance and strengthening rule of law are not likely to make much noise in the current climate of mutual mistrust and hostility, but they are still there. As the fighting continues, the task of those who would promote the development of an Angolan regime that respects the rule of law, human rights, and the constitutional liberties of its citizens is to find effective and appropriate ways to encourage these potential reformers, without putting them at risk.

Over the past four years, the Angolan government, UNITA, the United Nations (UN), and a number of Western powers have been engaged in an often circular struggle to implement the Lusaka Protocol, the peace agreement which formally ended the fighting that followed the country's first multiparty elections in 1992. The 1991 Bicesse Accords, which put an end to more than 30 years of civil strife, provided the backdrop for those elections.

Angola's peace process has been part of a dual transition: from war to peace and from single-party to multiparty rule. The linchpin of the peace process is the construction of democratic institutions and power-sharing arrangements at national, provincial, and local levels. Nothing in Angola's history has prepared either the general public or government officials to participate in a democratically based political system. Furthermore, the transition to formal democracy has in some senses advanced ahead of the transition from war to peace. A weak, formally democratic system is struggling to survive alongside an ongoing and increasingly acute armed conflict in which the combatants are also the principal protagonists in the new political system.

In this challenging environment, the NDI was asked to design a program that would help to bridge the gap between the new political system as envisioned and as practiced. The program sought to improve the quality of interaction between citizens and government in the new democratic political context by working at two levels: building the capacity of ordinary citizens to understand and interact with government officials, especially at the local level, and training local government officials in methods for improving local governance through a more active engagement with local citizenry.

Toward this end, NDI, in mid-1997, conducted the first comprehensive public survey on attitudes and knowledge of basic democratic principles and processes in Angola. The focus group research began with a basic premise: that the attitudes and behavior of ordinary citizens toward the political system will ultimately affect whether the system thrives or fails. Accordingly, focus group questions were designed to gauge citizens' attitudes toward and understanding of key aspects of the transition process and the new political system. The information gathered in this survey was intended to provide the basis for a large-scale civic education effort to be conducted at the grassroots level and through radio programming.

Primary topics covered included: the Government of Unity and National Reconciliation; the broader process of national and community-level reconciliation, the functions of local government authorities; and human rights and constitutional rights.

The results of the focus groups suggest first that Angolan citizens do not necessarily share in the assumption that citizen attitudes and behavior are of primary importance, instead placing much greater emphasis on the attitudes and behavior of political elites. They lay the bulk of the responsibility both for ending the war and for establishing a functioning, inclusive political system squarely on the shoulders of government and UNITA leadership.

Returning to our premise, however, an examination of citizen attitudes toward the new political system and the transition process suggests a sense of frustration not so much with the proposed democratic political system as a system of government as with the way it is being implemented in Angola.

After setting out the context in which these focus groups were carried out and the methodology followed, I present the results of the research, preserving as much as possible the voices of the participants themselves, ending with a brief discussion of the policy implications of the focus group results.

Historical Context

The roots of Angola's civil war reach to the period of its struggle for independence from Portugal in the 1960s. The 1960s and early 1970s were marked by tensions between three independence movements: the Popular Movement for the Liberation of Angola (MPLA), the Front for the Liberation of Angola (FNLA), and UNITA. While these engaged in shifting alliances with one another while fighting the Portuguese, all were vying for the right to take the reigns of government at independence. By 1975, the three movements had agreed to share power in an uneasy transitional government that never came off. By the date established for independence, 11 November 1975, the three movements had divided Angola in three, with the MPLA in control of Luanda, the capital. While the MPLA declared victory in Luanda, UNITA and the FNLA proclaimed the popular republic of Angola in the central province of Huambo. Essentially, the war between these movements that had begun before independence picked up after a momentary lull during which power was transferred from the Portuguese to the MPLA.

Angola's war became one of the prime Cold War proxy battlefields in Africa. Cuban troops were sent to reinforce the MPLA in its struggles against South Africa-backed and U.S.-backed UNITA. Finally, in 1991, the MPLA government and UNITA signed the Bicesse Accords, which led to the country's first multiparty elections in September 1992. Civil war began anew in the wake of those elections, however, as UNITA refused to accept the results. The most recent peace accord, the Lusaka Protocol, was signed in November 1994. Its future remains in question, as four years and three UN peacekeeping missions later, major provisions of the Lusaka Protocol remained to be implemented.

Mid-1997, when NDI's focus groups were carried out, was an especially challenging time in Angola. The peace process was making only halting progress, having been relaunched with the Lusaka Protocol two years after renewed civil war broke out following the country's first multiparty elections in 1992. Throughout 1996, key aspects of the protocol, including the creation of a Government of National Unity and Reconciliation (GURN), which would incorporate UNITA in the cabinet and at provincial and local government levels, the reseating of UNITA members of Parliament elected in 1992, and the unification of territorial administration, had been repeatedly put off. In April 1997, the GURN was established at cabinet level, although installation of government and local officials proceeded much more slowly and in some cases not at all. Seventy UNITA deputies took their seats in Parliament, and although UNITA's leader, Jonas Savimbi, declined to come to Luanda for the swearing-in of the new government, it was possible to sense renewed optimism regarding the outcome of Angola's troubled peace process.

Optimism proved unjustified. Just one month after the formation of the unity government, Angolan government forces and UNITA soldiers found themselves on opposite sides of the war in neighboring Zaire, where UNITA's longtime ally

Mobutu Sese Seko was soon to be deposed by the rebel troops of Laurent Kabila. The scenario would be repeated within a matter of months in Congo-Brazzaville, where another of UNITA's allies was routed with the help of Angolan government troops. Fighting between government and UNITA troops resumed in the diamond-rich provinces of Lunda Norte and Lunda Sul, and security in other areas around the central highlands was constantly in jeopardy.

These events of course foretold trouble for the peace process in Angola. More than a year later, the military situation is even more unstable. Fighting in the Lundas has spread to the neighboring provinces of Malanje and Uige, and some sources report that more than a million people are internally displaced. The peace process, no longer merely stalled as it was for much of 1997, now appears to be in full retreat. On 1 September 1998, the government suspended UNITA members of GURN as well as UNITA's 70-member parliamentary delegation. All but two of the GURN members and most members of Parliament were reinstated after the formation of UNITA-Renovada (UNITA revised/renewed), a UNITA faction that has severed links to Jonas Savimbi and is therefore "acceptable" to the Angolan government. This split appears to have occasioned serious tension among UNITA members in Luanda and served as a license for local government forces to step up persecution of UNITA officials throughout the country who have not sworn allegiance to UNITA-Renovada. Needless to say, other principal elements of the Lusaka process, including the extension of state administration to key areas of the country and the demilitarization of UNITA and its transformation into a legal political party, still face formidable obstacles. Official meetings between the government and UNITA to discuss the peace process are increasingly rare. The peace process has been severely complicated by the fact that there are now effectively two UNITAs, each claiming exclusive legitimacy.

In his October 1998 report to the UN Security Council, Secretary-General Kofi Annan announced plans to reduce significantly the number of UN peacekeeping personnel in the country unless real progress is made toward restarting the peace process.

Focus Group Methodology

Thirty focus groups were conducted, in both government and UNITA-controlled areas, in the provinces of Huambo, Bie, and Uige, and in Luanda. Focus group participants included male and female students 14 to 19 years of age; members of associations, churches, and other community organizations 20 to 24 years of age; urban and rural teachers; demobilized soldiers; women and young men marketplace vendors; urban and rural heads of family; urban and rural adult men of various professions; married women, farmers, internally displaced people; and the elderly.

The project began with broad consultations with Angolan sociologists and survey researchers on sample design and on the development of the discussion guide. NDI's partners in this phase were drawn from the Angolan Association for Rural and Environmental Development (ADRA-Angolana), the National Institute of Statistics, and Agostinho Neto University. From 2 to 4 July, the first focus group moderator training workshop was held in Luanda. Eighteen moderator candidates from Luanda and Huambo underwent two days of training and practical exercises, followed by a day at an internally displaced persons camp in which each trainee had the opportunity to moderate a focus group. Twelve moderators, of whom ten spoke one of the national languages of Huambo or Uige, were selected from this group to participate in the focus group research project.

Two weeks later, the twelve moderators experienced an additional day of training and orientation to the research project. In Uige, a two-day workshop was held to train additional moderators to work in that province. This was partly in response to the refusal of UNITA officials to permit "Angolans from Luanda" or any other part of the country to conduct this sort of activity in their areas. (This did not prove to be a problem in Huambo or Bie, primarily because the traditionally UNITA areas in which all the focus groups being conducted there had come under government control in the weeks before the groups were organized.) In Uige, the workshop was conducted in collaboration with the bipartisan Provincial Human Rights Commission, an organization that brings together teachers, lawyers, and other interested individuals from the city of Uige (government-controlled) and nearby Negage (UNITA's northern regional capital) to discuss human rights issues. The group has received substantial support from the United Nations Verification Mission Human Rights Unit in Uige. The focus groups were conducted from 7 July to 30 August 1997.

The findings of the focus group research are in two sections, the specifics of the political transition process and questions about permanent features of the political system, including the meaning of democracy and the peculiarities of its practice in Angola, the role of local government authorities, and the meaning and significance of human and constitutional rights.

The Transition Process

The End of the War

> *A radio diz que a guerra acabou mas nós não concordamos.* (The radio says the war is over but we don't agree.)[1]

> *A radio agita a guerra mas quando a radio e os jornais disserem que a guerra acabou, entao vamos acreditar.* (The radio agitates for war – when the radio and the newspapers say that the war is over, then we will believe it.)[2]

The war is by no means over according to the majority of people who participated in this research. The overwhelming majority said that, for them, the war would be truly over when there was freedom of movement and commerce. This is one of the key provisions of the Lusaka Protocol, and those who cited it usually adopted the "official" wording from the protocol – "free circulation of people and goods." Other protocol provisions mentioned were demobilization and reintegration of UNITA soldiers and unification of the army.

In the Lusaka Protocol, that phrase refers to unimpaired movement between government and UNITA zones. However, this does not necessarily mean that people are preoccupied with the implementation of one specific piece of the protocol. In fact, the focus group results caution against a strictly political interpretation of the phrase. For participants, free circulation has two important nonpolitical implications: goods continue to be artificially expensive, whether they are imported or produced within the country, as long as free circulation is impaired; and free circulation also requires that people not be hassled by the police as they go about their daily lives.

For example, free circulation was cited more frequently in Luanda focus groups than those in the provinces. This is surprising, since people in Luanda do not undergo the daily experience of having to cross between government and UNITA zones to see relatives or to buy goods not available in their area. The following comment, for one, is from a focus group with internally displaced people in Luanda.

> People are not living freely; there is not free circulation from one place to another . . . I myself was intercepted by the police and had to give them two million kwanzas, and I began to think that democracy is false in our country.[3]

The second most frequently cited indication that the war had really ended would be the arrival of Savimbi in Luanda. This answer came up most often in Huambo and Bie.

Finally, there was a good deal of emphasis in Luanda on the behavior of the police. One student said that the end of the war would mean "that the police stop mistreating the people."[4] The police are discussed in more detail below.

Reconciliation

For most individuals, the greatest obstacle to reconciliation is division caused by the war, principally the fact that people tended to be aligned or were perceived to be aligned with either one side or the other.

Reconciliation was understood as "forgetting about war," "the end of mistrust," "learning how to live together," "forgetting the past and pardoning our neighbors," "joining hands and singing with one voice," "recognizing that no one has been 'defeated' at the level of the family or the community." Others emphasized the importance of communication, of opening a dialogue in order for reconciliation to occur.

The overwhelming majority of focus group participants felt that reconciliation was the responsibility of the government or of the two warring parties, the MPLA government and UNITA. Most people distinguished between *national* reconciliation and reconciliation at the community level. At the national level, responsibility for reconciliation was most often attributed to the government. At the community level, it was *sobas* (traditional community leaders), church leaders, and "the people in general" or "all of us." The UN was also cited as one of the principal entities responsible for reconciliation in Angola. Only one person argued that the people themselves had to provide the momentum and the example for their leaders. "The people should send to their leaders the message of peace and national reconciliation."[5]

Those who had concrete suggestions for how to promote national reconciliation tended to favor one of two remedies: government intervention at the community level in the form of meetings and speeches about reconciliation and improved communication about the peace process.

Many identified the need to change mentalities in order for reconciliation to be successful. "There must be a revolution in the mind of each person. I cannot stop talking to someone just because his father is from UNITA."[6] Others emphasized the importance of communication, of opening a dialogue in order for reconciliation to occur. As one participant put it, "Communication is necessary in order for people to unite."[7] More concretely, the media should play a role in promoting reconciliation. "On both sides there are people who want war, and the media should broadcast messages against war."[8]

There was a strong perception that reconciliation would be easier at the grassroots level than at the political level. "In politics there is no such thing as reconciliation."[9] On a social level, however, people were able to cite numerous examples of informal reconciliation. One participant cited the following example of reconciliation in practice at the community level:

> Here there is a neighborhood for UNITA members of Parliament where a party was organized two weeks after they arrived, a so-called National Reconciliation Celebration. And no one asked if your father was from the MPLA or from UNITA. At these small parties people start to become friends and the separation ends.[10]

In addition to political differences, people underscored ethnicity and differences in living standards as factors causing separation or division in their communities.

GURN and the Extension of State Administration

> On April 11, when the GURN was inaugurated, I was very happy, I thought that it would mean big changes. But until now nothing has changed because we see that those in government only want to fill their pockets and those of their families, to make up for lost time.[11]

The vast majority of focus group participants had heard of the Government of National Unity and Reconciliation and knew what it was. Those who had never heard of the GURN or who had heard of it but didn't know what it was were distributed fairly evenly between Luanda and the provinces. Typical descriptions of the GURN follow.

> The GURN is the union of people from many parties.[12]

> The GURN is a government constituted by members of various parties.[13]

> The GURN is a group formed by people from all parties to be able to lead the country.[14]

> It is to see whether in fact Angolans can achieve reconciliation.[15]

Most people had heard about GURN through radio, television, or friends and neighbors. Other important sources of information were newspapers and local religious leaders and government officials. In general, the less people knew about GURN, the more they were inclined to be optimistic about it. As one participant put it, "I don't know anything about the GURN, but it seems that it will resolve the problems of the people."[16] Among those who said they knew what GURN was all about, feelings about what GURN could do were mixed, although the great majority was cynical about the likelihood of any positive impact. Those who did believe that GURN would be able to deliver thought it would bring an end to the war and promote reconciliation, but that this would take time.

> I think that we cannot construct a life from one day to the next. When you get a job, on the first day you commit many errors. Those who are in the government now don't have experience. We have to give them time to improve their work.[17]

GURN was:

> a positive step, a sign of hope for a better Angola.[18]

> That's where we can end all the talk that we have heard, about war.[19]

The majority of the participants, however, saw in GURN business as usual. Their responses reflect not so much an opinion of the performance of GURN itself, which had been functioning for only a few months at the time of the research, but a profound skepticism about the abilities and intentions of government in general.

> [GURN is] lard, and only those who are there are going to get fat and not us.[20]

> [GURN] is not going to resolve the problems of the population, and it is going to create an economic crisis because of the purchase of luxury cars [by government officials] and because [those in government] only think about themselves.[21]

> The GURN will resolve the problems of the government and not the people.[22]

> The GURN is not resolving anything; it puts nothing in practice; there are even new threats of war.[23]

It came to make our problems worse, since now there is enmity and distrust [within the government].[24]

From the information that I have, the GURN met and then did nothing.[25]

I don't see reconciliation – they just point fingers; that's what I know about the GURN.[26]

The GURN will only have value when it is understood that governance means providing services to the people.[27]

The simple fact that we have ministers from four parties in government doesn't mean reconciliation. Are they the only Angolans? If so, then we will also make our war.[28]

Others would be more positive about the potential positive effects of GURN, if only it functioned the way it was envisioned, if only it was for real.

[GURN] might bring us good intentions, but we want them to be put into practice.[29]

We don't see evidence of their work. Lots of promises, little practice.[30]

And finally:

There is hope, but only Dr. Savimbi knows for sure.[31]

Extension of State Administration

In Quibala, the GURN was beat up.[32] [The first exercise in extending state administration ended in failure at Quibala after reaching only a few munici-palities. Members of GURN were severely beaten when they arrived in Quibala to swear in new municipal officials.]

Focus group participants were surprisingly well informed about the process of extending state administration. Most knew not only what it was but some detail about it, either where administration had already been extended and why or when it was stopped. Many gave reasons for the failure of the process.

It is difficult now for someone who fought for twenty years against a regime to accept a new flag.[33]

If [the leaders] were thinking about the people, state administration would already be extended all over the country.[34]

UNITA doesn't want extension of state administration, because UNITA wants to stay at war.[35]

Several people emphasized the importance not only of extending the state physically but of changing people's attitudes toward the process and educating them about it. "We have to create the right mentality for a real reestablishment of the state."[36] As another participant put it:

We don't believe in extension of state administration because all of the forces of society are not in agreement that this process should be carried out, so we simply have vandalism by one side against another.[37]

Democracy, the Role of Local Authorities, Human and Constitutional Rights

The Meaning of Democracy

> *Estamos a pagar pla democracia muito mal dada.* (We are paying for democracy poorly done.)

A strikingly high proportion of focus group participants demonstrated at least a basic understanding of the term "democracy." In only one group did members say they had no idea what democracy was or fail to provide examples of basic democratic principles.

For the majority of participants, democracy was most closely associated with freedom of expression. Freedom of movement, tolerance, and mutual respect were also cited as key aspects of democracy. Freedom of expression, however, was far ahead of the others in terms of the number of times it was cited. Linked to the issue of freedom of expression was the idea that in democracy, citizens' voices should have an impact on governance.

In neither respect, however, did democratic theory and practice coincide in Angola, in the minds of the participants. For example, most of them believed that, in a democracy, people are free to speak their minds without fear of reprisal. They then went on to explain that this was not the case in Angola. Those who cited freedom of expression as a fundamental part of democracy usually ended the phrase with the words "without fear of reprisals" or simply "without fear." One group pointed out that "people call in to radio shows to express their opinions and ideas, but they have to request anonymity to protect themselves."[38]

Similarly, in terms of accountability of government to the people, Angola does not qualify as a democracy in the minds of most focus group participants.

> In a democracy, the government should listen to the ideas of the people who elected them, but in this democracy [in Angola], this provision does not exist in practice.[39]

Another participant reinforced this view, saying there is no democracy now because "the population does not have a voice."[40]

A surprisingly high level of understanding of the basic values of democracy is matched by high levels of frustration and cynicism regarding the wide gap between the theory and practice of democracy in Angola.

> Our leaders want to show the people that democracy means to rob, kill, and
> do whatever you want without being punished.[41]

There is also a strong link in people's minds between democracy and the functioning of specific government institutions – people understand that in a democracy there are certain government institutions which ought to work in a certain way. The behavior of the police, for example, is for many people contrary to basic notions of democracy:

> When I hear the word *democracy* I get irritated because it is a word that is
> used very often but does not exist in practice. . . . Someone comes and steals
> my wallet, my watch, and the police do nothing.[42]

> Government institutions do not function the way they should and are not
> accountable to citizens.

This was particularly true in the case of the police and not simply because they are unresponsive to citizens' needs. If there was one theme that ran across region, gender, age, occupation, and educational level, it was a preoccupation with police abuse. Although the discussion guide did not contain a separate section on the police, the discussions elicited so much comment on them, almost all of it negative, that I think it is important to highlight these expressions here.

According to one young community activist:

> It is much better these days to come across a petty criminal than to come
> across the police.[43]

Others agreed:

> Our security is always at risk; the police who should protect us turn out to be
> more dangerous than the criminals.[44]

> The police very often contribute to disorder.[45]

Interestingly, despite the fact that most people said they believed the police were responsible for causing at least as many problems as they resolved, nearly everyone named the police as the entity that guarantees their personal safety.

Another intriguing twist is that most people, when asked what they would do if they suffered police abuse, said they would complain to an officer's superiors. This would seem to indicate a certain amount of faith in the institution of the police, if not the individual members with whom people come in contact.

A minority of participants voiced despair with the system as well.

> We have no recourse; there are no courts; if the authorities abuse us, to
> whom can we complain?[46]

Or :

> We are always suffering abuse and there is nothing we can do. The system
> allows these abuses to multiply.[47]

Most, however, had concrete solutions for police abuse. Asked what they would do, most answered along the following lines:

> Try to find [the police officer's] unit and inform them.[48]

> We should go to the appropriate authorities of his squadron and if that doesn't work, go directly to the tribunal.[49]

> If going to his squadron didn't resolve the case, one would go immediately to the Provincial Command of the Angolan National Police to see if they can resolve it or not. If not, one would go to the institutions of military justice, since he is part of the military.[50]

There is a widespread perception among the groups surveyed that a double standard is in effect in Angola's political system. Cynicism was expressed in general terms as well as through specific examples. For example, two common responses were:

> In other countries it means freedom, but in Angola democracy is only for "the haves."[51]

> The word *democracy* is only for those who eat well.[52]

A group of teachers in Luanda gave a more specific example, which highlights the responsibilities rather than the rights associated with democracy.

> Democracy extends only to the masses, it doesn't reach elites. For example, if a high-level person kills someone, nothing happens. Justice doesn't reach this person; he takes the law into his own hands. For democracy, everyone must be equal under the law.[53]

Two other issues were closely associated with democracy in participants' minds. These were peace and an improvement in living standards. Democracy is not possible without peace, and peace and democracy will bring about improvement in people's well-being.

Local Government: Who Is in Charge?

This question was first posed as "Who are the local authorities here?" or "Who is in charge here?" Moderators then presented a series of hypothetical problems and asked how the group members would go about trying to resolve them. The resulting answers were put into the form of a diagram of the local hierarchy of authority. In some cases, each focus group participant made his or her own diagram. In others, the moderator drew the diagram on the basis of what the group said.

Virtually all focus group participants in Uige, including demobilized soldiers and male and female students, described the hierarchy as follows: provincial government, Angolan Armed Forces (FAA), police, the people.

In some cases, FAA and the police were at the same level of authority. This perception of the police and military and paramilitary units as intermediaries between the government and the people was also present in Luanda but less prevalent. In Luanda, the police figured most prominently for younger participants aged 15 to 25. Since Uige focus group participants weredisproportionately young compared with Luanda, Huambo, and Bie, age may play a part. Also important may be the fact that the city of Uige is seen by the government as an island in a sea of UNITA, which very likely translates into tighter security and a larger role for the police and defense forces.

In Luanda, the police figured less prominently in people's diagrams but were still present. Two of the nine groups that said they had a clear idea of who the local authorities were named the police in second place, right after the local administrator. The diagrams drawn in Luanda were less uniform than those in Uige. As a rule, the Luandans gave more detail about formal structures at the local level. For example, most people named not only the local administrator but also the neighborhood administrators and heads of residents committees.

In Huambo and Bie, there was more emphasis on the governor, the four vice-governors, and traditional authorities. There was also a very clear separation between urban areas and rural areas. Two kinds of organizational diagrams were typical: (1) urban areas: governor, vice-governors, government officials, traditional authorities; (2) rural areas: *soba,* coordinator, *seculos* – assistant *sobas.*

Traditional authorities were hardly mentioned in Uige and in Luanda, no doubt because focus groups took place primarily in urban or periurban areas there.

In addition to seeking to understand people's notions of the hierarchy of local government authority, the focus groups raised specific examples of various kinds of problems to get a general idea of how people viewed the role of various government and nongovernment actors in resolving the challenges they face daily.

For the most part, people appeared to have low material expectations of the government, but they retained faith in government institutions. When a community required social services, for example, in very few cases was the solution simply to go to the government and seek support. Usually, as in the instance of rehabilitating a school or a clinic, people said that they would try to organize members of the community to do the required work, that they would get together and buy medicines to supply a clinic, or that they would turn to NGOs for help.

At the same time, however, people across the board had very clear ideas about which authorities were supposed to deal with which kinds of problems. If participants almost never invoked the government in general as provider of their needs, they almost always named a specific government department responsible for resolving a range of problems, from conflicts over housing and land to teacher corruption. For example, almost everyone responded that if a problem arose over conflicting claims to a house, they would demand documentation from the other claimant and direct the problem to the Department of Housing. In the case of teachers demanding bribes from parents to allow their children to study, the most common answer was that they would speak to the director of the school, and if that didn't work they would speak to the local or provincial delegate for education. Similarly, in the situation of a maternity hospital that was surrounded by mines, most people had concrete suggestions as to whom to ask for help: usually the police or the local army unit, and in one case INAROI, the Angolan national agency responsible for land mine removal, was identified.

No one, however, said that the government was satisfying their needs, and when the question "Does the government succeed in satisfying your needs?" was posed directly, most of the answers were extremely cynical. The following are some typical replies.

> There is not support from the government, and they satisfy our needs when it suits them.[54]

> The government might do some things, but it is not enough. NGOs help us more.[55]

> Years ago, the government had the capacity to satisfy our needs, but today it doesn't and is considered incapable. Now we get some help from NGOs, who help us in the construction of schools, clinics, etc. That's how the people survive.[56]

> Local government doesn't meet the needs of our families. We only survive with the help of NGOs and the church.[57]

> The local authorities don't succeed in meeting anyone's needs because they are only interested in the well-being of themselves and their families.[58]

> The government hasn't helped the people in a long time. On the contrary, it is the people who help the government.[59]

Traditional authorities play an important role in meeting community needs and resolving conflicts at the local level. For most people contacted in Huambo and Bie, *sobas* are the first and most important line of authority at the community level. In general, *sobas* appear to be most influential in solving problems within the family and in disputes over land. People tended to distinguish between *sobas* and local administrators in terms of the origins of their authority:

> Government authorities receive orders from the government and resolve issues on the basis of government law. Traditional leaders work on the basis of traditional law; their orders come from tradition.[60]

Human Rights

A surprisingly high number of focus group participants, across age groups, region, and occupational and educational status, are familiar with the concept of "rights" and have a basic notion of the meaning of human rights.

> They are the rights of citizens.[61]

> Human rights means to treat others as human beings.[62]

> Respect for life, the rights of others.[63]

> To have the right to live, to do what you know how to do without the
> interference of anyone.[64]

> Human rights means that every Angolan citizen should feel free, should not
> be oppressed.[65]

> It is to feel at peace, and to have everything that you work for.[66]

> It is to walk freely without fear of stepping on land mines.[67]

Equally striking is the sense of the participants that human rights, as they define
them, are not systematically respected in Angola.

> Human rights is freedom of movement, personal liberty, in sum everything
> that no one has been able to achieve up until now.[68]

> Many die and are killed because these [human] rights have been taken
> away.[69]

> [Citing the fact that crimes are provoked by police and their commanders,
> and nothing is done about them, that there are no jobs for returning students
> from abroad, and so forth:] There are no human rights in Golfe.[70]

In addition to the conventionally defined concept of human rights, for the focus
group participants those rights also included socio-economic claims to housing,
employment, decent salaries, and education.

> Human rights are all of those rights that a person should have for their
> social, economic, and cultural well-being.[71]

> There are no human rights because we have trouble just getting enough to
> eat; we are very limited in financial terms.[72]

> It is to enjoy a little bit of all the riches of the country. Right now we are
> stagnating and no one enjoys the riches of the country and this is not human
> rights. Human rights is to have everything you need to live.[73]

One group pointed out that it is incorrect to think that human rights violations
are committed only by the police. All forms of deprivation – for example, absence
of electricity, water, salary – are violations of human rights. Asked what were the
most important individual rights, participants again highlighted freedom of expression and freedom of movement. The following were most frequently cited: freedom of movement, including free circulation between government and UNITA
zones and freedom to move about town and between their homes and fields without being harassed; socio-economic rights – work, decent salary, education, home,
health care; freedom of expression. One participant summed up freedom thus:

> To be able to leave here and go anywhere at all without fear and talk about
> the problems that afflict us without suffering reprisals.[74]

One of NDI's goals in this section was to ascertain whether people had a notion of rights being accompanied by duties and whether "freedom" also implied responsibilities. The answer was a resounding yes. Virtually everyone was careful to make the distinction between liberdade *(liberty) and* libertinagem *(libertinism). For the focus group participants, laws, and the duty to uphold them, made the difference between liberty and anarchy.*

> Sem leis, todos andam na libertinagem. *(Without laws, we are all just libertines.)*[75]

Most noted that liberty must also imply respect for others.

Law

For most people, laws exist to preserve order and to organize the life of the community.

> Without laws, the people do not advance . . . without laws no one has respect for anyone else.[76]

Once again, however, the participants expressed the sentiment that while this was true in the ideal, it was not true for them.

> The law exists, but it is not enforced.[77]

> The law is just, but it is not followed.[78]

Another recurring theme reemerged in this section, the notion of a double standard in terms of the way elites and ordinary people are treated. Earlier, someone noted that democracy was for the poor, meaning only ordinary people were subject to the limitations of the law and other democratic institutions. Here the same idea resurfaces.

> Law is for the poor.[79]

This group went on to give an example of a general, now an ambassador, who killed someone and never went to prison for it. Another group cited a similar example involving a local military commander and an ordinary citizen.

Most people know that the law comes from "the government." A slightly smaller number of people were able to identify the Parliament as the country's chief legislative organ, although given that most bills originate in the executive and must pass through the Council of Ministers before going to Parliament, perhaps the government, in the sense of the executive, is the most accurate answer. The minority responses were the most interesting in this section. The third most frequent answer to the question "Who makes the laws?" was "the police". Other answers included local administrators, *sobas,* and the courts. One person answered that the people make the laws.

The Constitution

As for the constitutional law, the numbers of people who had and had not heard of it were about evenly divided. Those who ventured an answer to its definition were for the most part correct in their perceptions. The following are sample answers.

The constitutional law is the guidelines drawn up by government which the people should follow; it is a statute or regulation that we can all follow.[80]

It's an order that establishes what must be done in a country.[81]

Others had heard of it but were disinterested or disgusted.

We have heard of the constitutional law but we don't pay any attention, we are not interested in it.[82]

It has no practical utility – they are always changing it.[83]

We have never heard or seen a copy of the constitutional law; I think it must not be widely distributed.[84]

Looking back, the 1997 focus groups provide a rough portrait of a country caught in limbo between a partial and increasingly fragile peace and a return to all-out war. They capture the prevailing sense of instability and record the widespread conviction that the war was not yet over. For most participants, the removal of barriers to movement and commerce throughout the country, which had consistently been erected by both sides, would be the most important sign that peace had truly arrived. The second most frequently cited indicator of war's end would be Jonas Savimbi's installation in the capital. Clearly, in the minds of most participants, the remaining barriers to peace were coming from the top, not from ordinary citizens.

Focus group participants demonstrated a high level of both general awareness and specific knowledge about key aspects of the peace process. They also understood some of the basic principles of both democracy and human rights. At the same time, they were keenly aware that these principles were systematically violated in Angola. Two fundamental liberties were identified over and over again as being both the most important democratic freedoms and the most difficult to exercise under current conditions: freedom of expression and free circulation of people and goods. It is important to note that while participants evinced strongly negative and cynical feelings toward government in general, these same negative feelings were not applied to democracy as such. Frustration was with the fact that "real" democracy was not practiced in Angola rather than with democracy as a system of government.

People were fairly well versed in how local authorities are supposed to help them resolve the problems they confront in their daily lives. Most, for example, were able to cite specific government departments designed to resolve particular problems. However, people also felt very sharply the government's inability or unwillingness to address their most pressing problems.

While participants had an intuitive notion of what government should and should not be doing, there was a much lower level of understanding about the law, particularly the constitutional law that sets out the basic rights and responsibilities of citizens as well as the formal limits on the state. In some areas, notably Uige and to a lesser extent Luanda, there is also a general perception that the police, the Angolan Armed Forces, and civil defense forces are the principal intermediaries between the people and the government. This perception is probably firmly rooted in local reality. Many people believe that the police themselves make the laws. Again, for all intents and purposes this may be true in some locations.

While the focus groups suggest that there was and is important work to be done to empower individual citizens and advocacy groups to make Angola's exemplary democratic constitution effective in practice, they also point up sharply drawn limits to what can be achieved from below, from outside the state and the formal political system. First, the matters of most concern to citizens are those over which they have the least control. Achieving a measure of political stability, freedom of movement, freedom of expression and association, all depend to a great extent on the ability of the government and UNITA to put a decisive end to their conflict. Ongoing low-intensity controversy, such as that which has marked the Angolan peace process from the outset, offers almost limitless opportunities for human rights violations and myriad extra-judicial activity under cover of "legitimate" defensive action. The most well-informed activist and courageous citizens are obviously no match for the combined repressive powers of a government and armed rebel movement at war with each other.

Second, the focus group results suggest that even after an effective political settlement is achieved between the warring parties, civic education efforts should focus not on ordinary citizens alone, but on civic education and training to improve the capacity of those parts of the Angolan government that come in direct contact with Angolan citizens, particularly on issues related to human and constitutional rights. These include the police, the armed forces, and local judicial and administrative officials. For many focus group participants, government is not a bewildering maze but a place with known departments that are meant to resolve specific problems. The difficulty is that when people go to these departments, when they interact with the individuals who represent government in their daily lives, their needs are not met and their faith in the system is continually eroded. This is demonstrated in the striking contrast between what people say about how they would resolve concrete problems and their attitude toward the government as a whole. They say they would go to a specific department, yet their expectations that their needs would be met there are close to zero.

How useful are these focus groups in helping us to understand the downward spiral away from a successful political settlement to Angola's long-running conflict? Do they provide important insights into the troubles with the Lusaka Protocol then looming large on the horizon? In conveying a sense of uncertainty and instability about the peace process, in insisting that the war was not yet over, they are certainly consistent with what was to come. But they are also important on another level – they reinforce the notion that there is a disconnect between those who are responsible for bringing about peace and structuring the new political system and the majority who must live according to its rules, and they highlight the yawning chasm between the stated goals of the Lusaka process – peace, national reconciliation, effective multiparty democracy – and reality.

Notes

1. Mutilados de guerra, male (hereafter M), 20–30, Kilombo, Huambo.
2. Youth, M, 17–25, Camussamba, Huambo.
3. Deslocados, M, 35–47, Luanda.
4. Students, female (hereafter F), 15–19, Cazenga.
5. Market women, 35–55, Kunge, Bie.
6. Community activists, M, 20–24, Golfe, Luanda.
7. Teachers, M/F, 26–37, Golfe, Luanda.
8. Students, M, 25–30, Kuito, Bie.
9. Men, 50–59, Operario, Luanda.
10. Community activists, M, 20–24, Golfe, Luanda.
11. Youth, F, 22–26, Golfe, Luanda.
12. Catequists, Chivela, Huambo.
13. Students, M, 25–35, Kuito, Bie.
14. Teachers, M, 25–35, Chinguar, Bie.
15. Women, 59+, Operario, Luanda.
16. War-disabled veterans, M, 30–59, Kilombo, Huambo.
17. Youth, F, 22–26, Golfe, Luanda.
18. Students, F, 16–18, Uige.
19. Deslocados, M, 45–59, Benfica, Luanda.
20. Students, F, 16–18, Cazenga, Luanda.
21. Youth, M, 19–25, Uige.
22. Students, M, 14–18, Uige.
23. War-disabled veterans, M, 20–30, Kilombo, Huambo.
24. Students, F, 16–18, Uige.
25. Students, F, Cazenga, Luanda.
26. Community activists, M, 20–25, Golfe, Luanda.
27. *ibid.*
28. *ibid.*
29. Women, 59+, Operario, Luanda.
30. Students, F, 16–18, Uige.
31. Demobilized soldiers, M, 19–32, Uige.
32. Employed men, 25–59, Golfe, Luanda.
33. Community activists, M, 20–24, Golfe, Luanda.
34. War-disabled soldiers/community leaders, M, 30–55, Kilombo, Huambo.
35. Deslocados, M, 45–59, Benfica, Luanda.

36. Community activists, M, 20–24, Golfe, Luanda.
37. Women, 59+, Operario, Luanda.
38. Teachers, M/F, 26–37, Golfe, Luanda.
39. Secondary school students, M, 25–35, Kuito, Bie.
40. Teachers, M/F, 26–37, Golfe, Luanda.
41. Students, F, 16–18, Cazenga, Luanda.
42. Youth, F, 22–26, Golfe, Luanda.
43. Community activists, M, 20–24, Golfe, Luanda.
44. *ibid.*
45. Students, F, 16–18, Uige.
46. Youth, M, 19–24, Uige.
47. Community activists, M, 20–24, Golfe, Luanda.
48. Deslocados, M, 45–55, Benfica, Luanda.
49. Youth, F, 15–19, Cazenga, Luanda.
50. Women, 59+, Operario, Luanda.
51. Community leaders, M, 30–55, Kilombo, Huambo.
52. Deslocados, M, 25–45, Benfica, Luanda.
53. Teachers, M/F, 26–37, Golfe, Luanda.
54. Students, F, 16–18, Cazenga, Luanda.
55. Students, F, 16–18, Uige.
56. Women, 59+, Operario, Luanda.
57. Youth, M, 18–20, Operario, Luanda.
58. Students, M, 25–35, Kuito, Bie.
59. Catechists, M/F, 25–40, Chivela, Huambo.
60. Women, 59+, Operario, Luanda.
61. Youth, M, 18–20, Operario, Luanda.
62. Women, 59+, Operario, Luanda.
63. Youth, M, 19–24, Uige.
64. Students, F, 16–18, Cazenga, Luanda.
65. Demobilized soldiers, M, 19–32, Uige.
66. War-disabled veterans, M, 30–59, Kilombo, Huambo.
67. *ibid.*
68. Community activists, M, 20–24, Golfe, Luanda.
69. Students, F, 16–18, Uige.
70. Teachers, M/F, 25–36, Golfe, Luanda.
71. Students, M, 25–35, Kuito, Bie.
72. Community leaders, M, 30–55, Kilombo, Huambo.
73. Demobilized soldiers, M, 20–36, Huambo.
74. Community activists, M, 20–24, Golfe, Luanda.
75. Students, F, 16–18, Uige.
76. Demobilized soldiers, M, 19–32, Uige.
77. Youth, F, 22–26, Golfe, Luanda.
78. Youth, M, 19–24, Uige.
79. Men of diverse labor status, 25–59, Golfe, Luanda.
80. Teachers, M, 25–35, Chinguar, Bie.
81. Students, F, 16–18, Cazenga, Luanda.
82. War-disabled soldiers, M, 30–54, Kilombo, Huambo.
83. Community activists, M, 20–24, Golfe, Luanda.
84. Students, M, 25–35, Kuito, Bie.

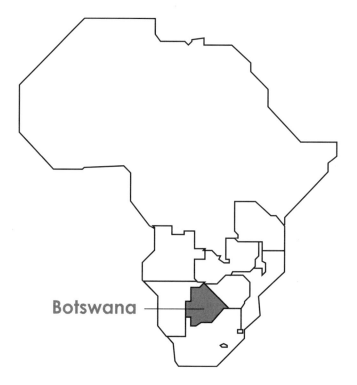

Botswana

Electoral Politics and Public Participation in Botswana

Patrick Molutsi and Tidimane Ntsabane

Botswana has been a multiparty democracy since its independence in 1966. The first multiparty election in which four political parties took part was held in March 1965. Since then elections in Botswana have been held every five years, namely, in 1969, 1974, 1979, 1984, 1989, and 1994. This year, 1999, is the eighth time general local and parliamentary elections are to be held. Botswana, unlike such countries in the Southern African Development Community (SADC) as Angola, Mozambique, Namibia, Tanzania, Zambia, and Zimbabwe, does not have a direct presidential election. The president comes automatically from the party with the majority of seats in the National Assembly.

After more than three decades of electoral and pluralist politics, Botswana has lessons to offer emergent democracies in the region and beyond. This essay focuses on the public opinions and perceptions of democracy in Botswana. The main source of evidence comes from a number of surveys conducted over the years by the University of Botswana– based Democracy Research Project (DRP). The surveys focused on awareness, knowledge, popular participation, and issues influencing party preference. They were first conducted in 1974 and subsequently in 1988, 1989, 1994, and most recently in April 1999. Several survey issues reveal much about the quality and depth of Botswana's democracy. The data cover, among others levels of popular participation, party affiliation, the electoral system, and the role of traditional political culture. The following sections provide an overview of debates and trends under each issue.

Dr Patrick Molutsi is Dean of the Faculty of Social Sciences, University of Botswana, Senior Lecturer and former Coordinator the University's Democracy Research Project for 5 years. A renowned writer in the areas of democracy and development in Botswana and southern Africa, he was a principal author of the SADC Good Governance and Human Development Report of 1999. Mr Tidimane Ntsabane is a lecturer in the Department of Sociology at the University of Botswana, having done postgraduate work at the University of Wisconsin-Madison. He is also a member of the University's Democracy, a multidisciplinary nonpartisan research group investigating the political life and institutions of Botswana.

Electoral Participation in the Past Three Decades

Generally, Botswana has enjoyed high levels of electoral participation. Except in the 1974 and 1984 elections, which recorded the lowest and second lowest voter turnouts — 33 percent and 58 percent, respectively — the average voter turnout for the other years was more than 65 percent.[1] The latter figures refer to turnout as defined by the number of people registered to vote versus those who actually vote. However, as Molutsi showed, when the number of eligible voters is used as the denominator, the voter turnout percentage in Botswana drops significantly to below 50 percent (see Table 1).[2]

Table 1

Election Statistics, 1965–1994

	1	2	3	4	5	6
Year	Potential no. of voters	No. of electorate registered	% of electorate registered	No. of electorate who voted	% of 4/1	% poll = 4/2
1965	243 365	188 950	78.0	140 789	58,0	74.0
1969	267 647	156 428	58.5	92 965*	34,7	59.4
1974	309 810	236 848	76.4	95 809*	30,9	40.5
1979	362 515	343 483	67.3	147 658	40,7	60.6
1984	416 996	293 571	70.4	227 756	54,6	77.6
1989	507 569	367 069	72.3	250 487	49,4	68.2
1994	609 000	370 356	60.8	281 931	46,3	76.1

* These figures include the registered voters from uncontested constituencies. We have treated the latter as if they all voted, which has inflated the poll percentage for 1969, 1974 and 1979. The actual poll percentages for these elections were 54.9; 31.2 and 58.4 respectively.

Interestingly, a recent survey of 171 countries across the world on electoral participation by IDEA showed that "overall participation in competitive elections across the globe rose steadily between 1945 and 1990.[3] According to IDEA, the number of voters who turned out to vote in each election between 1945 and 1950 represented 61 percent of the voting age population. This figure rose steadily to 62 percent in the 1950s, 65 percent in the 1960s, 67 percent in the 1970s, and 68 percent in the 1980s. IDEA observes, however, that by the beginning of the 1990s the figure had dropped to 64 percent because of rapid democratization in Eastern Europe and developing countries.

The question that needs an immediate answer is: Where does Botswana stand in this trend? After seven elections between 1965 and 1994 Botswana ranked 146th with an average voter turnout of 46.5 percent among the 171 countries. Compared with other African countries that had held two or more elections between 1945 and 1990, Botswana's voter turnout percentage was less than fourteen of those in the survey. These countries were Mauritius's 6 elections with 82.5 percent; Namibia, 2, with 80.4 percent; Comoros, 2, with 75.7 percent; Cape Verde, 2, with 75.6 percent; Madagascar, 4, with 72.5 percent; Togo, 4, with 69.3 percent; Lesotho, 3, with 65.2 percent; Benin, 2, with 60.1 percent; Zimbabwe, 5, with 58.8 percent; Cameroon, 3, with 56.3 percent; Gambia, 6, with 55.6 percent; Uganda, 3, with 50.6 percent; Nigeria, 3, with 47.6 percent; and Sierra Leone, 3, with 46.8 percent. Clearly, Botswana might be said to suffer from more entries than all these countries. However, considering the latest election alone, with a 44.5 percent voter turnout, Botswana still falls below that of Mauritius, Madagascar, Namibia, Togo, Algeria, Benin, Morocco, Zimbabwe, Tunisia, Lesotho, Cameroon, Gambia, Uganda, Nigeria, and Sierra Leone.

There must be some explanation for Botswana's apparent popular democracy on the one hand and low participation on the other. The results of the surveys suggest that the explanation may lie around issues of ignorance and low levels of literacy; low political mobilisation, control by the traditional leadership, and so on. The surveys demonstrated a great deal of ignorance of the system. Many voters are said to be reluctant to in every election because they had determined who should lead them at the very first election in 1965. In their view, you once elect or select a leader who remains in office until he or she dies. This tradition of choosing a chief is said to be an important factor limiting political participation in Botswana (BDP - Botswana Democratic Party 1974). Indeed, the close association between tribal chiefs and modern politics in Botswana has for many years caused this confusion. However, there is ignorance at another level: in the 1994 elections, for instance, there were reports of voters who displayed their party's slogan in the polling booth in spite of prior warning against doing so. Ignorance is also often revealed at two levels: (1) when voters give their registration cards to their candidates for "safe keeping" and (2) by the large percentage of spoiled votes. These issues are constantly discussed during Botswana elections.

Political participation in Botswana varies according to gender and age. More women than men tend to vote. Similarly, there tend to be proportionately fewer "young" votes. Tables 2 and 3 on page 52, based on the Democracy Research Project survey conducted on the eve of the 1989 elections, demonstrate these trends very clearly.

Table 2

RESPONDENTS BY GENDER AND CONSTITUENCY

Constituency	Sample		Constituency	
	Male	Female	Male	Female
Nkange	81(34.6)	145(62.0)	2563(29.4)	6153(70.6)
North East	84(35.9)	150(64.1)	3656(33.9)	7123(66.1)
Francistown	86(40.9)	127(59.1)	9037(53.6)	7813(46.4)
Selebi Phikwe	78(39.8)	118(59.9)	6492(55.3)	5256(44.7)
Mochudi	64(29.9)	147(68.7)	3675(42.4)	4990(57.6)
Lob/Barolong	97(47.1)	106(51.3)	7097(47.8)	7759(52.8)
Ngwaketse South	110(46.8)	119(50.6)	3523(37.7)	5825(62.3)
Kanye	85(37.5)	152(63.9)	5111(38.8)	8078(62.8)
Molepolole	99(39.6)	147(58.8)	4425(36.7)	7625(63.7)
Maun/Chobe	60(46.5)	66(51.2)	7501(46.0)	8802(62.8)
Kweneng West	106(42.7)	139(56.0)	3755(39.5)	5762(60.5)
Gaborone South	105(45.9)	122(51.7)	11505(61.4)	7221(38.6)
Gaborone North	109(45.4)	124(51.7)	6411(58.9)	4473(41.1)
TOTAL	1165(40.6)	1664(57.9)	74751(46.2)	86880(53.8)

Table 3

AGE DISTRIBUTION OF THE SAMPLE POPULATION

Constituency	Years				
	21– 30	31– 40	41– 50	51– 60	61– 70
Nkange	52(22.2)	64(27.4)	51(21.8)	28(12.0)	19(8.1)
North East	38(16.2)	58(24.8)	70(29.9)	29(12.4)	20(8.5)
Francistown	56(26.0)	64(29.8)	40(18.6)	27(12.6)	18(8.4)
S/Phikwe	58(29.4)	62(31.5)	54(27.4)	13(6.6)	3(1.5)
Mochudi	60(28.0)	39(18.2)	37(17.3)	19(8.9)	20(9.3)
Lob/Barolong	68(33.0)	59(28.6)	43(20.9)	21(10.2)	7(3.4)
Ngwaketse South	50(21.3)	65(27.7)	55(23.4)	24(10.2)	20(8.5)
Kanye	52(21.8)	69(29.0)	41(17.2)	29(12.2)	29(12.2)
Molepolole	55(22.0)	80(32.0)	55(22.0)	31(12.4)	15 (6.0)
Maun/Chobe	39(30.0)	36(27.9)	31(24.0)	11 (8.5)	5 (3.9)
Kweneng West	51(20.6)	71(28.6)	61(24.6)	20 (8.1)	16 (6.5)
Gaborone South	105(45.9)	62(27.1)	34(14.8)	17 (7.4)	5 (2.2)
Gaborone North	111(46.3)	56(23.3)	40(16.7)	15 (6.3)	7 (2.9
TOTAL	797(27.8)	785(27.3)	612(21.3)	284(9.9)	184(6.4)

Political Parties as Agents of Political Mobilisation

Political parties, as central institutions of electoral politics, are expected to organize the voters into registered party members. They are further expected to encourage the members to participate in political events, including elections. However, in Botswana, as in many developing countries, political parties remain weak and peripheral to mainstream politics. This is especially true of the opposition parties. Although they have elaborate constitutions which define party structure at the ward, constituency, regional, and national levels, Botswana parties are generally thin on the ground. Most of them have no offices, even at national headquarters. They operate from the private houses of some of their leaders. Only the ruling Botswana Democratic Party (BDP) and the main opposition, Botswana National Front (BNF), had a few offices across the country during the 1994 elections.

Currently, the political parties have very few registered members. None of the parties, including the wealthy BDP, can provide data on the size of its membership. In general, ward, constituency, and regional committees are set up only in an election year or in a year preceding an election. Various reasons have been advanced for low party membership. Literature has generally pointed to the lack of the financial and human resources required to develop political parties into living organs of democracy. Many parties have neither full-time employees nor vehicles they can use during campaigns, a situation that has enabled wealthy individuals to buy their way into political parties. Other observations relate to the generally low level of popular participation in Botswana organisations. Nongovernmental organisations, for example, the trade unions, women's organisations, youth organisations, and so forth, have generally low membership. The culture of low voluntary participation in Botswana's population may be a reaction to the colonial experience during which people were generally coerced by chiefs into participating in community projects.[4]

Finally, the weakness of political parties may derive from their traditional campaign strategies. Most parties still use the "freedom square" as their main strategy for attracting supporters. The more intensive house-to-house campaign strategy is less used. Structured and targeted meetings in community halls, for example, remain limited. In general, the political party is still not central to effective political mobilisation in Botswana.

The Effects of the Electoral System

Since independence, Botswana has practiced the first-past-the-post (FPTP) single member constituency electoral system. The FPTP has served the ruling party very well, as Table 4 illustrates. The results show that, on the whole, the opposition

Table 4

PERCENTAGE OF POPULAR VOTE BY PARTY, 1965–1994

Party	1965	1969	1974	1979	1984	1989	1994
BDP	80,4	68,4	76,6	75,2	67,9	64,7	54,5
BNF	-	13,5	11,5	12,9	20,5	26,9	37,3
BPP	14,2	12,1	6,6	7,4	6,6	4,5	4,1
BIP/IFP	4,6	6,0	4,8	4,3	3,0	2,4	3,6
Others	0,8	0,0	0,5	0,2	2,0	1,5	0,5

Table 4a

NUMBER AND PERCENTAGE OF NATIONAL ASSEMBLY SEATS
HELD BY POLITICAL PARTIES, 1965–1984

Party	1965	1969	1974	1979	1984	1989	1994
BDP	28	24	27	29	28	31	31
BNF	-	3	2	2	5	3	13
BPP	3	3	2	1	1	0	0
BIP/IFP	0	1	1	0	0	0	0
Total	31	31	32	34	34	34	44

% of seats

Party	1965	1969	1974	1979	1984	1989	1994
BDP	90	77	84	91	82	91	67,5
BNF	-	10	6,5	6	15	9	32,5
BPP	10	10	6,5	3	3	0	0,0
BIP	0	3	3	0	0	0	0,0

parties, which still command less than 50 percent of the popular vote, could nevertheless have obtained a somewhat better representation under a proportional representation electoral regime than the FPTP simple majority system. The electoral regime has therefore not helped to strengthen political parties. Instead, it has strengthened the already dominant ruling party.

Political parties have reacted to poor performance in elections by claiming that cheating has taken place. Throughout the 1970s and 1980s the opposition parties raised two issues relating to elections. First they argued that the elections had to be administered by a body that is not a government department. In 1988, the government responded to this demand by instituting a referendum, which resulted in the removal of the office of elections from the Office of the President to a separate one headed by a supervise of elections. The move, however was considered inadequate by the opposition parties, which continued to advocate for an independent electoral commission. This was finally established in 1998.

The second electoral issue over the years concerned lowering the voting age from twenty- one to eighteen years. The opposition parties, especially the BNF, which tended to attract young people to its rallies, felt that they could benefit more from 10 to 12 percent potential voters in the eighteen to twenty age group, which the twenty-one age limit excluded. The DRP survey conducted in 1989 showed the BNF controlling some 36 percent of the people aged twenty-one to thirty years compared with the BDP's 22.9 percent and the Botswana People's Party's 19 percent. The BNF believed that the statistics presented in Table 5 could be extrapolated into the lower age brackets. The lower voting age was only achieved in 1998, so its impact on party support will not be seen until the 1999 election.

Table 5

PARTY SUPPORT BY AGE

Age	Party							
	None		BDP		BNF		BPP	
	Number	Per cent	Number	Per cent	Number	Per cent	Number	Per cent
21– 30	51	37.2	334	22.9	270	36.8	39	19.0
31– 40	36	26.3	399	27.4	214	29.2	47	22.9
41– 50	23	16.8	354	24.3	127	17.3	51	24.9
51– 60	11	8.0	160	11.0	54	7.4	32	15.6
61– 70	5	3.6	109	7.5	32	4.4	21	10.2
71+	4	2.9	65	4.5	20	2.7	10	4.9
TOTAL	137	100.0	1457	100.0	733	100.0	205	100.0

The one issue which has still not gained popularity, especially within the ruling party circles, is changing the electoral regime. The opposition parties have raised it, but not as strongly as the previous two issues. This might, however, become a major issue for debate, given that both Namibia and South Africa, as neighbours of Botswana, have opted for some type of proportional representation. Similarly, the experience of Lesotho, where under the FPTP one party was able to win all the seats in the 1997, elections might signal the trend for change to proportional representation in the rest of the SADC countries.

The Role of Chieftaincy in Traditional Leadership

In Botswana, perhaps more than elsewhere, there is a very strong relationship between traditional chiefs and modern politics. The first president who was the son of a chief got his overwhelming support from his father's ethnic group and other main Tswana chiefdoms. The opposition BPP, which had been in existence earlier and was better connected regionally and internationally, lost the first election to the newcomer Botswana Democratic Party, whose leaders were generally from the conservative lower middle class. Different writers have largely attributed the BDP's popularity to the royalty of its founder and president, the late Sir Seretse Khama. Indeed, the recruitment of his son, who is the ordained chief of Bangwato into the BDP in 1998 and his straight move to the post of vice president of Botswana, says a lot about how parties have exploited the traditional element in politics. In 1969 the Botswana National Front also succeeded in wooing the late paramount chief of Bangwaketse, Bathoen II Gaseitsiwe. Again, Bathoen was able to win three seats for his party from his part of the country.

The negative aspects of chieftaincy, however, arise from non-chiefs who try either to stand against someone royal or against a party that enjoys the chief's sympathy. Many candidates have lost elections in this manner. Thus, except in urban areas where voters have reached a higher level of maturity and confidence, chieftaincy is a major factor in political mobilisation and public opinion in Botswana.

The Political Culture

Traditional leadership and party leadership are factors in political mobilisation within Botswana's complex political culture. Traditionally, political power, based on age, was centred around a person's social standing. Minorities, women, and young people were not expected to be leaders or to contest for leadership positions. This culture is still strong and influences the election of those who win political and civic offices. Members of political parties, nongovernmental organisations, and village and ward development committees know that it is much harder to be elected if one is of, say, San origin, a woman, or a youth. Indeed, the most recent party primary elections by the BDP and the Botswana Congress Party (BCP) returned 95 percent of the incumbents, who were predominantly elderly men.

Conclusion

The foregoing discussion of trends in Botswana politics relative to participation and public opinion says a lot about the level of democratisation in Botswana. It points to the following:

1. The need to develop a new political culture through promotion of merit and ability rather than social status.
2. The need to dislodge chieftaincy from politics.

3. The need to give financial support to political parties to enable them to democratise themselves and society in general.
4. The need to introduce a more rigorous political education.
5. The need to develop specific strategies to help women, youth, and ethnic minorities make a breakthrough in politics.

Notes

1. See Molutsi 1997. For full citation - contact author.
2. *ibid.*
3. IDEA, *Voter Turnout from 1945 to 1997: A Global Report on Political Participation* (Stockholm: Information Services, 1998).
4. M. Benson, *Tshekedi Khama* (London: Faber and Faber, 1960).

Bibliography

Benson, M. *Tshekedi Khama*. London: Faber and Faber, 1960.
Edge, W., and M. Lekorwe, eds. *Botswana: Politics and Society*. Pretoria: J. L. Van Schaik, 1998.
IDEA. *Voter Turnout from 1945 to 1997: A Global Report on Political Participation*. Stockholm: Information Services, 1998.
Holm, J., and P. Molutsi, eds. *Democracy in Botswana*. Athens: Ohio University Press, 1989.
Molutsi, P., and B. Tsie. "Political Mobilisation and Strategies for Elections: A Report of the Study of the 1989 Botswana Elections." University of Botswana, Democracy Research Project, unpublished report, 1989.

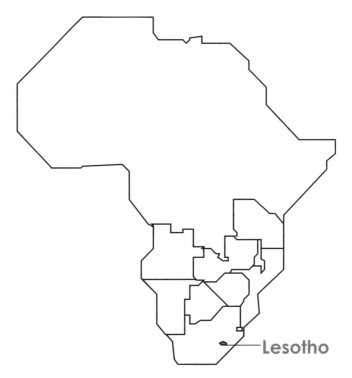

Lesotho

Will Lesotho Become a Democracy?

Chris Homan
Eric Happel

With a successful second election in May 1998, many believed that Lesotho had solidified its membership among southern Africa's nascent democracies. With post-election violence and intervening SADC troops, the distinction was lost. Lesotho's path to democracy has often been difficult and uncertain. The impoverished, landlocked nation gained independence from Great Britain in 1966 and adopted a constitutional monarchy with a Westminster-style parliamentary system of government. However, democratic rule ended in 1970 when the prime minister and Basutholand National Party (BNP) leader, Chief Leabua Jonathan, nullified the first post-independence election results. The ensuing two decades were marked by political instability, repression, and autocratic rule, which included several years of military rule following a 1986 coup.

With a parliamentary election, democratic civilian government eventually returned to Lesotho in 1993. The Basutholand Congress Party (BCP) won all 65 seats from the single-member districts. Following opposition allegations of fraud and mismanagement surrounding the 1993 election, many Basotho,[1] and particularly NGOs, advocated for a new independent electoral body. The government of Lesotho responded in April 1997 with legislation establishing an Independent Electoral Commission (IEC) to take charge of the country's election process. The IEC's responsibilities would include voter registration and education, election preparation, and regular consultations with political parties.

Amidst this positive development, political uncertainty mounted in June 1997, when Prime Minister Ntsu Mokhehle formed the new Lesotho Congress Democracy (LCD) party following a year of mounting internal differences within the BCP. Many BCP members and opposition parties questioned the move's

Chris Homan, a program officer at the National Democratic Institute for International Affairs, was a member of the international observer delegation organized by the United Nations Development Program. Eric Happel, a program officer at the National Democratic Institute for International Affairs, was posted in Lesotho for six months during its 1998 national election. Lhatoya Reed assisted in the editing of this article.

constitutionality and attempted to disrupt parliamentary proceedings. The legislature continued to meet until February 1998 when the government called for its dissolution in preparation for the May elections.

With the September 1997 swearing in of the IEC, the government of Lesotho took an important step in effective election administration and restoring voter confidence. The IEC faced a formidable task preparing every aspect of the election, with its mandate further complicated by a reduced voter age, from 21 to 18, and 15 new parliamentary constituencies. Despite time constraints and relative inexperience, the IEC, with international assistance, administered an effective national election in May 1998.

More than 832,000 of approximately 1.15 million eligible voters registered, and more than 72 per cent of those registered turned out to vote on election day. The ruling LCD party won 79 seats (60 per cent of the national vote), and the BNP captured one seat (25 per cent of the national vote). The other 10 parties and 28 independent candidates captured 15 per cent of the national vote, but did not win any seats. Over 400 international and domestic observers said the election met international standards and reflected public sentiment.

With an effectively administered election and a seemingly peaceful transfer of power, many believed Lesotho's democracy had passed the critical test of a second election. However, over the next several months opposition allegations of electoral fraud led to mounting political unrest. An investigating SADC delegation, while finding that administrative errors had occurred,[2] did not find evidence of fraud. Shortly after release of the delegation's report in September, SADC troops intervened at the request of the Lesotho government to stem a mounting military mutiny and civil unrest. The ensuing days were marred by widespread looting and arson, resulting in the destruction of much of the capital's central business district. With tensions high, SADC representatives negotiated an agreement between the ruling and opposition parties that called for another national election in 15 to 18 months and an interim body, the Interim Political Authority (IPA), to oversee the process. Each political party would have two representatives on this body.

Despite a successfully administered election, events in Lesotho are a reminder of the fragility of democratic experiments. As Lesotho embarks on yet another attempt to "get it right," there are significant lessons to be learned from the 1997–1998 election process. This article explores a few that are central to the process.

Were the People Ready to Vote?

The period between the 1993 and 1998 elections was marked by mounting public frustration that Lesotho's return to democracy was not rapidly solving economic and development needs. Basotho voters were caught between hope and despondency. They saw small changes around them, but their lives remained a struggle against hunger and for education of their children. They were fighting against the sentiment that voting would never bring the desired difference to their lives. Comments made in the 1997 focus group study of the NDIincluded: "they forgot about us;" "they do nothing for us;" "there is no difference because of the vote."[3]

Low morale and disillusionment with the impact of voting was the biggest threat to voter participation in the 1998 election. However, several notable events helped create renewed interest and trust in the upcoming election, the most important being the establishment of an independent electoral body. Only a year before the election, few would have predicted the strong public turnout both to register and to vote.

Cooperative Development of the Independent Electoral Commission

Attempts to develop a democracy in Lesotho have constantly been reversed over the last 30 years. The prospect of establishing democratic institutions and practices are, at best, uncertain. The 1993 election results were challenged by opposition allegations of fraud and inadequate administration. Public frustration and lack of confidence in the political process was in part related to these issues.

Amidst these sentiments, in 1995 Lesotho's NGO community conducted a national dialogue that addressed many civil society concerns, including election administration. Participants included representatives from NGOs, churches, opposition parties, and the government. One of the most significant ensuing recommendations was to create an independent electoral authority. Later in 1997, the Lesotho government passed legislation establishing the Independent Electoral Commission (IEC), as well as a new electoral law.

Over the following year, the government of Lesotho worked with political parties to nominate commissioners to the IEC. Candidates were vetted through the second chamber of Parliament as well as the king. Three candidates were eventually chosen and sworn into office in September 1997. Despite its relative inexperience, the short period before the election, and serious logistical challenges, the IEC conducted the May 1998 national election in an effective, professional, and credible manner. The election earned praise from more than 140 international observers and the majority of domestic observers.

The collaborative manner in which the IEC was established is noteworthy and serves as a model for addressing election system frustrations that contributed to recent unrest. NGOs, government, the monarch, political parties, and other members of civil society all worked together toward a common objective. The inclusiveness of the process added credibility to the final product and served as a model for addressing difficult public policy matters. Given the importance of establishing a neutral independent body, the process of creating it was particularly crucial. Unfortunately, despite these efforts and those of the IEC to work neutrally with all parties, it often fell victim to government intransigence and opposition criticism.

Delimitation of Boundaries

Lesotho's 1993 national election included 65 constituencies. With the decrease in the voter age to 18, several thousand additional electors were expected in 1998. In anticipation, Lesotho amended its electoral law to provide for 80 constituencies. One of the IEC's first tasks was delimitation of these new boundaries into constituencies with a nearly equal number of voting age citizens. The IEC conducted this task in January and February 1998. The process was open to public and political party involvement.

The number of voters per constituency was evenly matched, with one exception. An urban setting known as Stadium Area had almost twice as many registered voters as the other constituencies. This occurred because several smaller villages nearby mistakenly used Stadium Area as their village name during the registration period. The preliminary voter list was complete by the time the problem was discovered, and reregistration would have been required to correct it. Because the error and possible solutions were discussed with the parties, few later expressed serious concern. The IEC recognized in retrospect the importance of finalizing delimitation before voter registration.

Voter Registration and the Voter List

Voter eligibility requires Lesotho citizenship and attainment of the age of 18 prior to election day. Disqualifying criteria include conviction of crimes punishable by death under Lesotho law and certain other crimes and expression of obedience to any foreign power. Registration is mandatory under Lesotho law, although voting is not. Once registration is closed, a preliminary voters' list must be displayed for a period of 15 days. During this time, registered voters are expected to check the voters' list for accuracy and report errors to the IEC. Finally, once corrections have been made and objections processed, a final voters' list, which must go to each political party and to the polling site, is printed. Each polling site is issued the section of the final list appropriate to that polling district. To help with the process, the IEC hired the British firm De La Rue to provide registration materials and train registration supervisors in December 1997.

Registration of electors began on 5 January and concluded on 10 March, 1998. While the registration process was only seven weeks long, approximately 840,000 of an estimated 1.1 million eligible voters registered, a success largely attributable to an effective process established by the IEC. The process went smoothly, with relatively few complaints reported to the IEC. Upon arrival at the registration sight, a potential voter would first have his or her identity verified by the village chief or elder. Temporary registration staff processed the application and provided a voter card that included a picture and signature or thumb print.

There was a notable lack of registration opportunities for those working outside of Lesotho, which drew criticism from the international community. A sizable number of Basotho work in the South African mines, but could register only by returning to a home village. Surprisingly, political parties drew little attention to this shortcoming. It is not known how many mineworkers were able to return to Lesotho to register.

The next steps, compilation and verification of the voters' list, encountered a number of difficulties. For various administrative and political reasons, computers donated by South Africa arrived late. The preliminary voters' list was completed and displayed for verification on 13 April. The list was displayed for six days at each registration sight, although the election law calls for 15 days. The list was 20,000 pages long and required almost 14 hours to print, making it nearly impossible to provide hard copies to all the political parties as the parties requested. The IEC said it would provide the preliminary list to any party that provided 20 disks. Only one party provided the disks and received the list, an issue that later came under scrutiny during the post-election investigation.

It was later discovered that the preliminary list had several flaws, including duplication, underage electors, incorrect addresses, and what seemed to be an implausible distribution of birth dates. Once the approximately 20,000 reported errors were corrected in the database, several other steps were taken to purge any remaining mistakes. Underage and duplicate voters were identified and removed. Mistakes found after the printing of the final list were corrected in the supplementary list, which was printed and distributed shortly before the election. Nonetheless, the list remained a source of contention before and after the election.

These problems can be traced to several factors. First, the data capture occurred over a brief four-week period. The IEC hired 180 clerks to work in three consecutive shifts for almost 28 days. While the database software was designed to force the clerks to enter essential information twice, the unfamiliarity of the process and rapid pace undoubtedly allowed for some errors. Furthermore, due in large part to time constraints, the registration staff received only minimal training, in turn creating additional risk of error.

There were also some problems with the data supplied by registrants. Many Basotho told the IEC that they did not know their exact date of birth, a common occurrence in African cultures. In these cases, a dummy date was used, for example, 1 January. This decision likely led to later opposition complaints of implausible birthdate distribution.

Even though Lesotho does not maintain an official village list, polling districts were based on village names. Some registrants would identify a particular village by the name of the largest family, while others would group the same village with its adjacent neighbor. This discrepancy created confusion throughout the election process, including polling day.

Finally, international consultants were brought in at three different points in the election process. The first consultant departed soon after the preliminary list was printed. The second overlapped with the first for two days and left shortly before the final list was printed. The last overlapped with the second for two days and stayed until after the election. While each consultant was skilled and helpful, the turnover created a lack of continuity in skills and knowledge transfer for the IEC and its staff.

Registration of Political Parties and Independent Candidates

According to the election law, only registered political parties could endorse candidates. Each political party also had to submit a petition with at least 500 signatures and register a party symbol clearly distinguishable from others. Twelve parties eventually registered and endorsed candidates. Twenty-eight independent candidates also registered and either selected their own symbol or allowed the director of elections to assign one.

Several political parties charged that other parties submitted fraudulent registration petitions, specifically alleging duplicate signatures for multiple parties. This allegation may have been true, given that election results indicated that some of the smaller parties received fewer than 500 votes. While there is nothing in the election law prohibiting the practice, the IEC has suggested that multiple endorsements be prohibited in the future.

Nomination of Candidates

According to Lesotho's election law, nomination may begin once the election period commences and closes between 30 and 60 days before polling day. The official nomination occurs in each constituency. When the nomination process is completed, the returning officer from each constituency notifies the director of elections.

Nominations officially closed on 20 April, 1998. As is the case in most elections that are triggered by the dissolution of Parliament, almost all candidates were nominated on 20 April. A total of 438 candidates were nominated in the 80 constituencies. On 19 and 20 April and several days after the election, the IEC received several interim court orders related to internal political party disagreements about their own nominees in six constituencies. Once the ballot papers, being printed in Canada at the time, arrived in Lesotho, IEC staff had to paste stickers with corrected nominees on affected ballots. In Constituency 6, the matter was not resolved until four days before the election and would have caused a further change to the ballot in this constituency. However, it was too late to correct and redistribute that area's ballots. Fortunately, this relatively minor case involved only one individual challenging his own party over the nomination of its candidate.

Polling Districts and Polling Stations

The election law stipulates that each constituency be divided into polling districts with a similar number of voters. Within each polling district, the polling stations were created according to the number of electors in that area. The 80 constituencies were divided into approximately 1,000 polling districts with 2,300 polling stations, with a maximum number of 500 registered voters per polling station.

In Lesotho, several challenges made the division of polling districts and stations an extremely difficult task. First, registration and delimitation occurred simultaneously. Therefore, delimitation set up certain boundaries while registration officers unknowingly may have grouped certain villages that straddled two constituencies. Second, some registration officers chose to group several villages under one name while others at adjacent registration sites chose to use less inclusive, smaller village names. Third, returning officers had to find appropriate polling sites within the polling districts. However, the short time between the creation of the voter list and polling day made it difficult to anticipate how to allocate the polling stations within a district based on numbers. Until the week before the election, returning officers were coming to the IEC to move, merge, or create polling stations. In fact, on election day, some polling stations were moved, merged, or created owing to immediate logistical problems. Lesotho's poor communications infrastructure and mountainous terrain lengthened and complicated this process. The IEC often had to send a messenger to the remote returning officers to ask them to come to IEC headquarters to clarify certain polling divisions or polling stations. Additionally, several returning officers, unfamiliar with computer-generated lists of polling divisions and stations, did not recognize the discrepancies until they sat with IEC officials and were questioned about the polling divisions and stations.

Despite these difficulties, there were very few reports on election day of names being at incorrect villages or villages incorrectly allocated to polling districts. This process was eased by displays of 80 sets of IEC posters explaining where each village should vote.

Ballot Papers

The IEC carefully followed bidding procedures to procure ballot materials and stated that all necessary steps were taken to ensure the quality and security of the ballot papers. The selected firm, Code Incorporated of Canada, delivered all ballot papers correctly and on time.

In Lesotho, the quality and security of the ballot paper were important issues. Following the 1993 election, there were rumors that magic paper allowed ballot marks to be switched from one party to another. Similar rumors were again circulated in 1998.

Voter Education

Lesotho is one of the most literate countries in Africa. According to a study conducted by the Lesotho Distance Learning Center in 1995, 70 per cent of the women and 46 per cent of the men had basic indigenous language literacy skills. However, people do not bring these skills to work, inasmuch as reading habits have not been developed.[4] Therefore, when potential voters were polled regarding their preferences for receiving information about the election, they were unanimous in their opinion about the need for systemic process messages contained in photographs and diagrams with limited texts.[5] In addition, voters were very clear about those who should be conveyers of the message and the style of the presentation. They wanted a "neutral" agency to conduct interactive workshops with direct personal contact.[6]

The election law delegated voter education to the Independent Election Commission, whose publicity and training office was composed of three staff members. From February to April 1998, the IEC worked with the NDI, United Nations Development Program, and the United Nations Educational, Scientific, and Cultural Organisation to train area electoral officers, returning officers, and presiding officers. The small IEC training staff, under significant time constraints, administered a limited program to educate voters about registration and election day procedures and the importance of participating in both.

Technical assistance to NGOs from NDI, Irish Aid, the Commonwealth, and others complemented the IEC's voter education efforts. However, the NGO community failed to fully implement many of its planned voter education activities. Many shortcomings were addressed by international technical assistance from NDI and the Commonwealth. While many workshops and community gatherings (*pitsos*) were conducted, significantly more time and effort were needed to reach a greater percentage of the population.

In addition to holding voter education workshops, the IEC worked closely with NDI and the Commonwealth to produce a large number of training and voter education materials to distribute to the broader population. The IEC provided training materials to the NGO community as well as supplemental manuals to electoral officers, returning officers, political party candidates, presiding officers, and party agents. The IEC also provided materials to the general public almost exclusively in Sesotho, including three tabloid newspapers and 100,000 pamphlets on each of the following topics: registration, the campaign period and inspection of the voter list, and polling day. The IEC further produced and distributed approximately 10,000 of each of the following ten posters: description of the IEC; how to register; where to register; ten commandments for voters; tolerance of others' views; how to inspect the voters' list; how to choose a candidate; how to cast a vote; the secrecy of the vote; and announcements on where and when to vote as well as who the candidates were. Three different pamphlets were printed: how to register (10,000); how to choose a candidate (50,000); and how to vote (100,000).

The IEC used an effective distribution method for these materials. The country's ten area electoral officers would come to IEC headquarters at least once each week for regular meetings and to collect new voter education materials. All the materials were in turn delivered to the returning officers who distributed them within their respective constituencies. Election observers reported seeing the voter education materials throughout the country.

The IEC also used government-owned Radio Lesotho, which reaches most of the country, to educate voters. The station ran several public service announcements indicating when to register, when to inspect the voter list, and when to vote. It also broadcast several interviews and call-in programs with IEC personnel, members of political parties, and government officials. The station worked with the IEC to allocate equal time to each registered political party, including the government party. The IEC also hired a local production company, Liatla Productions, to produce ten dramas and ten documentaries on several different election-related topics. Because of its reach and popular appeal, radio was one of the most effective voter education mediums in Lesotho.

Lesotho's NGO community conducted numerous voter education activities. Organisations held voter education workshops, produced materials, and led the country's first candidate forums. The Lesotho Council for Nongovernmental Organisations (LCN), an umbrella organisation of NGOs, distributed funds from an Irish Aid grant to approximately 12 member NGOs to conduct voter education activities as well as participate in election observation. With NDI's assistance, the NGOs began with a workshop to discuss how each would approach voter education. Consequently, with the member NGOs, the LCN created a voter education plan that was to cover most of the country, using workshops and community groups as the principal medium for education as well as a plan to deploy national observers. The LCN produced several materials including two posters, two pamphlets, and a comprehensive manual for domestic observers. It should be noted that several organisations did not adhere to original plans and as a consequence many areas were not covered by the NGOs. Still, the NGOs' contribution was significant. Through their efforts and those of the IEC, many people in the country did receive sufficient voter education as indicated by the relatively large number of registered voters as well as the 72 per cent voter turnout on election day. Another indication of the effectiveness of voter education efforts was the small number of spoiled ballots, estimated to be less than one per cent.

Logistics

Each of Lesotho's ten administrative districts had its own warehouse for storage of election-day equipment, with the exception of Maseru, which used the primary IEC warehouse. The district warehouses were government-owned buildings that returned to government use after the election. Because Lesotho is a mountainous country, it was necessary to distribute as much of the polling-day equipment to the districts before election day as possible. This included items such as empty ballot boxes, polling booths, and tents to be used for polling stations.

In addition to these larger items, each polling station received a general polling kit and a security kit. Both kits, packed at IEC headquarters, were delivered one to three days before election day. Polling station kits included all the standard, nonsensitive items, including forms, pencils, envelopes, stamp pads, and lanterns. The security kits included all the sensitive materials such as ballot papers, voter lists, indelible ink, official envelopes, stamps for the ballot papers, and padlock seals for the ballot boxes. In remote areas, some materials had to be delivered by helicopter. In all areas, the materials were delivered to the responsible IEC staff members.

Absentee Voting

The election law provided absentee voting for public officers employed in other countries and their dependents, defense and police officials, candidates and their agents, and IEC officials. One polling station was set up in each constituency for absentee voters and returning officers served as the presiding officers. On 19 May, absentee voters were required to vote in their home constituency or Maseru, where a special polling station was set up for any absentee voter. These ballots were kept separately under guard and eventually sent to the respective constituencies on 22 May. The absentee ballot papers were sent to a polling station in each constituency and intermixed with those cast at that particular station. A total of 9,386 registered voters applied and were accepted as absentee voters. Of this number, 7,477 actually cast absentee votes.

Absentee voting was not without controversy. The national observers complained to the IEC that they were not included as eligible to vote in absentia. Several drivers of the international and national observers made similar complaints.

Election Day

Polling
Despite several administrative mistakes, international and national observers noted that election day was peaceful and well managed. The overwhelming majority of

the more than 2,300 polling stations opened on time and operated without incident. Empty ballot boxes were shown to the crowd and party agents before voting began. In the morning and early afternoon, many stations experienced long lines and a slow polling process. Nevertheless, the public exercised tremendous patience and those in line by closing time were allowed to vote in accordance with the election law. At least one party agent was present at each polling station, with agents from at least the three major political parties at many sites.

Despite Lesotho's mountainous terrain and underdeveloped infrastructure, the majority of difficulties were dealt with in an appropriate and timely manner. Often radio was used to reach polling staff. For example, difficulties included initial confusion about whether voters could use their own pens or pencils, delayed opening of some polling stations, minor errors on the voter lists, a few improperly sealed ballot boxes, and in some cases, a shortage of supplies. In a few isolated instances, polling sites did not conduct voting until the following day. Also, the balloting procedure was unnecessarily cumbersome: the voter received a ballot paper with one of two numbered stubs removed, marked the ballot, folded it, returned it to the polling official to remove the matching stub, and then placed the ballot in the box. However, the majority of the polling staff followed proper training. No pattern of intentional misconduct was evident, and it was deemed by observers that none of the shortcomings undermined the integrity of the election.

The Ballot Count
The initial vote count took place in each polling station immediately after closing. Ballots were counted in full view of polling staff, party agents, and observers. Upon completion of the count and agreement on the results, the ballots were placed in a special envelope, and polling staff and party agents both signed across its seal. The results were similarly logged and approved by signature on specific "A45" forms. These sealed envelopes and accompanying forms were immediately delivered to that constituency's returning officer who in turn filled out the "A47" form which tabulated all the A45 forms from a given constituency. Some errors occurred because polling staff sealed A45 forms inside the envelopes containing the ballots. This administrative error later explained why some envelopes had been opened and resealed or why some A45 forms were "missing," when they were in fact still in the ballot envelopes.

During the course of the SADC investigation, it became clear that there were some discrepancies between the A45 and A47 forms. For further explanation, see "SADC Investigation" below.

Result Reporting
The night of the election, some of the constituencies closest to Maseru compiled all their polling station results. The returning officers then provided IEC headquarters with results, the timeliness depending on access to

telephones and location. As soon as results were submitted, the IEC reported the pre-liminary numbers over the radio. By the end of the following day, most of the results had been reported. However, due to the remoteness of some areas and the slowness of some of the counts, it took four days for the remaining constituencies to report to headquarters.[7] Actual ballots and polling station materials were stored in each district and brought to the Maseru headquarters over the two months following the election.

Observers
Lesotho election law allows for both long-term and short-term election observers. Under this law, the IEC invited several countries as well as international and national organisations to observe the election.

Lesotho's election drew significant international and national attention from those hoping to observe the event. More than 140 short-term international observers were organized under the auspices of the United Nations Development Program. A number of countries and organisations, including the Commonwealth and Ireland, also contributed long-term observers. An additional 400 national observers, including members of NGOs and churches, were deployed throughout the country. Most of the national observers were organized and deployed by the Lesotho Council of Nongovernmental Organisations. The international and domestic observers re-leased a joint statement that, while noting minor administrative and logistical errors, praised the election as meeting international standards. Several international organisations, including SADC and the Commonwealth, also released independent statements applauding the election.

On 24 May, the joint election observer group's statement was released after some controversy. The plan was to develop the statement over two sessions and release it to the press at a third. The first session served for two representatives of each country or organisation to draft the statement. At the next session, all observers were to meet to approve the statement. However, members of the press arrived during the second session and were permitted inside. In a discussion about the terms used to describe the election, SADC members, who had not attended the first session, strongly recommended that the words *free* and *fair* replace "according to international standards" in the draft statement. A discussion ensued in which some observers worried that "free and fair" was too ambiguous. Some in the media mistakenly understood this to be an argument over the nature of the election as opposed to a disagreement about semantics.

Post-Election

The Immediate Post-Election Environment
Opposition protests alleging electoral fraud began immediately after the election and led to mounting political unrest over the next several months. In early June,

largely peaceful opposition supporters held rallies in the streets protesting the election results. Opposition parties also lodged approximately 20 formal complaints with the Independent Electoral Commission and pursued some complaints further through the courts. To support their case, they hired a South African auditing firm to investigate the preliminary voter list and several other matters. The court cited administrative errors that the IEC had committed, but nothing serious enough to doubt the election results. After the opposition parties lost their post-election court case, street protests became more frequent and disruptive.

On 5 August, a substantial protest closed much of the capital. Thousands of angry opposition supporters crowded the streets and began a vigil at the king's palace that lasted for more than two months. The supporters wanted the king to dissolve Parliament and call for a new election. In the second week of August, the protests grew increasingly obstreperous and all shops on the main road in Maseru closed. Five opposition and ruling party supporters were killed in August clashes.

The SADC Investigation into Allegations of Post-Election Fraud

South African Deputy President Thabo Mbeki went to Lesotho on 11 August to help resolve the growing discontent. During his one-day visit, he met with the opposition and the ruling party as well as the IEC. According to Mbeki's statement following the meetings, they all agreed to allow a SADC task force to investigate the opposition parties' allegations of election fraud. The opposition parties later said they did not agree to the task force. The SADC task force arrived on 15 August with Honorable Pius Langa, Deputy President of the Constitutional Court of South Africa, as the chair. The nine-member task force included three representatives each from South Africa, Botswana, and Zimbabwe. The Botswana representatives were election officials while others were judges, lawyers, or accountants. Their terms of reference included investigating the registration of voters, the voter lists, election day activities, the vote count, and the results.

Upon arrival, the task force immediately began plenary and private sessions that included the government, opposition parties, and the IEC. Also present at the plenary sessions were Commonwealth and Organization of African Unity (OAU) observers, an NDI staff member, and representatives from national NGOs as well as the general public. Despite tremendous involvement of observers and international consultants in the election process, the task force did not accept any input from these sources. The opposition alleged several irregularities, including "ghost" voters on the registration list, military involvement in the transport of election materials, improper counting, poor quality ink, discrepancies in the announced results and the number of voters, an unnatural birthdate pattern on voter lists, unqualified voters, IEC noncooperation with opposition parties, the printing of extra ballot papers, condonation of irregularities by the first director of elections (who was eventually dismissed), two instances of abandoned election materials, an unnecessarily close relationship between the IEC and government, and several other items that surfaced during the investigation.

The Langa Commission, as it came to be known, also investigated the IEC's documentation, including the A45 and A47 forms. While examining these two sets of forms, the Langa Commission found several discrepancies between the totals yielded by A45 forms (one per polling station) and those of the A47s (one per constituency). When the IEC conducted its own investigation, similar errors were found. However, in some cases the IEC discovered that the Langa Commission's numbers were incorrect as well. These discrepancies occurred for several reasons, all administrative in nature. For example, most differences were less than 250 votes in total and likely attributable to math errors. Many polling stations where sums were totaled lacked electricity or calculators and polling station officers had been awake for more than 24 hours.

Approximately one-quarter of the constituencies had differences of 250 to 1,000 total votes. These errors were likely attributable to both misplaced A45 forms and math errors. The IEC headquarters did not know how many polling stations there were in some areas, and consequently was uncertain how many A45 forms there should have been. Furthermore, in the 20 constituencies that experienced larger errors, polling stations were changed the day of the election to respond to the needs on the ground. This also made it difficult to track the number of polling stations and consequently the number of A45 forms that should have been submitted. In several instances, polling station officials inadvertently sealed the A45 forms in envelopes intended for ballots only, rather than sending them to the returning officers as required. It is likely, however, that polling station officials called in the information contained on the A45s to the returning officer.

A week after the Langa Commission completed its investigation of the IEC documentation, the IEC submitted a paper that attempted to explain the discrepancies in totals and unaccounted-for A45 forms. Errors were likely related to the IEC's short preparation time before the elections, the inexperience of the IEC, and the rural, underdeveloped nature of Lesotho. It is important to note that in only one instance did the errors seem to affect the outcome of a race. Winners in most constituencies were victorious by thousands of votes. Even in those constituencies with smaller margins of victory, the errors were not great enough to affect the outcome.[8] However, the administrative errors and opposition's grievances ultimately led the Langa Commission to recount the votes from most of the constituencies.

This phase of the investigation, discussions and review of documentation, was completed on the evening of 26 August, at which time Deputy President Mbeki returned to Lesotho. He spent most of the previous night negotiating with the opposition and ruling party. Before leaving the next day, Mbeki made a public statement that the investigation would continue. He emphasized that no allegations of fraud had been substantiated or dismissed.

The recount was conducted from 29 August to 1 September by South African students from Qwa-Qwa and Free State universities as well as officers from the South African Defense Force. The recount included 66 of the 80 constituencies and was supervized by the ten-person Langa Commission, while the parties, the government, and the IEC acted as observers.

The Langa Commission Report

The investigation concluded in early September, and the final report was released on 18 September. The opposition alleged that the delay allowed for tampering with the report, and political unrest began to build. The Commission did not find the fraud allegations to be credible nor did it call for new elections. Instead, the report documented many administrative errors.

The report began with some background information and outlined the Langa Commission's terms of reference. The next few pages described the election process as prescribed by Lesotho law. Then the report described the Commission's methodology, which involved plenary sessions, written submissions, investigation of IEC documents, and a recount of the ballots cast. The next two sections outlined and discussed the allegations made by the opposition parties. The following section discussed the validity of each allegation. All allegations were either dismissed or deemed inconclusive. Had it ended there, the report would simply appear to be critical of several IEC administrative mistakes. However, the next section, "General Remarks," is ambiguous enough that almost any conclusion can be drawn:

> In considering the way forward, we feel it would be appropriate to mention the following: it has been suggested that a new general election should be held on the basis that the irregularities cast doubt on the fairness of the 1998 election. We are unable to state that the invalidity of the elections has been conclusively established. We point out, however, that some of the apparent irregularities and discrepancies are sufficiently serious concerns. We cannot however postulate that the result does not reflect the will of the Lesotho electorate. We merely point out that the means for checking this has been compromized and created much room for doubt.

In the final section, the Langa Commission makes several recommendations to all parties involved, emphasizing the need to restore confidence in the IEC, ensure that the IEC has sufficient resources, adhere to the election law, train all those involved in the election, keep better records and controls, manage the election materials carefully and completely, and examine "the wisdom of using one or other electoral system" in Lesotho.

The Langa Commission's report was ambiguous and inconclusive in many sections, which made it possible for both the opposition and the ruling party to publically claim vindication. Of particular significance were the lack of substantiation for fraud allegations, no call for a new election, and the assertion that administrative errors did not change the election outcome. The report also conceded that the IEC had only seven months to prepare for a difficult election and recognized that the method for allocating seats required greater attention.

SADC Military Intervention

Throughout the months after the election, there was sporadic unrest in Maseru. The unrest resulted in several deaths, dozens of injuries, and a long-running protest in front of the king's palace demanding the king's intervention and a new election. On 11 September, factions within the military seized this opportune time of unrest to mutiny. The mutiny was brought under control by Basotho authorities who remained loyal to the elected government.

Political parties were to meet on September 20 to work out a settlement to the dispute. However, the meeting did not occur and opposition dissatisfaction escalated. On 20 September, 70 to 80 per cent of the military effectively rebelled. This rebellion could not be brought under control by those who continued to defend the government. Under an active SADC treaty, the government called for SADC military intervention, which occurred on 21 September. The SADC forces, initially disorganized, met unexpected resistance. Looting, arson, and rampant lawlessness overwhelmed the capital. While order was slowly returned, the capital was in ruins with damage in excess of $200 million. There was also looting and killing in outlying areas of the capital.

Call for a New Election

During the month of October, more than 3,500 South African and Botswana troops were deployed in Lesotho to help keep peace. On 14 October, an agreement was reached between the ruling and opposition parties. The parties agreed to the establishment of the Interim Political Authority (IPA), which was sworn in on 9 December. The IPA has two members from each of the country's 12 political parties and will appoint an Independent Electoral Authority to prepare for new elections in 15 to 18 months. The IPA has the authority to review the Electoral Code of Conduct and the electoral structure and recommend changes to the law.

NDI Involvement in Lesotho

The NDIs first conducted a survey mission in Lesotho in March 1996. The mission sought to gauge opportunities for an NDI program to solidify and advance Lesotho's democratic gains. The mission found that while the Basutholand Congress Party's dominance of Basotho politics had been less than impressive in advancing the needs of the country, the NGO community is a strong and impressive component of Basotho civil society with great potential to influence the political process.

NDI therefore initially developed a U.S.Agency for International Development–funded program that focused primarily on strengthening Basotho civil society, particularly through indigenous NGOs, to facilitate more effective participation in the nascent democratic political process and forthcoming national elections. NDI also conducted some early activities with the Independent Electoral Commission, including a study mission to Namibia (see below).

Later, through a grant from Irish Aid, NDI began additional work with the IEC to strengthen its capacity for administering the upcoming national elections. NDI's program aimed to help the IEC overcome its challenges as a new institution with major responsibilities in an often tense political environment. NDI activities focused on three areas: staff training, technical assistance, and information dissemination/voter education. NDI opened a short-term field office to provide day-to-day assistance to NGOs and the IEC. To date, NDI assistance has included the following.

Electoral Budget Assistance to the Government of Lesotho

At the request of government ministers, NDI arranged for a visit in June 1997 by Namibia's director of elections to aid in the preparation of the Lesotho general election budget. He also provided several suggestions for the successful establishment of the IEC and its ensuing work. This assistance allowed the government of Lesotho to gain a more accurate picture of what was required.

Focus Group Research

In late June and early July 1997, NDI conducted a series of countrywide focus groups with the help of the NGO community and South African and Basotho academics. The results are being used to help NGOs design voter education programs and materials and were expected to generate greater interest in issues of concern to the electorate. The results indicated, among other things, the following:

- a low level of understanding of the upcoming election and voting process;
- frustration with democracy's inability to solve chronic difficulties such as unemployment and limited access to affordable education;
- a sense of unfulfilled promises and feelings that politicians have abandoned their constituents; and
- a desire for responsive government and democracy, but a loss of hope and trust in the democratic process.

These results were integrated into voter education programs carried out by NGOs and the IEC.

Voter and Civic Education Training for NGOs

The Basotho NGO community requested NDI assistance to improve their capacity to effectively undertake voter education programs. NDI provided periodic training, with the NGOs conducting and planning the bulk of the actual voter education.

In late August 1997, NDI organized a two-day NGO training program in Lesotho. The objectives of the seminar were to expose the NGO community to comparative voter education models; help them analyze and understand public opinion about the elections; and guide them as they begin to create strategies for conducting a coordinated voter education campaign in Lesotho. Attendance throughout the two days averaged 30 leaders and activists from various local NGOs.

In January 1998, NDI organized another three-day training program. This voter education training workshop was led by Michael Weeder, NDI consultant and former director of South Africa's Project Vote. The event, which included participation of IEC senior staff, helped to coordinate and implement voter education activities of the IEC and NGO community. Weeder and NDI staff continue to provide in-country direction and assistance in the preparation of voter education materials.

Assistance to the Independent Electoral Commission

In November 1997, two of three IEC commissioners participated in a four-day study mission to Namibia. The program, sponsored by NDI and organized by the Namibian Directorate of Elections, was headed by Professor Gerhard Tötemeyer. Other meetings included the Speaker of the National Assembly, the former Director of the Namibian Broadcasting Company, the Chairman of the Namibian Electoral Commission, and the Director of the Namibian Institute for Democracy. All attendees shared insights into the various challenges and approaches to conducting a legitimate election process.

In another effort to help the IEC consider how other electoral bodies have approached challenges, NDI sponsored a visit for three experienced electoral commissioners to Lesotho. The delegation comprised the Chairman of the Ghanian Electoral Commission Dr Afari-Gyan, the president of the Electoral Tribunal of Panama Dr Guillermo Marquez, and former Sierra Leone Electoral Commissioner

Almami Cyllah. They met with the IEC, donors, government officials, diplomats, international consultants, IEC staff, and election officials. The visit helped focus attention on outstanding electoral issues. The delegates presented to the IEC a list of recommendations that included a revised election timetable; improvement of relations with the government; establishment of a dispute mechanism; and encouragement of an inclusive and transparent process with the parties and media.

In March 1998, NDI Senior Consultant Ed Brown helped the IEC organize and participate in a two-day workshop for political parties and civic organisations. The workshop provided information of which political parties and NGOs, as potential election observers or monitors, should be aware for pre-election and election day activities.

NDI assisted the IEC in developing and printing voter education materials and official documents. Along with representatives of the NGO community, NDI assisted the IEC in publishing a voter educator's manual designed to be used as a handbook for IEC staff and NGO community workers who were to lead voter education sessions around the country. NDI also provided computer training to IEC staff and trained electoral officers.

Through a grant from Irish Aid, NDI assisted with the following voter education materials and productions.

- 10,000 posters that described the IEC, including its roles and responsibilities;
- 10,000 posters on how to register;
- 10,000 posters announcing where to register;
- 1,500 voter education manuals;
- 8,000 pamphlets on registration;
- 100,000 tabloid newspapers on the registration process;
- 10,000 posters with the Ten Commandments for Voters;
- 10,000 posters on the topic of tolerance;
- 100,000 tabloid newspapers on the campaign period and inspection of voter list;
- 10,000 posters on inspection of voter lists;
- 10,000 posters on the campaign period;
- 100,000 tabloid newspapers on voting day;
- 15,000 posters on the voting process;
- 10,000 posters on the secrecy of the vote;
- 50,000 pamphlets on how to choose a candidate;
- 100,000 pamphlets describing how to vote;
- 10,000 posters announcing the election and where to vote;
- 1,500 Sesotho versions of the candidate agent manual; and
- 20 radio dramas and documentaries.

Subgrant to the
Church Community

With a small subgrant from NDI, the African Methodist Episcopal Church in Lesotho had designed a pamphlet entitled "Why We Must Vote." Not only was the pamphlet approved by the IEC, but the Commission also asked that more be printed and made available for wider distribution. The church also emphasized the importance of voting through its countrywide network of churches and schools. In addition, the church conducted candidate forums in the weeks before the election to allow voters to engage candidates face-to-face on pertinent issues.

NDI helped arrange American representation in a United Nations international observer group. More than 140 international observers were deployed around the country for the 23 May election. Several countries, including Ireland, also provided long-term observers that helped assess the pre-election environment. While a joint statement commending the election was released, several groups, including the Commonwealth and SADC, released their own positive statements.

Post-Election Roundtable
Discussion in Maseru

Five days after the elections, NDI organized a roundtable discussion to identify both successes and lessons learned from the 1998 elections. There were two panels of speakers in sessions lasting approximately one and a half hours. NDI Program Officer Chris Homan moderated, giving each panelist five to ten minutes to speak. After each presentation, Homan accepted questions from the audience. Panelists for the first session were IEC Chairman Sekara Mafisa, IEC Director of Elections Mphasa Mokhochane, U.S. Deputy Chief of Mission Raymond Brown, Commonwealth Consultant Sam Graham, and UN Consultant Frank Vassallo. The second panel was composed of LCN Voter Education Coordinator (Ms) Puleng Lenka, Irish Observer (Ms.) Marie Meegan, NDI Voter Education Consultant Rev. Michael Weeder, Transformation Resource Center representative (Ms) Moets'eoa Senyane, and Christian Council of NGOs representative Rev. Mqethezane. Approximately 60 people attended, including representatives of the political parties, media, NGO community, international observers, diplomatic missions, and other interested persons. This session was recorded, and tapes were given to the IEC to release to the national radio station because many aspects of the election were discussed that would have been of interest to a wider audience.

Several recommendations by the participants and audience members were discussed at the forum. Many were general, but they highlighted areas that need further discussion. Suggestions made during the discussion follow.

- Improve the process of registration and regularly update the voters list; make electoral laws easier to understand;
- Allow more time for inspection of voter lists;
- Allow a two-phased nomination process: first, nomination papers should be presented for the public to view the lists of names and have an opportunity to object, upon which the electoral commission would decide; second, if the candidate or individual opposes the commission's decision, it could be appealed in court;
- Carry out an aggressive voter education program between elections, including:
  - voter education as a part of school curricula;
  - encourage NGOs to carry out voter education with clear strategies;
- Provide voter education for presiding officers as well as other polling station and IEC staff, even before providing training on their specific official roles;
- Extend the categories of individuals allowed to vote in absentia;
- Improve and simplify the voting process; for example, eliminate second counterfoil at the top of the ballot (the one that the presiding officer must remove);
- Improve the system of securing ballots that are being taken to polling station;
- Publicly fund political parties;
- Improve the construction of polling sites; for instance, avoid tents serving as polling stations;
- Involve NGOs/civil society in lobbying efforts to improve the voting process, and encourage debate on electoral systems;
- Ensure that civil society and the IEC provide more accurate information;
- Create a permanent election machinery, an institutional infrastructure so that issues can be regularly and effectively addressed; and
- Generate general public discussion on the electoral system, in which the IEC can be instrumental.

Post-Election Roundtable Discussion

On 13 October, NDI held a roundtable discussion in Washington, D.C., to discuss the Lesotho elections and the events that followed. The goal of the discussion was to continue to keep those interested in Lesotho informed while also deepening their regional understanding. Several persons concerned with Lesotho participated, including Ambassador Dr Eunice Bulane, Kingdom of Lesotho; Deputy Chief of Mission Ndumiso Ntsinga, Republic of South Africa; Ambassador Archibald M. Mogwe, Botswana; Ambassador Bismark Myrick, U.S. Ambassador to Lesotho (1993–1998); Frank Vassalo, long-term United Nations Development Program consultant to the Lesotho IEC (via video link from Australia); and Sam Graham, long-term Commonwealth consultant to the Lesotho IEC.

Conclusion

Recent events in Lesotho demonstrate not only the fragility of many new democracies, but the importance of developing a democratic culture as well. While many in Western democracies take for granted the peaceful transfer of power and the dignity of conceding defeat, such concepts are often elusive in many emerging democracies. While legitimate questions could be raised about Lesotho's first-past-the-post election system, opposition parties initially did not look to an established national dialogue process to address such concerns. Furthermore, losing parties did not view upcoming local elections as an opportunity to build their political bases or influence.

The 1998 election raised important questions. First, one must ask why the presence of party agents as well as international and domestic observers did not help quell opposition claims of fraud. Agents from the major parties were present at a majority of polling sites and none lodged complaints on election day. Furthermore, over 140 international and 300 domestic observers, including a number of long-term international witnesses, gave near unanimous praise to the election. While one can speculate that post-election events could have been worse without this validation of the election, ultimately such statements did not deter opposition claims of being cheated.

One then further wonders whether a technically good election is sufficient if the losing parties believe they have been unfairly excluded from power. Lesotho's election commission is far more independent than others in the region. Its administrative errors were minor compared with the enormous undertaking of conducting an election with only seven months' preparation. Furthermore, no allegation of fraud was ever proved in court or to the visiting Langa Commission. A technically good or "internationally validated" election, it seems, is not sufficient to ensure stability. There must also be popular acceptance of the concept that one can accept defeat and fairly and honorably compete next time. These are important challenges to address in Lesotho's future democratic evolution.

Notes

1. The people of Lesotho.
2. Immediately after the May 1998 election, the NDI sponsored a post-election roundtable comprised of IEC officials, international consultants and observers, and representatives of the diplomatic community. Many administrative errors and suggested remedies were publicly discussed. None of the errors was claimed to have had any substantive impact on the election results. Evaluation of a proportional model was also discussed as a partial solution to continued one-party dominance in the Parliament.

3. In 1997, Street Law, a South Africa nongovernmental organization, and Susan Booysen, a political scientist at Rands-Afrikaans University, conducted focus group research throughout Lesotho.
4. *Lesotho's Long Journey,* a report by Sechaba Consultants.
5. Focus group study.
6. *ibid.*
7. Constituency 65, Moyheni, did not hold its election until August because of the death of a candidate after nomination day.
8. As this article was being written, it was believed that one constituency being reviewed by the court might reveal a miscount resulting in a different winner.

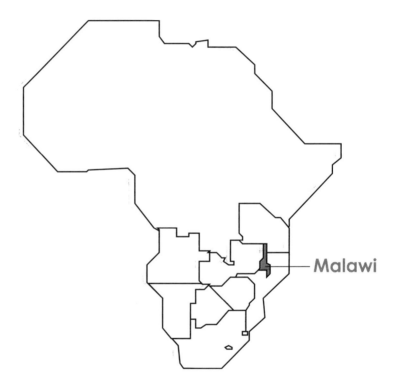

Malawi

Malawi's Transition to Democracy

Foster Mijiga

Malawi, a southern African country with an estimated population of 10 million people, is bordered by Mozambique, Zambia, and Tanzania. Malawi held its first democratic elections on 17 May, 1994. Eighty-seven per cent of the Malawian population lives and works in rural areas; the survival and economic growth of most Malawians depend entirely on agriculture.[1] Unfortunately, Malawi's food and agricultural industries have been hit by three successive droughts within the past six years. Life expectancy has declined to under 45 years. The infant mortality rate in Malawi is 134 per 1,000. On the international scale, Malawi is rated as one of the poorest countries in the world with a per capita income of approximately $100. Additionally, more than 80 per cent of the population is illiterate.[2]

The outcome of the 1994 election marked the first change in the control of government in Malawi after 30 years. Out of eight officially registered parties, three received the majority of the votes. The United Democratic Front (UDF) won 85 seats in Parliament, the Malawi Congress Party[3] (MCP) won 55 seats and the Alliance for Democracy (AFORD) won 36 seats. In the presidential race, the current president, Bakili Muluzi, gathered 47 per cent of the votes, while former president, Kamuzu Banda, came second with 33 per cent. The leader of the Alliance for Democracy, Chakufwa Chihana, came third with 19 per cent.[4]

The 1994 elections were a result of negotiations and increased progress toward democratization that began after the end of the Cold War. This process, coupled with increased pressure from the international donor community, the Commonwealth countries, the 1991 Harare Declaration, and the 1992 pastoral letter issued by Malawi's powerful Roman Catholic bishops, gave rise to the demand for fundamental political changes in Malawi. The release of the bishops' letter precipitated demonstrations and calls for multiparty democracy throughout the country.

Foster Mijiga, a program officer at the National Democratic Institute for International Affairs in Cape Town, South Africa, manages a legislative training program at the School of Government, University of the Western Cape.

This unrest, accompanied by the international donor community's withdrawal of all but humanitarian aid to Malawi, encouraged an intransigent President Banda to call for a national referendum in June 1993 on one-party versus multiparty rule.

During the referendum, Malawians voted by more than a 2:1 margin in favor of instituting multiparty democracy. Following the referendum results, the government repealed constitutional clauses declaring Malawi a one-party state and legalized other political parties. The government also formed a National Consultative Council (NCC) and a National Executive Council (NEC), both comprising representatives from all registered political parties. The NCC and the NEC were assigned the task of proposing legislative reforms and facilitating the multiparty elections that took place on 17 May, 1994.

Expectations

A focus group study report, *Dziko ndi Anthu* (The Nation Is the People), conducted by the National Democratic Institute for International Affairs (NDI) two months prior to the May 1994 elections, revealed a number of important themes that were common among the electorate throughout the country. One recurring theme among most Malawians was that candidates and ultimately their members of Parliament, if elected under the democratic dispensation, would be coming to their villages to meet the electorate and to hear for themselves what the needs of the people were.

Participants in the focus group studies stated a long list of developments and problems they hoped the new political order would address. The increasing desire to find solutions to their daily social, political, and economic problems was a clear motivating factor among most Malawians, who were eager to participate in the elections. Most participants in the focus group studies believed that once a democratic government was elected, it would be able to:

- reduce the price of maize seeds and fertilizer;
- provide medicines in hospitals;
- increase salaries and provide employment opportunities;
- control and regulate prices;
- alleviate poverty;
- reintroduce TEBA (work in South African mines);
- provide good houses;
- provide decent clothes;
- provide loans for starting small-scale businesses; and
- facilitate equal distribution of wealth, and so forth.

From this list, it is clear that most Malawians associated democratic governance with social and economic progress. In other words, they were supporting the democratic system as a solution to the problems they experience in their daily lives.[5] To follow up on people's expectations, participants in the studies were asked what they understood by the word *democracy*. The average participant described democracy as:

- food;
- better prices for farm inputs;
- better prices paid for their produce;
- real freedom;
- being able to do what you want;
- people don't get diseases;
- to be able to form many political parties;
- the freedom of agreeing and disagreeing;
- the freedom for villagers to sell farm crops;
- equal distribution of wealth;
- discussing the truth;
- staying freely without conflict;
- living in harmony;
- respect of one's views;
- democracy is people and government; and
- the abolishment of compulsory party membership cards.

Participants in the 1994 pre-election focus group studies viewed political and economic change as one process. They believed that a new democratic government would solve what they described as "chronic daily problems." Their eagerness to participate in the new multiparty political system was based on the understanding that it would provide them with an opportunity to elect a person of their choice who would have a clear understanding of their daily problems and concerns. One participant described the role of an elected representative as similar to that of a messenger who facilitates communication between the electorate and government.

Between the 1993 referendum and the 1994 general elections, there was great enthusiasm for democracy among most Malawians. They patiently endured the lifting of authoritarian practices, and many had eagerly registered to vote. More than 80 per cent of the eligible voting population registered to vote in the parliamentary and presidential elections.[6]

After the election it was reported that more than 80 per cent of the registered voters turned out on election day. The official results also showed that Malawians knew how to vote, posting only a 2 per cent spoiled ballot rate.[7]

Early Experiences in a Democratic Malawi

Three months after the general elections, NDI Malawi embarked on a second research project composed of 14 focus groups across the country. This research was conducted to assess the perceptions of Malawians toward the democratic process after the 17 May general election.

The September 1994 focus group study revealed that people in most areas of Malawi recognized and welcomed the political change that had taken place. The most important change among the participants was the removal of what they regarded as the most unpopular aspects of the one-party regime, such as forced purchase of party cards, the poll tax, forced gift giving, and several others. Many participants in the study cited the end of these practices as positive political changes since the election. Others mentioned the reduction of political intimidation and the greater freedom of expression as significant political changes brought by the multiparty era.

While Malawians appreciated the political change, economic change was more important to most participants. When asked to identify the most pressing problems, participants almost invariably mentioned *chakudya, madzi, feteleza* (food, water, fertilizer). The author of the NDI September 1994 report made the following observation:

> Participants view the transformation of the Malawian political system as incomplete. Malawians say that the most unpopular aspects of the one-party regime have been removed, but their everyday life remains unchanged. It seems likely that Malawians will make future political judgements based less on the presence of civil liberties or freedoms than whether or not basic quality of life has improved.

The September focus group study was a clear indication that people's expectations of the new government and the new democratic political system remained high. Almost all participants felt that government should provide basic social services and infrastructure in their areas. Most people also believed that the government has a responsibility to solve their everyday problems and help them meet their basic needs. Participants wanted the government to provide food, fertilizer, employment, even shoes and bicycles. Women, in particular, wanted the government to provide credit facilities for small businesses.

The litany of requests was remarkably consistent throughout the country. Most of these expectations were augmented by promises made by politicians during the pre-election campaign period.[8] The extent of people's expectations was best illustrated by a participant from the central region district of Nkhotakota, who defined multiparty democracy as "the assurance of people's happiness by the government."

The September study also revealed that the election campaign messages had been overwhelmingly exaggerated, and people were beginning to develop a negative attitude toward their elected representatives. Participants in all areas stated that "*campaign ndi bodza*" (campaign is a lie). During the campaign, people were promised free food, free fertilizer, shoes, clothes, houses, bicycles, employment, and the resumption of TEBA (migrant labor to the South African mines). Participants who had eagerly participated in the 17 May democratic elections described the political and economic trends during the four-month period between the electon on 17 May, 1994, and the September 1994 focus group studies as unsatisfactory. While some participants were willing to give the government more time to follow through on its more realistic promises, there was a general atmosphere of skepticism and bitterness over what participants described as *atinamiza* (deceitful behavior of politicians).

The Democratic Process in Malawi

The skepticism revealed in focus group studies as early as four months after the election increased to record levels during the third round of focus group studies conducted by NDI in September 1995. While participants continued to view Malawi's political transition positively, most felt that the government was failing to address their problems adequately.

However, despite the economic hardships experienced by most participants, the majority virtually felt that the democratic system of government was the only hope for improvement in their quality of life. Notably, the negative view of the post-election period among most Malawian people had not translated into a negative view of democratic governance. People still reacted positively to words such as "democracy and multiparty," and none of them suggested that a return to a one-party state would solve the economic problems. A woman from the lakeside district of Mangochi said that the government was doing the best it could under the difficult economic circumstances within the short period that the new government had been in place. She referred to a common proverb: "A child cannot run in one day."

The NDI conducted a fourth round of focus group studies in August 1996. NDI targeted the same geographical areas where previous groups had been held in 1994 and 1995. About 35 per cent of the participants during thc August 1996 study had participated in previous NDI surveys.

The results of the 1996 survey showed that economic concerns were still paramount. A majority of the participants continued to view the post-election period as a time of deteriorating economic and social conditions. Most people said that they were worse off in 1996 than they were before the advent of democracy.[9] Concerns about corruption, violent crime, and insecurity increased dramatically during the 1996 survey and participants cited these as symptoms of a breakdown of law and order in the country.

On the other hand, Malawians remained enthusiastic about democracy and continued to cite positive changes. A village headman from the southern district of Mulanje said, "Now we are living freely without buying compulsory party membership cards, we do not have to pay poll tax, and the new government has introduced free education." Another gentleman, from the southern region district of

Mwanza, said, "Today we can discuss anyway we want, we can even criticize the government, no problem. In the past you couldn't discuss anything concerning the government"

During the 1996 survey, the appreciation of new freedoms and the end of oppression cut across political affiliations, gender, and ethnic backgrounds. However, economic concerns resurfaced in every discussion, in fact, many people described terms such as "freedom" and "democracy" in economic rather than political terms. An old woman in the central region district of Nkhotakota said, "Democracy is when a person finds the things that he or she needs, such as food and money, without difficulties." Another middle-aged man from the lakeside district of Mangochi said, "Freedom means eating good food, wearing good clothes, and sleeping in good houses."

In general, most Malawians echoed the same economic and social concerns that had been raised in the previous years and reiterated that democracy had no meaning unless these concerns were addressed.

Democracy and Election Campaigns

Economic issues dominated every focus group discussion conducted by NDI before and after the 1994 elections. During the group studies, it was clear that most people had a positive view of democracy as a solution to their economic problems. This view was reinforced by campaign messages that preceded the election by parties and candidates contesting the elections. Candidates promised voters that once voted into power, they would address all the concerns and issues raised. A man from the central region district of Salima said, "I was paraded barefoot on stage at a campaign rally, and told that if I voted wisely, I would be given shoes. It's more than three years, and now I'm not only barefoot, but I am walking barefoot on an empty stomach." While research showed that most Malawians already had high expectations of the democratic order, the promises made by politicians before and after the general elections did nothing other than substantially increase people's expectations.[10]

Focus group studies conducted by NDI in 1997 and 1998 revealed a substantial increase in popular discontent with the democratically elected government. These two studies went beneath the dissatisfaction that participants had raised in previous studies to identify the real causes and underlying issues of the substantial increase in public dissatisfaction. In both studies, participants cited the deteriorating standards of living, which they attributed to a sharp increase in the cost of living as the key problem.[11]

Throughout NDI's research, participants defined democracy and multiparty politics as systems that "improves the quality of life." This definition dates back to the first NDI study conducted in 1994. The study revealed that in the minds of most people, government's failure to improve the quality of life meant that "democracy has failed." This perception, whether true or false, remains a popular perception cutting across political affiliations and ethnic and gender backgrounds.

Since the 1994 elections, there has been record voter apathy during parliamentary by-elections and runoffs in Malawi. Of 23 parliamentary seats contested in separate by-elections, the turnout of registered voters has been on average less than 30 per cent; when all eligible voters are taken into consideration, the numbers are embarrassingly less than 15 per cent. As they prepare for the second democratic parliamentary and presidential elections scheduled to take place during the first half of 1999, there is a growing division of opinion among Malawians. One group feels that the 1999 election offers the opportunity for change in the government, or at least government policy, while another group feels that politicians are liars and therefore not worth their vote. A third group is considering voting for female candidates under the assumption that women will not be as corrupt as men, and a fourth group is considering voting for independent candidates and doing away with political parties all together. There is some body of opinion which holds that the current government needs more time, but these people also would like a better explanation of how changes are going to be effected. Notably, unlike the September 1995 focus group study, the 1998 focus groups revealed that the negative view of the post-election period was leading to a negative view of democratic governance.

Focus group participants in 1998 were disgruntled with political parties, their activities, and what they say. Virtually all participants were not interested in what political parties say or do, referring to them as opportunistic interest groups with nothing to offer, but always in conflict with one another and consequently dividing the masses.

Irritated Malawians in the country's largest township, Ndirande, in the southern district of Blantyre, said that political parties have failed to serve the interests of the people, and that instead, the masses should be educated to vote for a candidate in his or her own personal capacity and not on a political party ticket. All the people who participated in the Ndirande focus group said that the representative system no longer represents them and that they will use the 1999 election to take control of their own lives from a leadership which has failed to deliver but instead has become richer than before.

Conclusion

The rising discontent with political parties, coupled with the people's previously mentioned dissatisfaction with democratic governance in general, raises a significant challenge to the prospects for democratic consolidation in Malawi.

Several factors have been offered to explain the problems currently being experienced in Malawi, such as lack of commitment on the part of politicians, corruption of leaders, the legacy of the previous one-party regime, inadequate government resources, the International Monetary Fund and World Bank policies, and a whole list of other factors.

While some of these points seem to be potential contributing factors to the current political, economic, and social conditions in Malawi, the extent to which they affect the consolidation of democratic governance varies.[12] According to focus group participants, democratic governance has not addressed their daily problems as was expected, and they attribute this to inefficiency and lack of commitment on the part of their elected representatives. On the other hand, the elected representatives cite, among other factors, structural adjustment programs, the legacy of the one-party regime, and foreign debt repayment as some of the underlying factors making it difficult for the government to deliver on its promises.[13] But whatever the case, the bottom line is that participants in the 1998 focus group studies strongly felt that the democratic system has failed because their lives have not improved, a perception that was not present during the September 1995 study.

When considering this perception, one needs to reexamine this perception in the context of the 1994 focus group study, particularly the definition and expectations of a democratic government and the multiparty system. Among other definitions and expectations, the NDI focus group conducted two months before the May 1994 election revealed that Malawians defined democracy as food, alleviation of poverty, creation of jobs, and being able to do what one wants to do. The 1998 studies have revealed that most Malawians who are eager to participate in the 1999 election will use it as an opportunity to begin to hold future representatives accountable. "They want candidates for election in 1999 to tell them truthfully if they will be able to solve local problems and to give them assurance that they will stay in close touch with their constituents if elected," reports the author of the 1998 NDI focus group study report.

Virtually all focus group studies between 1994 and 1998 have revealed that democracy has no meaning in Malawi unless the welfare of the electorate is improved. In one of the 1998 focus groups, when asked whether he was going to vote in the 1999 election, a middle-aged man from the southern district of Mulanje said, "I don't think so; I will either be ill or dead by 1999. There is no food to eat and no medicine in the hospital."

In all 14 focus group studies conducted in October 1998, increasing food shortages and high prices of farm inputs were highlighted as the most pressing issues, both being priority issues raised by participants in 1994 before and after the May elections. During the studies, it became clear that Malawians still acknowledge the political freedoms that have come with the multiparty era; however, people have openly stated that they will use this freedom through the electoral process to remove "ineffective leaders" and elect a new leadership that will improve their quality of life and provide food.

The disappointment with elected representatives cuts across both the ruling and opposition parties. The 1998 study also revealed substantial consensus among the participants of disinterest in political parties. These people said that the increasing conflicts between political parties, the daily accusations and counter-accusations, simply demonstrate that there is something wrong with the political system as a whole and political parties in particular.

The outcome of the focus group studies has revealed that the historic election of 1994 was a significant milestone in Malawi's political history. However, this major event did not take place in a vacuum. The election was a result of a variety of factors, some of which have been raised by participants in the focus group studies, most relating directly to social-economic issues.

While the 1994 election facilitated the installation of formal multiparty democracy in Malawi, the installation of an elected government was just the beginning of a long process.[14] The NDI study provides an overview of the perceptions prevailing among Malawian citizens toward democracy before the 1994 elections and after. These perceptions, whether true or not, are opinions that people in the studies hold with conviction. Participants feel that politicians have used them for personal gain.

According to the 1998 study, when asked about their view of "politics," participants disassociated themselves from politics and expressed their disappointment over what politicians do. The word *politics*, which in vernacular language is called *ndale* (tripping up an opponent by the use of one's leg) reminds Malawians of the mudslinging and abusive exchange of words they hear on the radio and all the negative campaigns they read in newspapers.[15]

The 1998 focus group report repeats the popular view among Malawians that democracy is a system of government intended to ensure economic well-being and goes on to identify different perceptions across Malawian society. While one group remains committed to participate in the 1999 election with the view of removing the current set of representatives, a second group feels that not voting is actually a vote.

The different motivating factors for participation in the election provide an overview of the status of the democratic process in Malawi since 1994. However, by looking at the different definitions of democracy and the expectations that arise from that definition, the question arises as to whether democracy was instituted in the first place and whether what has failed was indeed democracy. The second question that arises is whether the failure to address and fulfill the expectations of Malawians would be considered the failure of a new democratic system of government.

The current views and motivating factors for Malawians to participate in the 1999 election derive from, and are determined by, the problems they have experienced over the years. According to participants in the NDI focus groups, government as a vehicle has not been driving very well since independence in 1964, and so far Malawians have identified the drivers, not the vehicle itself as the major problem and hence the need to replace them. This obvious but very important illustration is crucial for the future and sustainability of democracy in Malawi, for as long as the problem is unclear, there can be no solution.

It is unclear from the results of the focus group studies whether democracy has really been on the agenda after the elections and whether it is realistic to consider democracy as the only solution to the social and economic problems that participants in focus groups face, although democracy creates a conducive environment for solving social and economic problems.[16] The progress of the transition to democracy in Malawi cannot therefore be determined merely by the improvement in the social and economic status of the people in Malawi, although this criterion of assessment is relevant.[17] Neither can the democratic progress be determined by assessing the commitment and efficiency of the leadership alone.[18]

If democracy is to prevail in Malawi, the people must view themselves not as end consumers but as the means and agents of this system. And if the people are the means and agents of democracy in Malawi, democracy must be institutionalized from the grassroots level. Democracy in Malawi as a means of survival and a solution to social and economic problems has thus far proved to be unsustainable, leading to an increased desire to replace drivers of this government machinery.[19] Participants in the 1998 study talked about democracy in economic and social terms rather than as abstract political rights, citing economic opportunities, the social prosperity of the masses, and a vibrant welfare system as priority issues.

In conclusion, an assessment of the democratization process in Malawi is incomplete without a clear answer as to whether democracy was ever institutionalized in Malawi after 1994 or whether the 1994 historical event was just a one-time "free and fair election." Focus group participants repeatedly referred to the disconnect between the electorate and the representatives, which is often revitalized during election time. This relationship has reduced democracy to multiparty electoral competition which, according to the participants, has often been exploited as a strategy for accumulating power and wealth.

To a large extent, this illustrates why Malawians view democracy as a solution to social and economic problems and see themselves as consumers rather than agents of the democratic process. Many reports have claimed "low human development" in Malawi (United Nations Development Program [UNDP, 1997 Report]), ignorance of rights and the meaning of democracy (Centre for Advice, Research, and Education on Rights [CARER, 1994–1995]), so it appears that there is little which could be rightly attributed to the knowledge of ordinary Malawians in terms of their understanding of the abstract concept of democracy, when they never had the opportunity, even in historical times, to live the democratic way in order to experience and learn it.

Finally, the 1998 study has revealed that Malawians will use the ballot as a bargaining tool during the 1999 election. As one female participant from the southern district of Mulanje put it, "Voting just enriches the elected officials, leaving the electorate suffering." A gentleman from the southern district of Blantyre summarized it by saying, "Only those candidates promising truthfully to address the people's needs will be voted into power."

Notes

1. United States Agency for International Development (hereafter USAID), "Congressional Presentation, Financial Year 1997."
2. USAID, "1997 Report."
3. The former ruling party under the one-party Constitution.
4. Malawi Election Commission.
5. National Democratic Institute for International Affairs (hereafter NDI), "Focus Group Report" (*Dziko ndi Anthu*), 1994; John Roche, *Malawi Beyond Banda*, 1993.
6. NDI, "Final Report: Political Party Training and Voter Education, National Election," May 1994.
7. Malawi Election Commission.
8. See *Daily Times,* 25 May 1999; Melinda Ham and Mike Hall, "President Bakili Muluzi, Building Democracy," *Africa Report* 39 (1994); Francis A. Korngay, Jr., "Chakufwa Chihana, Dissident for Democracy," *Africa Report* 39 (1994).
9. NDI, "Focus Group Study Report," August 1996.
10. Both the United Democratic Front and the Malawi Congress Party manifestos prior to the1994 elections outlined extensive welfare and economic policies. A lot of emphasis was placed on poverty alleviation.
11. See World Bank Reports, 1993–1998, "GDP Growth and Inflation Rates: Changes in the Consumer Price Index."
12. Robert Putnam with Robert Leonardi and Raffaella Y. Nanetti, *Making Democracy Work: Civic Traditions in Modern Italy* (Princeton: Princeton University Press), 7–14.
13. See J. Bayo Adekanye, "Structural Adjustment, Democratisation and Rising Ethnic Tensions in Africa," *Development and Change* 26 (1995): 355–374; *Business Malawi,* 8 September 1997; Guy C.Z Mhone, ed., *Malawi at the Crossroads: The Post-colonial Political Economy* (Harare: SAPES Books, 1992).
14. See Bruce Cohen, *Malawi's Magic Carpet Ride to Democracy,* August 1994; John Roche, *Malawi Beyond Banda;* Michael Chege, "Between Africa's Extremes," *Journal of Democracy* 6, no. 1 (January 1995): 44–51.
15. NDI, "Chibwenzi Cha Nkhwangwa Chokoma Pokwela: A Report on Focus Groups and Structured Interviews," 1997, 7–15.
16. See Claude Ake, *Democracy and Development in Africa* (Washington, D.C.: Brookings Institution, 1997), 135–142.
17. See Putnam, *Making Democracy Work* .
18. See Forrest David Mathews, *Politics for People: Finding a Responsible Public Voice* (Urbana: University of Illinois Press, 1994).
19. See Thomas H. Carothers, *Assessing Democracy Assistance: The Case of Romania* (Washington, D.C.: Carnegie Endowment for International Peace; distributed by the Brookings Institution, 1996).

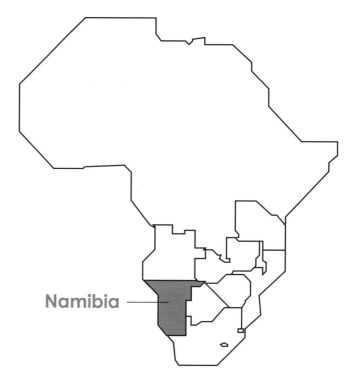

Namibia

Democracy in Namibia:

Wind of Change

or Withering Breeze?

Vezera Bob Kandetu

Historical Context

Namibia, like virtually all African states, derives her recorded political history from the Berlin Conference of 1884. At it the European states of the time converged to carve a *modus operandi* that would enable one and all to stake their claim to the already acquired and projected spoils on the African continent. Subsequent to Berlin, Namibia was among the territories that were claimed by or given to Germany, as the case may be, to become Deutsch-Südwestafrika (German Southwest Africa).

After World War I, in 1918, European and North American states that were party to the war effort gathered in Versailles, France, in the aftermath of Germany's defeat, to draw a model according to which the state would be treated. A long story indeed. But the short of it is that on 28 June 1919, the Versailles Peace Treaty was signed; Article 119 held that Germany would cede all its rights and titles to its former colonies to the principal allied and associated powers that were set to dictate the path of events for decades to come. And so did Namibia pass on from colonial Germany to the League of Nations without an opinion having been sought from the Namibians themselves.

Debates ensued within the League of Nations on whether the German colonies would be annexed or treated separately. In the end, a compromise was reached in terms of which nonannexation and international accountability were accepted for all the former German colonies, Southwest Africa included. These principles were embodied in the mandate systems provided by Article 22 of the Covenant of the League of Nations, which in part reads as follows:

Vezera Bob Kandetu, dean of students at the University of Namibia, headed the independent monitoring unit for the Council of Churches during the election that inaugurated Namibian independence.

> To those colonies and territories which, as a consequence of the late war, have ceased to be under the sovereignty of the states which formerly governed them, and which are inhabited by peoples not yet ready to stand by themselves under the strenuous conditions of the modern world, there should be applied the principle that the well-being and development of such peoples form a sacred trust of civilisation and that securities for the performance of this trust should be embodied in this covenant.[1]

The best method of effecting this principle is that the tutelage of such peoples be given to advanced nations, which by reason of their resources, their experience, or their geographical position, can best undertake this responsibility "and that this tutelage should be exercised as mandatories on behalf of the League of Nations."[2]

South Africa was by virtue of this arrangement mandated in 1920 over Southwest Africa on behalf of the League of Nations, under what came to be termed class C mandate. Unfortunately not much was done by South Africa towards the realisation of the League's sacred trust of civilization, and successive South African regimes would entrench their rule, transfer their citizens to the territory as settlers, and flout any propositions of the League and its successor the United Nations (UN), much to the disappointment of the international community and disillusionment of the Namibian people, who were never consulted at any point during the scheme of things.

It stands to reason, therefore, that Namibia's political history has not known democracy and none of the country's proposed mentors and midwives have attempted to show that by example. The passing of Southwest Africa from imperial Germany to South Africa in 1920 with no opinion sought from Namibians is a living testimony. Whatever attempts at democratization must depart from this fact and be predicated on the reality that the independence of Namibia was a product of efforts by Namibians themselves based on their own methods, and the movement to democracy may have to develop along this path at a pace perhaps slower than expected. This will call for patience on the part of those nations of the world, and their citizens, that wish Namibia well.

The mandatory arrangement did not work for Namibia. Instead of adhering to the letter and spirit of the Covenant, South Africa encouraged white settlers and, in fact, in 1946 South Africa requested the UN Organisation (UNO) to allow it to incorporate Southwest Africa as a fifth province of the Republic of South Africa. The UN declined. In 1948 the Afrikaner-dominated Nationalist Party came to power in South Africa and was more aggressive than the party of General Smuts which preceded its rule. In 1950 the wrath of the South African National Party was effectively felt in Namibia through its apartheid regime. The new government denounced the mandate and proclaimed the treatment of Southwest Africa as South Africa's colony or its fifth province. The UN strongly resisted this move, but, unfortunately, could not stop South Africa's schemes in Namibia.

Needless to say, the arrival of the Nationalist Party regime in South Africa and its policies *vis-à-vis* Namibia, polarized the political arena in both South Africa and

Namibia and contributed to a large extent to heightened international tension, culminating in the Cold War between Western Europe, including the United States, and Eastern Europe. In 1966 the International Court of Justice (ICJ), reversing its earlier interlocutory decision, ruled that it had no jurisdiction to give a binding and enforceable decision on South Africa's mandatory position over Southwest Africa. This decision did not help to defuse the tension that was fast building between the Namibian people and the South African regime in Namibia on one hand and between the UN and South Africa on the other. Appeals for South Africa's better wisdom came to nothing. Diplomatic efforts were fielded and remained ineffective as South Africa remained intransigent. The world increasingly became impatient with South Africa.

Against this backdrop of realities, the Namibian people, who hitherto had worked peacefully and patiently to support the world's efforts in persuading South Africa, became impatient to the point of contemplating organized action against the regime and its apartheid policy,[3] which by this time was fast entrenching itself in Namibia. Different political formations had started to take shape by the mid-fifties, varying from labor groupings, traditional leadership, and modern political trend initiatives. Their appeals and protests did not persuade South Africa and instead encouraged the regime to unleash violence against them, in the form of persecutions and detentions.

By the late 1950s, the Southwest Africa Peoples Organization (SWAPO) had been formed and in time took it upon itself to face the South African regime's might in Namibia. Virtually all the organisation's leaders had to leave the country to avoid ongoing detentions, but they went primarily to aid the efforts of the international community through lobbying and petitioning regional, continental, and international organisations as well as mobilizing international public opinion (later efforts helped to galvanize a nongovernmental/liberation support movement, perhaps second to none in the history of struggles for justice in the world).

When in 1966 the ICJ ruled against progress, the SWAPO leadership, which was operating from all over Africa, convened a conference in Tanganyika, now Tanzania, where the movement had its headquarters. It was held at Moshi on 18 July 1966. This somewhat soul-searching *indaba* culminated in one of the most important decisions that came to serve as the cutting edge of modern political thought. The conference concluded that in view of the ICJ ruling, the people of Namibia were left with no option but to take arms against the apartheid regime. On 26 August 1966, the first shots were fired at Ongulumbashe near Tsandi, northern Namibia. For the first time in the history of the UN, Namibians had declared war on the South African regime in Namibia. The following are details of what came to be one of the most painful chapters in the history of political conflicts.

In 1969 the UN Security Council confirmed, through Resolution 269 of 1969, the revocation of South Africa's mandate and recognized the legitimacy of the struggle of the people of Namibia against South Africa's presence in their country. In 1971 the ICJ, in one of its advisory opinions, ruled that the revocation of South Africa's mandate was valid, that South Africa's presence in Namibia was illegal, and that its acts on behalf of or concerning Namibia were invalid. All these in place, the onus lay on South Africa to respond. The world waited with bated breath in anticipation of what South Africa Prime Minister John Vorster would say. When the moment came, Vorster made a statement that reverberated around the world, "We shall continue to administer Southwest Africa." By then the battle lines were drawn and the fate of Namibia would be sealed in blood for the close to 20 years that followed.

Negotiated Settlement

In 1977, two North American – Canada and the United States – and three West European countries – France, West Germany, and Great Britain – sponsored a plan that was intended to facilitate a negotiated settlement for Namibia's independence. They started intensive negotiations with a broad spectrum of interested parties to include SWAPO, South Africa the (southern African) Frontline States, and political groupings in Namibia.

The plan provided for a transitional process whereby Namibia would attain independence through elections supervized by the UN and conducted by a South African-appointed administrator general (AG) who would also run the country in the interim. The process would be inaugurated by a cessation of hostilities between the warring parties, South Africa and SWAPO. And it provided for free and fair elections under the joint supervision and control of the UN and South Africa through the Special Representative of the UN Secretary-General and the administrator general.

This was the first plan of its kind that attempted to pull the warring parties to the table and to move the process towards a settlement. After extensive negotiations, the idea was finally encapsulated in a UN plan that came to be known as the UN Security Council Resolution (UNSCR) 435 of 1978. Unfortunately, it took 12 years of negotiations, punctuated by intermittent hostilities in the region and an ongoing war between SWAPO and South African forces. Finally implemented in 1989, it ushered in Namibia's freedom and independence as a unitary and democratic state.

The Transitional Process and Beyond

The proposition that UNSCR 435 be implemented in 1989 left many Namibians with mixed feelings, partly because of the time it had taken and partly because of the war climate in the southern Africa region. South Africa was ablaze; Angola was sealed in blood; in Namibia the war was more and more real in the metropolis areas with bombings increasing and state repression through detentions intensified. Also, South Africa continued as if desperately to play her hand at various administrative experiments, jumping from Interim Government through Transitional Government, to Transitional Government of National Unity. Military manoeuvres continued, pulling the Cuban soldiers into the forefront of the Angolan conflict. But negotiations intensified and South Africa was increasingly pushed to the negotiating table. All these developments led a church leader to remark:

It all seems real but it looks remote. South Africa is talking in the right direction, yet going into the wrong direction . . . the war in the north is increasing, not decreasing.[4]

The implementation of UNSCR 435 was scheduled to start on 1 April 1989, and everybody waited in anticipation. The UN Transitional Contingent had started to arrive, albeit in small numbers. But they were visible in the minds of the average Namibian who watched television and read the newspapers. There was concern about their proposed numbers because the UN had trimmed their size owing to financial problems in the organization. Still, their arrival had boosted the morale of the Namibians. Observer groups had also started to arrive. The Frontline States had set up an office and the international media turned up in numbers at every event in town. The churches had started to organize observer groups through the international ecumenical community and other friends.

Consultations across the seas were the order of the day in many ways. SWAPO and her allies, the labour and student movements, were riding high and the parties opposed to SWAPO were increasingly sharpening their knives and positioning themselves to square it out with the liberation movement. But it was already evident that SWAPO was the front runner. Morale was sky-high among the party's supporters, and with the recent release from prison of leaders (Niko Bessinger, Daniel Tjongerero, Hendrik Witbooi, John Pandeni, Ben Uulenga, Asser Kapare and others) the mood among SWAPO supporters was ecstatic and reminiscent of Michael Jackson's upbeat song of the late seventies, "Ain't No Stopping Us Now." It was countdown to 1 April.

Enter the tragic events of 1 April 1989, which kept everybody convinced that the process was to be aborted as it was about to start. Whatever led to the painful events of that fateful day will still be told by those in the know. The fact is, war broke out and, unfortunately, many lives were lost again. The long and short of it all is that the crisis was arrested, thanks to shuttle diplomacy, global goodwill, and the commitment of Namibians to make the process work. But the three weeks or so that marked the events of 1 April were nerve-racking.

Elections came and Namibians were able, for the first time in history, to elect their own leaders, on a proportional basis, to a Constituent Assembly (CA) that would write the first ever Constitution of the Republic to be. The CA was inaugurated on 21 November 1989. The various leaders of the elected parties made moving statements, in a somewhat pensive mood, in a tense and rather hostile environment with (political) swords against SWAPO not yet parried. All these played against the backdrop of the regime of the South African transitional administrator general, who himself was rather hostile to the CA or elements thereof. His tacit approval for funds to some separatist white groups to establish whites-only schools during the session of the assembly bears testimony to the said hostile attitude. Thanks to the vigilance of Namibia's just elected leaders, the move was stopped when the CA unanimously condemned this act and forced the South

African authorities in Namibia to reverse this decision. And this is where it all started: with the will to rally together around the notion that Namibia will be a free, democratic, and unitary state.

The rest are details of history that, for the purpose of this article and its envisaged space, will not be considered.

Democratic Institution Building

Development of Parliament

> We expect a great deal, not only from the Executive in the implementation of policies, but also from our Legislators in crystallising ideas, by debating issues of national importance. This spirit of finding solutions through debate and consultation has served us well in the past, and it is my hope that both Houses of our Parliament will bring new vigor to this approach this year and beyond.[5]

The stage for the development of Namibia's Parliament was set by the development of the CA. The UN Security Council Resolution 435 set forth that, departing from the premise that, legally, South Africa was illegally occupying Namibia, South Africa had an obligation to withdraw from Namibia and by so doing to hand over power to the people of Namibia. A proper mechanism for this transfer had to be worked out. During the UN-supervized and South Africa-administered elections of 1989 held in Namibia, a 72-member CA was elected and charged with three basic tasks: (1) to draft a constitution for the proposed republic and to adopt it by two-thirds of the members of the CA; (2) to select and agree on a date for the independence of Namibia; and (3) on the basis of the new Constitution, to declare independence and to form a government.

All these expectations were accomplished with minimum delay and by and large in record time. The elections of the CA were held from 7 to 11 November 1989, through proportional representation whereby voters cast their ballots for political parties of their choice and each political party was allocated seats in conformity with the percentage they received in the popular vote. On 21 November 1989, the CA met for the first time to deliberate on the task at hand. On 9 February 1990, the CA unanimously adopted a new constitution. Since there was consensus on the transitional mechanism among the political parties representing the Namibian people in the CA, the process of moving from CA to the National Assembly became a formality. And on Independence Day, 21 March 1990, the CA became the National Assembly and assumed the responsibility of setting up a new political order in the rather politically divided and economically underdeveloped nation-state.

The National Assembly
and the National Council

The National Assembly constituted the unicameral or one-chamber legislature at independence whose role would be to promulgate legislation as initiated by the executive, the cabinet, or through private member initiatives or bills. The Constitution provided for and thereby required the establishment of the second chamber, the National Council, in order to complete Namibia's Parliament. The role of the second chamber is to review all legislation, whether initiated by the executive or by private members of Parliament. Legislation originates from the cabinet (the executive) and comes to the National Assembly in the form of bills. The National Assembly, after normally extensive debate, approves a bill and passes it on to the National Council for review. The National Council debates the piece of legislation; once approved, it is sent to the president for signature, in accordance with the Constitution.

The National Council is elected directly by means of a simple majoritarian system by the electorate in the constituencies and the 13 regions throughout Namibia, unlike the National Assembly, which is elected on the basis of proportional representation through the party list system. The National Council consists of 26 members, two from each region. The members are first elected to their respective regions' councils from which they are elected by the regional councillors to the National Council for a term of six years; the term of office for the National Assembly is five years. Each region elects a governor. Proposed legislation, however, provides for the governors to be appointed by the head of state from among the members elected to the regional councils. Both chambers of Parliament have a leader and a deputy of the House; the National Assembly elects the Speaker and Deputy Speaker, while the National Council elects the chairperson and vice-chairperson.

An important development in the Namibian Parliament is the formation of the Women's Caucus comprising female members of Parliament from political parties across the floor. The aim in forming the caucus was, in the context of contemporary national and global expectations, to promote gender sensitivity in parliamentary politics and to enhance the role of women in the Namibian Parliament.

Parliament does not operate in isolation. Its political party representatives provide the backbone and should normally serve as the lifeblood in the process of legislation. Each party has a chief whip who coordinates the position of the party *vis-à-vis* the legislative process as proposed or tabled in Parliament. Each party has a caucus through which it coordinates individual party members' positions in consultations. Each caucus meets regularly as determined by the parties themselves. In addition, each party has a leader in Parliament, who may not necessarily be the chairperson of its caucus or its chief whip.

The National Assembly has a fully functioning committee system that conducts hearings, convenes media briefings to articulate their work, and MPs travel around the country to consult with the public about issues of concern to them, such as corruption. The committees also invite ministries, for example, public accounts committees, to explain the activities of their various departments. MPs have developed the necessary capacity to study proposed legislation, to investigate policy issues, and to receive expert and other testimonies for consideration. The committee system of the National Council, still in its infancy, has kept the NDI on its feet for the past 18 months in attempts to help develop a functioning organization. Plans are under way to send committee chairs on observation visitations, which would expose them to functioning committee systems in similar institutions in other countries. One must concede, however, that the development of the committee system in the National Council has moved rather slowly. The Council needs to review its strategy so as to give impetus to this undertaking.

Development of the Executive

The Namibian Constitution provides for a three-tier form of state governance. It consists of the Executive – the head of state, called president and the cabinet; the legislature – the Parliament consisting of the two chambers and the Judiciary, the courts and the legal system.

By virtue of the Constitution, the Executive is drawn from the elected members of Parliament, including six appointed by the president. The Executive, effectively the government of the Republic of Namibia, is responsible for governing the country, initiating laws in the form of bills and tabling them in Parliament for that body's consideration and promulgation into law.

Appointment of the members of the Executive is the prerogative of the president, who is directly elected, by virtue of Namibia's supreme law, by the electorate, and as such is an executive president. The president is the chair of cabinet.
Members of the Executive, known to Namibia as members of the cabinet or cabinet ministers, head ministries and are collectively responsible for running the country under the leadership of the prime minister. Elected by their respective parties as members of Parliament, they have the obligation to attend to parliamentary requirements and expectations in addition to running their respective ministries. As it is now, Namibia's Parliament is dominated by the Executive, much to the discomfort of the rest of the members and more so from the opposition benches. There are currently 98 elected MPs. An additional 6 are appointed by the president. Of these, 40 are ministers or deputy ministers; the remaining 38 are back-benchers. The Namibian cabinet holds its formal meetings once a week on Tuesdays, and the Minister of Information and Broadcasting briefs the media on cabinet decisions every Wednesday.

The People and Their Democratic Institutions

Voices, Hopes, and Anxieties

> I know no safe depository of the ultimate power of the society but the people themselves and if we think them not enlightened enough to exercise their

control with wholesome discretion, the remedy is not to take it from them, but to inform their discretion.[6]

The advent of democracy in Namibia is a new development particularly considering the fact that the process itself was born out of a violent conflict situation. When the new state ushered itself into independence, Namibians readied themselves to establish a democratic state, albeit with mixed feelings. (Always present in South Africa was the threat of sabotage; of a civil war propelled by South Africa; of discontent leading to disagreements in the CA *vis-à-vis* the model Constitution that would finally be adopted. Still, Namibians moved along with serious business and adopted their Constitution in less than three months. The new nation-state then settled down to reality and started to develop the different political and other institutions, primary of which were the legislature, the Executive, and the Judiciary. This experience may have led the Speaker of Namibia's National Assembly to exclaim:

> Parliament is the forum for reconciling different opinions in the interest of the country, and its task is to bring out the human element in politics which leads to greater tolerance among politicians for each other's position. The obstacles with which our fragile democracy were faced could be seen in the workings of the country's first independence parliament. . . . A culture of tolerance and healthy, constructive debate is taking root in Namibia . . . It is both the responsibility of the ruling party and the opposition to see to it that Namibia's democracy is nurtured, otherwise it runs the risk of stagnation and ultimate decline.[7]

This is the democracy to which Namibia's well-wishers committed themselves to help nurture. The NDI is one of the organisations that moved along to develop democratic institution-building programs in support of Namibia's Parliament. NDI's work in Namibia has gone a long way in assisting to enhance the capacity of Parliament through a number of programs, which produced a storehouse of information that assists MPs and parliamentary staff, as well as political parties and regional authorities, to face with confidence the challenges of having to conduct the business of state.

Such information is in the form of analysing proposed and passed legislation, and survey findings of different players such as civil society and professional groups. It included focus group research, interviews with members of Parliament, and studies and reviews of the national budget. It is therefore expected that it will form the basis for examining the attitudes of Namibians, their expectations, and whether these expectations have been fulfilled or disappointed.

Studies and Their Conclusions
Much has been done to study public opinion about political developments and Namibia's transition to democracy for the past nine years of independence. For the

sake of brevity, this article focuses on the process of democratic institution building. For democracy to become meaningful in Namibia, citizens should be free to participate in the process and they must have free access to and influence on the process of developing national laws and policies. Parliament must be the constitutionally defined forum where citizens can have an effect on the legislative process. Outside of Parliament the citizens can participate in the democratic dispensation through civil society: NGOs such as the labour movement, women's associations, student bodies, and civic groups such as ratepayers' associations.

Since independence a number of studies and opinion surveys were undertaken by NDI or with its sponsorship to look at various issues on democracy in Namibia, and some were analysed in this process.

Democratic and Political Institutions:
Popular Conceptions

What good can democracy do if it is not about the development of people? People cannot be developed. They must develop themselves, given the necessary tools and resources. The least that elected leaders can do is to create and enhance the political environment in which people's self-expression and self-actualization can take place. This is where the need exists occasionally to quiz the people on the extent to which they keep a finger on the pulse, to gauge continually whether democracy is on course.

Focus Groups

Perhaps the most dynamic tool in attempting to find out how people relate to the political system in Namibia is the use of focus group research. A focus group is an extended discussion between members of the public about specific issues.[8] The group usually has a moderator who introduces topics in a specific way and guides the discussion. The data-collection process differs substantially from survey research methods in which questions are issue-specific and concise. Focus group questions are open-ended and respondents are encouraged to state their opinions frankly. Focus groups also have the advantage of eliciting complex responses from informants, and they are often used to help define major issues that can later be measured more accurately through the use of questionnaires and in-depth interviews.

One limitation of focus groups is that, by their nature, they produce data that could be subjective and difficult to interpret accurately as a representative measurement of perceptions towards society, political institutions, and the democratic process since independence. But to the extent that the people's voices speak for themselves, they can be a helpful tool in gauging their mood and, if applied carefully, can go a long way in providing a bird's-eye view of society.

This section concentrates primarily on two focus group surveys that were commissioned by NDI since independence, one in 1996 and the other in 1998, six and eight years, respectively, after independence. During the 1996 survey, 15 groups were conducted by two researchers from the University of Namibia from different locations around the country. They intended to study societies' perceptions on issues such as feelings about democracy, change, economic and educational opportunities, crime and discipline, democratic participation, Parliament, hunger for information, and the roles of the National Council and the National Assembly and others.

The 1998 study looked at 24 groups spread around the country, representing about seven political regions and focusing on the same issues as the 1996 study with gender equality, attitudes toward the Constitution, multiparty democracy, and ethics as additional issues. The two studies are appraised interchangeably.

The first study presents results of the 15 focus group discussions held between March and April 1996. The theme of the discussions was perceptions about democratic political institutions, with a focus on Parliament, six years after independence. Generally, a positive mood obtained about Namibia. Respondents appreciated a democratic form of government for the freedom it provided and the manner in which the ruling and opposition parties interacted in dealing with contentious issues in and around Parliament. Need was expressed for a strong opposition. Perceptions about Parliament were also voiced; they were generally positive and reflected an understanding of the nature and the roles of both chambers. The groups maintained that there was a need for communication among the key players, regional councils, the National Council, the National Assembly, and the government. The groups expressed a general desire for enhanced communication between Parliament and communities in the regions. In this regard, the groups crystalized some recommendations on enhancing communication. These consisted of more frequent meetings between MPs and citizens in all areas of the country; more effective means of transmitting parliamentary debates, including live broadcasts; better education on the role and nature of all governmental structures in Namibia.

The 1996 focus group study concluded that in general, democratic institutions in Namibia are healthy and that there is a need for a strong political opposition to balance the views of the ruling party. This need was expressed strongly, even in areas where the ruling party commanded up to 90 per cent support. There was a widespread view that the Constitution is a basic document that should be amended only after very careful deliberation. The study found that Namibians had a positive outlook toward their country and that they were increasingly enthusiastic about the democratic process.

The argument is advanced that this generally positive trend could be adversely affected by issues such as the sluggish economic development and the problems of discipline and crime. Concerns were widespread about the economic decline, much as there was appreciation of the fact that a wide range of factors such as the reform of the South African Customs Union, drought conditions over which the government had no control, the discovery and development of extractive natural resources, worldwide economic performance, and so forth, played a role. The focus groups held by and large that the youth of society lacked discipline, which was seen to exacerbate the problem of crime in the country.

It was argued that the police in free Namibia did not seem to have the wide-ranging, all-encompassing powers they wielded under apartheid. They had to respect the rights of all individuals, even suspected criminals.

The study found that knowledge of Namibia's Parliament was widespread. Most of the groups distinguished between the two houses and were able to discern the relative functions of the National Assembly and the National Council. In the final analysis, Namibians were eager to know more about their Parliament. They wanted factual information about the duties and responsibilities of each house. Namibians are also keen to have more face-to-face meetings with their legislators, especially with those from the National Assembly. Many respondents expressed the wish to hear their MPs speak in Parliament and wanted to hear detailed reports about parliamentary debates. Rural communities were marginalized, partly due to their limited access to electronic media and partly to language factors. Therefore, the need was expressed to enhance the standards of the indigenous language services on radio to raise the level of information flow to communities.

The second focus group study looked at and presented the results of 24 discussions that were held throughout Namibia between February and April 1998. This was intended to be a follow-up to the 1996 study and aimed at assisting Namibian political leaders to enhance the transparency, accountability, and efficiency of the political system, and those of the legislature in particular.

Some of the survey questions follow.

- Have the attitudes of Namibians toward their political institutions changed since the first focus group research of 1996?
- Have trends observed two years before become consolidated?
- If there are changes, what are they?

The study concluded that after eight years, Namibians recognized the country's political institutions as their own. Whether or not they agreed with all aspects of the political system, Namibians from across the political, and racial spectrum and gender divide expressed a strong sense of ownership of the country's political institutions.

The following issues were among the findings of the study.

- The decline in voter participation in recent elections is a phenomenon that deserves serious attention. Focus groups' comments on the tendency indicated that Namibians vote for change and become disillusioned if they did not experience change in their communities and in the country.
- Accurate information on the country's political system in general and Parliament in particular persisted in being lacking to a large extent. Only a minority of rural dwellers knew the statutory roles of the Parliament, and many urban residents had a vague understanding of the functions of the two chambers of Parliament, with the review functions of the National Council virtually unknown and the second house mostly perceived as a body in

which legal and regional concerns may be raised and brought to the attention of the National Assembly and the central government.

- Respondents across the country complained about the insufficient contacts between parliamentarians and the electorate and the lack of information about the workings of Parliament.

The study made the following recommendations.

- Members of Parliament should establish regular and predictable contacts with constituencies;
- Parliamentarians and political parties should engage in community-based voter (civic) education that extends beyond the times of electoral campaigns;
- Voter (civic) education should be included in various curricula of formal and non-formal education;
- The media, especially the Namibia Broadcasting Corporation's language services, should provide space for voter education programmes and consider extensive coverage of parliamentary debates.

The study, for the most part, asked participants to state their opinions on the same topics as those of the 1996 research, with the addition of two new topics, namely, the possibility of amending the Constitution and ethical issues. That is, how do the respondents feel about generous salaries and perks for political office-bearers, and what do they think about tendencies toward corruption and nepotism?

Generally this focus group study concluded that Namibians by and large believe that the country is a better place to live in than it was ten years before, with respect to the political situation in the country. Participants pointed to the difference between the former and current political dispensations. They felt that despite the changes brought about by independence and democracy, much still needed to be done, and the government and a broad spectrum of society needed to guard against complacency. Also, the degree of satisfaction the people expressed varied considerably. The younger participants were far more critical than their older compatriots.

Similar to the 1996 survey, most participants felt that democracy enabled people to participate in political decision making, particularly through voting. Apart from democracy as a political system, to many respondents democracy means a way of life, extending beyond the confines of political institutions, restoring a broader meaning to the concept by including freedom and human rights, particularly the freedom of speech. This is what some of the participants had to say.

- Female Katutura resident, central Namibia: "Democracy means freedom to vote for any political party you wish to vote for, without intimidation from anyone."

- Male Walvis Bay resident, western Namibia: "Democracy is to be free, to be free to speak, to be free from everything that oppressed us."
- Hoachanas resident, southern Namibia: "I see democracy as peace and cooperation . . . I do not think that it means that you can do whatever you want. Respect, tolerance, understanding, and living for each other; this is how I understand it, also as caring for and loving each other."

Many participants felt that while democracy was in the real sense a good concept, it was widely misunderstood in Namibia as a licence to unlimited freedoms. And calls demanding that the concept be explained more clearly to the people abounded.

Namibians have by and large come to accept their political institutions and feel ownership of them. They are critical of shortcomings and perceived wrongdoing and failings, but remain committed to the institutions. They are not found wanting when it comes to defending these institutions and would jealously guard against anything that seems to denigrate Namibia's democracy. There is an unsettling suspicion among many Namibians that a number of those in authority are abusing their powers and are out to enrich themselves while holding political office. Even at that, criticism would be devoid of making unbridled generalizations and would avoid blanket statements, while deeply rooted in a sense of respect for high office, personal discipline, and integrity. But they remain concerned about the need to move cautiously over some of the sensitive issues, such as the Constitution. They continue to appeal for the defense of democracy and want a strong opposition to check the ruling party, not necessarily a different ruling party.

It is instructive to note that while the socio-economic hardships increasingly draw average Namibians to a point of despair, they still find solace in the political institutions of their land and see themselves continually appealing for economic reform and abstinence from unethical habits. What is yours is yours, they say, and no one can take it from you.

Members of Parliament from both sides of the house expressed their views, hopes, and anxieties about the future of the country, the need to strengthen democracy, to enhance the economy, to improve education and living standards, to reduce government spending by, *inter alia,* checking the expansion of the civil service, and curbing corruption. There were, in the final analysis, words for the defense of democracy and the need for a stronger opposition. And while there were voices, especially from opposition benches, against amending the Constitution because they felt that it would set an unfortunate precedent, two characteristics prevailed that by and large pulled a thread through the views of parliamentarians across the floor. One, there is tremendous respect for Dr Sam Nujoma, the incumbent president, and virtually all MPs would go out of their way to praise or to record a word of appreciation for his political qualities and his role as a unifying figure. Two, there seem to be limited aspirations from the opposition benches to one day govern the country, and opposition parties seem content with being opponents – and to this the MPs of the ruling party agree – if only Namibia can have a stronger and much more effective role in keeping the ruling party in check. There, however, have been new developments underway urging the opposition parties to field presidential candidates.

The Struggle of Political Parties
in the Democratic Environment

Virtually all of Namibia's political parties are products of the apartheid regime. They were formed, starting from the late 1950s, either to oppose South Africa's occupation of Namibia and its concomitant policies (Southwest Africa People's Organization [SWAPO], Southwest Africa National Union [SWANU], National Unity Democratic Organization [NUDO], et al.) or, like the Democratic Turnhalle Alliance (DTA) and others, they were formed by, or in collaboration wit,h the South African regime in Namibia, to oppose the liberation movement spearheaded by SWAPO.

The prospects for Namibia's imminent independence ushered in a new political complexion and as time drew closer to the implementation of the UN Security Council Resolution 435 of 1978, which agreed to the terms for the independence of Namibia, new formations and counterformations were created, leading to a plethora of coalitions. What was striking during the transitional period was the fact that all political parties and coalitions which were organized and restructured for the purpose of contesting the first-ever Namibian elections had one target in mind, SWAPO.

By December 1988 it was evident that elections were destined to take place and that SWAPO would participate. It was also evident that South Africa had finally agreed to the settlement plan and that the Transitional Government of National Unity, which was midwifed by the South African regime in Namibia through the South African-appointed administrator general, would be history in a matter of months if not weeks. All these were playing against the backdrop of the fact that SWAPO and South Africa had to sign a cease-fire accord, which would facilitate SWAPO's participation in the elections, and everybody knew that by then it was only a formality. The stage was therefore set for the parties to prepare for elections and, with the exception of SWAPO, virtually all the parties entered into one form of coalition or another in order to be in a better position to stake a claim during the elections.

Before this period, Namibia boasted, theoretically speaking, more than 40 political parties, most of which were essentially family formations and by and large existed only in name. But the fact is that ten parties registered for and took part in the 1989 national elections and seven of them were elected, on the basis of proportional representation, to the CA. During the 1994 national and presidential elections, eight parties contested and five were elected and formed the second Namibian Parliament. Still, most of the parties that did not make it to Parliament continue to exist and some would occasionally enter some regional or local authority elections, only to recede into obscurity when things did not work all that well.

Five political parties are currently represented in the Namibian Parliament. They consist of the ruling party SWAPO, comprising more than two-thirds of Parliament; DTA, the main opposition, controlling 15 seats in the National Assembly and four in the National Council; UDF with one seat in the National Assembly and one in the National Council; and the Democratic Coalition of Namibia and the Monitor Action Group, each with one seat in the National Assembly and none in the National Council.

Since independence, Namibia has witnessed an organic association between the growth in strength of the ruling party and the decline of the opposition parties. During the 1989 elections, the ruling party won 42 of the 72 seats and the rest were shared among the elected parties. The 1994 national and presidential elections saw SWAPO gaining 53 seats in the National Assembly, and the trend has continued steadily in both houses of Parliament as well as in the regional authority elections. What will happen during the 1999 elections remains to be seen and it is only a guess as to how many of the current political parties in Parliament will be returned by the electorate.

The conundrum characterizing Namibia's political party spectrum defies wisdom and, in the absence of scientific studies, such enigmas can only rely on public views, speculations, and opinions. The following are among the questions that have occupied many minds.

- What is responsible for the decline in strength of opposition politics in Parliament?
- From what does the ruling party continue to derive its popularity?
- In what way will the decline in opposition politics affect Namibia's democracy? Will this be positive or negative?
- If this trend continues, and indications are that it is likely to, are we on our way to a "one-party dictatorship?"
- What must happen or be done for there to be a strong opposition to "check the ruling party" in Namibia?

And many more.

I submit that a number of factors are accountable for the state of political parties in Namibia, among them, seriousness of purpose, organisational capacity, constituency building, financial and other resources, and the ability to operate in the current, at times unforgiving yet lethargic socio-economic and political environment. These factors affect all political parties including those that are extra-parliamentary.

Seriousness of Purpose: Before Namibia's independence, the driving force for parties was independence and the purpose for engaging in political activity was driven by the wish to speed up independence. During the post-independence era, the driving force seems to be the determination to keep the gains, hold on to the seats in Parliament, or gain more. Or it may be the wish to win a seat in Parliament. As a result, most of the manifestos that proliferate during elections seem to be ends in themselves and are hardly ever an extrapolation from serious policy manifestos, intended to be blueprints to one day govern the country. Also, during the struggle, political parties had membership drives that were marked by ongoing fund-raisers and political activity.

The post-independence era has seen several political parties that primarily consist of activists and for whom membership drives and political activity are restricted to electioneering rhetoric. This trend does not seem to reflect seriousness of purpose. I assume that the ultimate aim of a political party is to one day govern the country and, unless the party has an ongoing political program, it is hard to imagine how this can be possible.

Organizational Capacity: Using the above argument as a point of departure, an organisation can be successful if there is the capacity to organize, campaign, and mobilize understanding of and support for its aims and objectives. Most of the political parties currently in and outside of Parliament have no regular offices and with the exception of SWAPO and the DTA, none have regular staff. It therefore stands to reason that most political parties in Namibia cannot be expected to perform any differently from the current status.

Constituency Building: One way for a political party to grow and develop is by constantly building the strength of its own constituencies and by making forays into new ones. Limited seriousness of purpose and limited organizational capacity serve as obvious barriers to constituency building, and most of the parties continue to rely on traditional constituencies for their continued existence and survival.

Resources: Financial and other resources play a pivotal role in the life of political organizations and serve as the cutting edge to success. During the struggle political organizing depended to a large extent on party membership contributions and deliberate ongoing fund-raisers. With political apathy creeping into the country, it goes without saying that parties are struggling with membership fees and, consequently, little political organizing is going on. Little wonder that Namibia's democracy is running the risk of being paralyzed by voter apathy and stay-aways throughout the country. As a result, a situation is fast growing whereby popular administrations will be elected by a small percentage of the electorate, while everybody is apportioning blame on everybody else and the directorate of elections is increasingly hard-pressed to explain to the people why the nation is abdicating its hard-won right to vote and its obligation to remain politically relevant in difficult and rather politically unpredictable times. It must be said, however, that the political parties in Parliament receive funding from the government, albeit on a sliding scale. As the real answers to the questions posed above remain elusive, the conundrum characterizing Namibia's political party spectrum will remain intact.

The Long View
In *No One Can Stop the Rain,* George Houser recounts an experience he had in Zimbabwe in 1983, three years after that country's independence. Zimbabwe was going through difficulties. A crippling drought had damaged crops and the country

was importing corn, unlike in normal years. There was an anti-government uprising in Matebeleland followed by a heavy-handed reaction from government
troops. Relations between the Zimbabwe African People's Union (ZAPU) and the
Zimbabwe African National Union-Patriotic Front (ZANU-PF) were strained, and
the patriotic front was about to break down. Houser spoke to Garfield Todd, then a
senator in the Zimbabwe Parliament. He asked Todd where Zimbabwe was going.
Todd must have responded, somewhat thoughtfully, "You've got to take the long
view." After this exchange, Houser reflected his perspective in the book:

> By taking the long view of Africa, looking at its past and its future, as well
> as its present, I try to put developments in some perspective. It must be
> recognized that the long period of foreign occupation from which Africa is
> just emerging has contributed heavily to its present problems. The colonial
> powers were devoted to serving their own best interests. They were not
> essentially seeking progress for the people of the Lands they controlled.
> Whatever advances were made, were incidental.[9]

The development of democracy in Namibia, in Africa, in the formerly colo-
nized world, have to be appraised in the context of the long view. While global
accords reached in international forums such as the League of Nations and its
successor the UN may have been pronounced with honourable motives, in favor of
guiding those nations which were hitherto unable to navigate their own course, the
fact is that these noble intentions did not work, and in the end the secondary
nations had to struggle their way to freedom and self-determination, albeit with
international solidarity and material support. It stands to reason, therefore, that to
the extent that Namibia's political history has not known democracy because the
country's perceived mentors and midwives through the years have not attempted to
show that by example, to that extent it will be inconsistent to view the development of Namibia's democracy through the prism of a country that has known
justice and democracy for decades. The independence of Namibia is primarily a
product of efforts by Namibians themselves based on their own methods and the
movement towards democracy may therefore have to develop along this path, at a
pace perhaps slower than expectations would have it.

With this in place, it is safe to say, also as corroborated by studies, evaluations,
surveys, and the discussions contained in this article, Namibia's democracy is far
more than a withering breeze, and the country can be proud of having a democratic
system, albeit with attendant problems, that is fast establishing a democratic
culture and a free society. But the need for the political leadership and the nation at
large to keep a finger on the pulse as far as issues of citizen participation, political
apathy, crime, corruption, and so on, are concerned, remains pronounced and quite
a challenge to Namibia's democracy.

Notes

1. "Essential Documents of the United Nations' Independence Plan, 1979–1989" (London: Namibia Communications Centre, 1989).
2. *ibid.*
3. P.H. Katjavivi, *The History of Resistance in Namibia* (London: James Curry Publishers, 1988).
4. Dr Abisai Shejavali: CCN Secretary-General, Media Conference, April 1989.
5. Speech by H.E. Dr Sam Nujoma at the opening of Parliament after a recess, 1996.
6. President Franklin Delano Roosevelt, quoted by I. Kaulinge at a media workshop, Windhoek, 8 July 1998.
7. Speaker of the National Assembly, "Parliament Handbook," 1998.
8. Report on focus group research in Namibia, March–April 1996.
9. George Houser, *No One Can Stop the Rain* (New York: Pilgrim Press, 1989).

Bibliography

Bruhns, P., and H. Becker. "Popular Perceptions of Political Institutions in Namibia." National Democratic Institute for International Affairs (hereafter NDI) Focus Group Research. Report, Windhoek,1998.

Centre for Democracy and Governance. "Handbook of Democracy and Governance Program Indicators." Washington, D.C., 1998.

Du Pisani, A. "State and Society under South African Rule." Windhoek, 1998.

Houser, G.M. *No One Can Stop the Rain*. New York: Pilgrim Press, 1989.

Hull, R.W. *Munyakare: African Civilisation before the Batuuree*. New York, London, Sydney, Toronto: John Wiley, 1972.

Katjavivi, P.H. *The History of Resistance in Namibia*. London: James Curry Publishers, 1988.

Keulder, C. "Bill Analysis: The Budget 1997/1978." NDI Report. Windhoek, 1997.

Keulder, C. "Political Perceptions and Opinions of Namibian Students. Survey Findings." NDI Report, 1998.

Namibia Communications Centre. "Essential Documents of the United Nations Independence Plan, 1976–1989." London Office,1989.

NDI. "Report on an Ethics Questionnaire, Regional Consultative Workshops." August 1998.

NDI. "Consolidating Parliamentary Democracy in Namibia." Windhoek: NDI, 1998.

NDI. "Strengthening the Parliament in Namibia." NDI Project Documents, Windhoek, 1995.

NDI. "Voices of Reconciliation: Angolans Speak on Peace and Democracy," Occasional Paper no. 1. Windhoek: NDI, 1998.

Sachikonye, L., and I. Mandaza. *Democracy, Civil Society and the State*. Harare: Sapes Books, 1995.

U.S. Agency for International Development Mission to Namibia. "Strategic Objective Number 4." Windhoek: USAID, 1996.

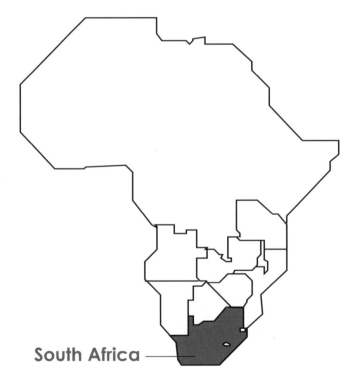

South Africa ———

South Africa:
Reflections on the
Miracle

Padraig O'Malley

*T*he story is the stuff of lore: how South Africa's apartheid regime, under the leadership of F.W. de Klerk unbanned the African National Congress (ANC) and the South African Communist Party (SACP), released Nelson Mandela; how both the ANC and the National Party (NP) government committed themselves to a negotiated settlement; how negotiations took place in circumstances of increasing violence – "black-on-black" was the euphemism of choice – for which the ANC held the government accountable; how the white right-wing attempted to prevent the inevitable surrender of power and the reins of government to the black majority; how the roller-coaster negotiations nearly came to naught on many occasions; how General Constand Viljoen's decision, at a crucial moment, to forswear violence to achieve the Afrikaner volk averted possible civil war; how Gathsha Buthelezi's decision to throw his electoral hat into the ring at the last moment also averted possible civil war. And then, of course, there was the "miracle" itself – the election days of 23 and 24 April 1994, when South Africans of all races went to the polls peacefully and without intimidation, equal citizens according to the interim constitution all parties had agreed to, and elected the country's first black-led government. What many had confidently predicted – that the Afrikaners would hold on to power as long as they had the resources and firepower to do so – became, overnight, extant, reams of punditry consigned instantaneously to one of history's many trash bins.*

Padraig O'Malley is a Senior Fellow at the McCormack Institute of Public Affairs, University of Massachusetts Boston, US and editor of the New England Journal of Public Policy. He is particularly noted for his writing on democratic transitions and divided societies, specifically on Northern Ireland and South Africa.

* Author's opinions and comments appear in *italics,* usually in parenthesis; opinions and comments of the focus group participants and interpretations of focus group analysts are typeset in Century Gothic, usually in quotation marks; identifications typeset in Times New Roman 10pt are quotes from sources cited.

This essay examines the findings of a number of public opinion survey reports carried out between September 1992 and October 1998 with a view to ascertaining the dynamics behind the transition in South Africa and to probing the nature of transitions in emerging democracies to see whether there are conclusions we can draw and lessons we can learn that can be applied to other countries undergoing similar transformations.

It is important to bear in mind that social policy research is only as good as the data it draws on, the quality and experience that the researchers bring to their work, and that even the best of work refers to feelings and attitudes that exist at a point in time, and that extrapolation of findings without strict adherence to these considerations is foolhardy at best and erroneous at worst. With these caveats in mind, we will wander into the mysterious world of transitions, often unfathomable in their own genesis, and never predictable in their outcomes.

How does one begin to describe a country which appears to exist in some suspended state, where on the one hand one could reasonably argue that the fissures in the tissue of the nation are beginning to become an open chasm and on the other that the continuous practice of "living on the edge" has incubated an immunity to what, in other circumstances or other countries, might be regarded as impending signs of social breakdown.

But perhaps it is the fact that South Africa has always tethered on the brink of social breakdown that the unacceptable has by and large become tolerable, and a benign ennui, even in the face of mass protest and the like, has bred a passive indifference to unfolding misfortune.

After the abolition of apartheid, there was little attention given to such things as emerging markets, and a people having had their first taste of freedom and national sovereignty were not about to immediately surrender a significant part of both to the card-carrying cadres of the World Bank and the taskmasters of globalization.

Who, after all, would have thought a few years ago that economic collapse in South-East Asia would wreak its wretched havoc in South Africa, that South Africa would have little option but to stand idly by as wave after wave of currency depreciation in South Korea, Malaysia, Indonesia, and finally Japan – the world's second largest economy once synonymous with invincibility – would claim the rand as one of its victims in the financial backwash, and with it any hope of the economic growth so essential for sustaining the miracle that "delivered" South Africa in 1994? The economic crisis in Zimbabwe – South Africa's biggest customer in the Southern Africa Development Community (SADC) – led to a 22 per cent decline in exports and was the main contributor to a decline of 6 per cent to all SADC countries, which in "normal times" account for 17 per cent of South Africa's manufactured exports. Since the countries – the United States, Germany, Japan, and Britain – which collectively accounted for one-third of all South Africa's manufactured goods exports were beginning to feel the first pings of the

South-East Asia crisis and the deflation in global demand that accompanied it, the outlook for South Africa exports became increasingly hazardous."[1]

In October 1998, the deficit had soared to $85 million, even though imports fell, in contrast to the surplus in September of $24 million. Exports had plummeted by almost 6 per cent – more than enough to offset the trade benefit of decreasing imports. The economy was in recession, or at the very least had become unstuck; per capita income was falling, the business sector reeling under the pressure of forces beyond its control, and South Africa joined the list of emerging markets being crushed by forces beyond its control: the dream of "a better life for all" seemed more ephemeral than ever. Not that any of these considerations crossed the minds of the students at the University of the Venda who trashed their campus and reduced a university building to cinders because officials refused to provide them with free beer for a party – all they were looking for, to put matters in perspective, was R500,000 to purchase 30 cans of beer per student."[2]

And not that things were falling apart: for that to happen they would have to have been together in some way, and in South Africa they never were; once the repression that held the country together was removed, once the glue that held the separate bits of separate peoples together, they had gone their separate ways, each committed to the pursuit of its individuals, with little sense of a common cohesiveness other than a generalized selfishness in the face of the needs of others.

South Africa faced a crisis of inadequate administrative capacity: The rate at which its social and economic problems were multiplying exceeded the rate of its capacity to deal with them: the collapse of government in the provinces, the bankruptcy of municipalities, endemic crime, an overburdened, understaffed, and largely unprofessional police force, woefully inadequate to the task and as likely to be involved in committing crime as in crime-busting,"[3] a judiciary taxed beyond its capacity to cope and torn between adjudicating between the rights of the accused and the indignation of victims, the lack of delivery of basic services, growing rather than diminishing inequalities in the distribution of income, the power of the public sector unions, the constant carping of COSATU, the proliferation of a black elite more concerned with the benefits of self-enrichment than with the sacrifices of redistribution – redistribution, according to the rule of thumb, should always be at the expense of others rather than of self – the culture of entitlement so graphically illustrated by the students at the university of the Venda and replicated ad nauseam in countless, although less dramatic fashions perhaps, the continuing pervasiveness of nonpayment for services – the virtues of Masakane – help for each other – were no longer being pummeled into the ears of an unlistening populace, who for the most part had not the means to pay for the services they received, and a suspect willingness to do so even if they could – and of course the economy, but that crisis, at least, was not of the government's own making.

The performance of Bafana-Bafana, the country's soccer team in the World Cup, is perhaps the best analogy one can conjure up to describe South Africa today. Having barely scraped through the preliminary round, it descended on Paris with a hubris out of all proportion to its achievements. The members were going to strut their stuff. They were going to put South African soccer on the world map – no babes in the wood they, but seasoned men of the hard ball – anyone who underestimated their potential would be awestruck by their performances. New kids on the block or not, in their short life in the Big League they had proved themselves something special. But special they were not. On the world stage they behaved like amateurs. Designer clothing did not substitute for designer soccer.

One ignominious defeat led to the next; each defeat demanding an "enemy" on whom they could place the finger of blame on. First, the officials – obviously racist – who made all the unjustified calls against them; then the infighting among the players themselves – no national cohesiveness here; then the coach, French, had to be on the other side. This, after all, was France and where would his loyalty lie? And then the sense of grievance among the players themselves. After all, they were the best, and when some of the "best" were told to take a seat on the bench, the "best" couldn't accept the discipline and broke ranks. They wouldn't play for a coach who had benched them, especially not an oily traitorous French one who spoke English like a Frenchman, Francophone to a fault, whose only aim was to undermine them, Anglophiles, to a better fault – who, with their colonial powers, never cease to behave in pre-colonial ways.

Then, better still, all but one or two members of the team played for European clubs. How could they display the skills of African soccer if they had been "seduced" into the ways of European soccer. And so it went. Everyone was to blame except the players themselves, who vented their grievances in elegant Paris nightclubs or whatever nightclubs were in the vicinity of whatever city they were ensconced in. Discipline became a joke – better to party all night than to submit to the rigors of boot camp, and anyway, who should have the audacity to tell them how to behave since none of their misfortunes, ineptitude, lack of team spirit, and purpose had anything to do with them, but with enemies lurking in their sunglasses, agents of the Third Force, or even more sinister forces like a daiquiri at 3.00 am on the morning of a match, or perhaps even the games' officials themselves? Besides, it was all racism.

Having imagined the future, they are incapable of letting go.

The September 1992
Focus Group Surveys

In the period following the unbanning of the African National Congress and the opening of all-party negotiations at CODESA,[4] a number of focus group surveys (FGS) were conducted among blacks to get a more accurate picture of their opinions regarding the changes that were occurring in their lives, how the abolition of apartheid laws had affected them, if at all; what they thought democracy was all about, and what they expected once "their" government took hold of the reins of power.

These focus groups were carried out for the most part in the immediate aftermath of the Bisho massacre."[5] This massacre was preceded by a summer of widespread discontent. First, the breakdown of CODESA II,"[6] the massacre at Boipatong;"[7] the collapse of negotiations; mass mobilization on a large scale; the debt within ANC circles about the "Leipzig option,"[8] hard-liners and moderates in both the NP and the ANC battling for the middle ground, and finally the ill-fated march on Bisho.

The right wing was making noises, and the prospects for a negotiated settlement seemed dim, although neither side (NP and ANC) had reneged on its commitment to one. In KwaZulu-Natal the war between the ANC and the Inkatha Freedom Party (IFP) continued unabated.

As did the so-called black-on-black violence in the rest of the country.

In December 1992, the mood was decidedly downbeat among the participants. The feeling was one of disappointment, and participants were more likely to say that things had gotten worse rather than better since the release of Mandela. Again, it is not difficult to understand why participants would feel this way. What they thought would be a quick transfer of power to Mandela, after his release in 1991, had become a drudgery, a long-drawn-out process with no end in sight. People were not very aware of what was being negotiated on their behalf. There had been a massive increase in violence, economic deterioration, strikes, and confrontations, a government committed to change but change on its terms, a government determined to "manage the process," a government not yet fully aware of the enormous changes in store or, perhaps, too aware and so more determined than ever to put off the inevitable day of final reckoning.[9] The government had underestimated the power of the forces it had unleashed, and the talent of the opponents with whom it had chosen to negotiate.

Participants worried most about violence and blamed the government for the violence, or at least for the failure to control it, not the liberation movement.

Participants did not believe the government was the actual perpetrator of the violence, but they did believe that the government was the instigator of the violence and that it encouraged the violence, often by setting black against black and then standing aside when the violence occurred.

Thus, in spite of the changes that had taken place in the previous two years and the dismantling of much of the apartheid structures, the mood of participants was one of concern, not optimism. Even at this stage in the process, one can also see the seeds of early disillusionment among participants. They had become tired of the political posturing, glib talk, doublespeak – and nothing changing.

They were not without hope but they had seen their expectations dampened and had not seen any change in the quality of life in their communities. In many ways they found that their daily lives had become more difficult rather than easier.

(Given that a lot had happened since 1991, starting with the unbanning of the ANC and SACP, the release of Mandela, demonstrations on a scale hitherto unheard of, an end to detention without trial, the repeal of all apartheid legislation, freedom of association, and freedom of speech, people's memories were either remarkably short-lived, or they had suppressed their memories of apartheid, or they were in some kind of denial and had not yet "unrepressed" themselves, or because many of the "petty" apartheid laws had been flouted for years. Or because for the majority the repeal of apartheid laws was something abstract, something that had no tangible impact on their lives, that did not affect the way the way they lived in any substantial way.)

Liberation was proving to be a more complicated business than people had imagined, a state of affairs not helped by the ANC's failure to educate the masses regarding the intricacies of negotiation, and that it wasn't simply a matter of the Boers docilely handing over power. The people did not grasp the point that the liberation movement had not "won" freedom but had agreed to a negotiated settlement, the purpose of which was to ensure that there would be no winners and no losers, although power would pass to the black majority.

The FGS made it clear that there was a great need for voter education in South Africa. The black community was not eagerly looking forward to voting in a national election, even if free and fair, if for no other reasons than that it had little idea of what elections were, or because it was apprehensive, or because it thought elections would be accompanied by an escalation in the level of violence.

For most participants, voting was something they had seen only on the news; it was an intellectual construct, one removed from their reality. There was no democratic tradition among nonwhites in South Africa, and virtually no experience with voting. Thus, never having had the experience, they could not associate the act of performing it with any change in the circumstances of their lives. Participants did not see voting as something that would materially affect their lives.

Even those who had some past experience with elections had nothing good to say about them: "Waste of time," "Nothing changes." That these participants should have such attitudes is not surprising, since they were limited to voting in elections for black local councils, which were, of course, vehemently opposed by the liberation movement. Nor did participants make much connection between elections and the problems they faced. But again hardly surprising: they had either been exposed vicariously to white elections, which did nothing to help them, or to black local elections, in which those who ran were often regarded as traitors, corrupt, or, at the very least, tools of the apartheid government and enemies of the liberation movement, in short, as collaborators with the people's oppressors. If local council elections were all participants had to go by, their negative attitudes toward elections would be understandable, as would their apathy.

Thus the April 1994 election, miracle or not, was in many respects a paradox: the paradox of a people who struggled for decades for the right to vote, to have themselves recognized as citizens of the country they and their descendants had inhabited for innumerable centuries, but who at the same time believed that having the right to vote and participating in elections would do little to change the circumstances of their lives.

Having secured the right to the franchise they had fought for so tenaciously, it appeared that many were prepared to squander their hard-won victory by refusing to exercise their right. The liberation movement had blithely assumed that once the "masses" were freed, they would rush to vote on the designated election dates to cast their ballots for the government of their choice. It was, as is often the case where the obvious is so unquestioned, an assumption that in-depth probing of the would-be newly enfranchised electorate found to be false; that far from seeing elections as a panacea for their ills, the would-be electorate had either negative attitudes toward elections or tended to the opinion that elections did not change things so that there was little point in voting.

Therefore the first lesson the liberation movement had to learn: for the masses, there was no correlation between democracy and voting, or for that matter between freedom and voting, or between voting and change. On reflection, the lack of associations is not surprising. For most nonwhites, voting was an intellectual construct far removed from the realities of their daily lives. Never having had the experience of it, they could not associate the act of performing it with any change in the circumstances of their lives. Indeed, voter education programs had either been so lacking or so ineffective in the two years following the unbanning of political opposition that the focus group research among fourteen different social and economic strata of blacks concluded (this quotation, in a bold typeface, and all those which appear throughout this essay, are the thoughts and opinions of the participants):

"Without an extensive and effective voter education program, voter turnout among nonwhite South Africans in a national election held within the next year would likely be disappointingly low, perhaps not exceeding one in two potentially eligible voters."

The reasons? Lack of information about the voting process and how to vote, and a lack of commitment to voting as a way to bring about change.

(Since people's perceptions in 1992 were that elections made no difference in helping them get the things they wanted in life, is there a possibility of regression, of people feeling in 1999 that their earlier perceptions were in fact correct, that they were sold a "bill of goods" prior to the last election; that they voted and that they had not gotten many of the things they had been promised?)

One can determine the first glimmers of rising concerns about crime.

Political violence was the major reason people thought things had gotten worse. Also, the decline in the economic situation – lack of jobs and higher prices. Africans thought their children were too involved in political strife and worried that their absence from school would put them at a disadvantage with whites,

Coloureds, and Indians who went to school every day. Another lost generation seemed to be raising its defiant head.

Yet it would be grossly unfair to depict participants' feelings only in terms of negatives. They were very conscious of the greater freedoms they enjoyed in matters relating to political expression, freedom of movement, freedom to buy houses, unbanning of political parties, and so on.

(*Thus, when people said nothing had changed and the like, they were referring to the material conditions they lived with, and these, it would appear, were of more concern to them than the more amorphous benefits of, for example, free speech,. which once granted quickly came to be taken for granted.*)

The one outstanding constant: the hopes participants harbored for their children. Repeated references were made to education, for the need for better schools, better teachers, and equal education for all races. Participants talked about saving minds; the path of upward mobility ran through the schoolhouse.

(*One would have thought that this recognition would have formed the basis for a national cohesiveness among the people, a willingness to sacrifice some in the short run in order that their children could reap the benefits. Yet, when one looks at later years and the increasing demands that workers made on their own behalf, this idea, that we must all sacrifice together in the short run, even when the global downturn began to take effect, was not a rallying point.*)

The fears participants expressed also focused on education: that they wouldn't get the education they needed to get the jobs they needed to live a better life. Fear, too, of economic collapse, continued violence, and chaos, the creation of a "culture of violence," the failure to inculcate the young with the right moral values, coupled with a fear that their children would not be able to overcome their sense of inferiority.

(*The concern with the economy must be seen in the context of the precipitous decline in the South African economy during these years when uncertainty, the continuing squeeze of financial sanctions, escalating strikes, and political work stoppages. At one point Finance Minister Derek Keys laid it on the line to de Klerk and Mandela: If they didn't get down to serious business, there would be no business for the new South Africa to inherit.*)[10]

(*As regards participants' fears of a culture of violence becoming pervasive, they were prescient, as crime quickly filled the vacuum left by the decline in political violence, as the guns stored during struggle days were unpacked and sold to whomever could afford them, which unfortunately most could. In an almost subconscious way participants were seeing glimmers of the future, and they did not like what they were seeing. Most of their incipient fears became a reality.*)

There was widespread lack of trust in the National Party government and, therefore, in the integrity of the electoral process. Participants did not want to participate in a sham, much less in an election that legitimated a white South African government. In short, the governing party couldn't be both participant in the process of change and manager of the process itself.

(This focus group research was, of course, conducted before the Transitional Executive Council [TEC] and the Independent Electoral Commission [IEC] were formed in September 1993. At this point in time, for most blacks, elections were not about electing a democratic government; they were about the transfer of power from whites to blacks, about establishing the legitimacy of black rule. Had the NP somehow, most unlikely as it might seem, put together a coalition that emerged victorious in a national election, with De Klerk reassuming the presidency and the ANC legitimately losing because it had been unable to put such a coalition together, though it might have won a plurality of the votes, all hell would have broken loose. The ANC would not have accepted the validity of the results, there would have been screams that the elections had been fraudulent, and the problems encountered in the vote count and the administration of the election itself would have become sufficient grounds to declare the election neither free nor fair. The very criteria that were used to hail the results as legitimate would have been used to condemn them. Had the NP attempted to "win" the election, it would have triggered a genuine revolution among the masses and international opprobrium of the first order. In this sense, the first democratic elections in South Africa were different from "first" elections held elsewhere: the people's voice would not have been the determining factor in adjudicating "fairness;" only an outcome that would have legitimated the ANC as the people's voice would have been internationally acceptable.)

"The dominant symbol was democracy. More than anything else, this represented what the participants wanted from the political system."

Democracy was widely interpreted as the antonym for apartheid. It encapsulated the opposite of apartheid. The primary reason for democracy's motivating power was the way in which it represented for people the antithesis of apartheid. Participants did not see democracy as a means, but an end; not as a process, but as a set of goals, accomplishments, results. They thought of democracy in terms of the things it created, rather than as a means to bring them about. The concept of democracy not only conveyed to nonwhite South Africans the powerful imagery it does in other cultures, but it contained a number of specific reference points as the opposite of apartheid. As a result, apartheid had an emotional impact on perceptions of democracy as a cure-all and that went beyond the norm in other parts of the world.

With each association apartheid conjured up in their minds, democracy conjured up the opposite. Thus, oppression became freedom; discrimination became equality; segregation became unity; humiliation became respect; violence became peace; poverty became opportunity; white minority rule became majority rule. Injustice became the rule of law; inequality became equal rights; domination became the right to choose one's leaders.

What was troubling, however, was the perception that democracy would have a coattail effect, that the attributes people associated with it would become instantaneous realities, immediate replacements for the realities of apartheid. Because the realities of apartheid were so concrete and had been experienced, sometimes at terrible cost, by blacks, they expected the perceived realities of democracy to be as tangible and experiential.

But, besides the obvious, there is one other difference between apartheid and democracy. Apartheid existed not only as a set of rules and legislative statutes that divided people along racial lines in every aspect of life and set boundaries to control every action of the individual, it was also a living instrument of dehumanization, a systemic organization of society to bring the maximum amount of human degradation to every person whose skin color was not white. For the vast majority of South Africans, apartheid was "for nearly half a century . . . the warp and weft of their experience, defining their privileges and their disadvantages, their poverty and their wealth, their public and private lives and their very identity – the system itself was evil, inhumane, and degrading – amongst its many crimes, perhaps its worst was the power to humiliate, to denigrate and to remove the confidence and self-esteem and dignity of its millions of victims."[11]

"The face represented by authority," Justice Pius Langa, currently deputy president of the Constitutional Court, wrote in a memorable submission to the Truth and Reconciliation Commission (TRC) "was of a war against people, and human dignity was its main casualty."[12]

Democracy, on the other hand, is a process. It does not confer dignity or self-esteem. It does not eliminate disadvantage, abolish or even alleviate poverty, or act in ways that are always humane or nondegrading.

(Does the fact that democracy has not brought about the things the majority of South Africans wanted in any significant measure mean that people are becoming disillusioned with democracy rather than with the government? If democracy is associated with ends accomplished, and not the means used to get there, does this mean that people could sanction the use of undemocratic means to achieve what are perceived as desirable, even democratic, ends? Or in the past four years have people gradually been weaned away from the association of democracy with ends met and do they now associate them more with the processes that must be used to achieve desired ends? And in the event of failure to reach those ends, do they blame the processes for holding things up or do they blame those who are charged with implementing the processes?

If democracy continues to be associated almost exclusively with the opposites of apartheid, do people retain their adherence to democracy because they believe that in the absence of democracy apartheid will return? Hence, are whatever affinities they have for democracy the result of fear, of negative perceptions that to reject it would mean a return to the bad old days? Where are the positive reinforcements for their beliefs, especially if their beliefs are misplaced?)

Again freedom was associated with its opposite: oppression. But this is a very truncated view of what freedom is and has more to do with the absence of the concrete and experienced manifestations of oppression than with positive and tangible manifestations of freedom). One profound change, as we shall see, has taken place since 1992. People no longer regard democracy as the antithesis of apartheid, but as a means of delivery – of jobs, houses, safety and personal security, water and electricity, schools, infrastructure, a higher standard of living.[13] And the overwhelming preoccupation with education is gone.

Democracy has become a material thing, a quantitatively measurable commodity. Jeremy Cronin, Deputy Secretary-General of the SACP, once bitterly complained of how the "whiz kids" of the IMF arrived in Johannesburg: "They came into our offices with laptops, filled in each figure – for inflation, foreign exchange controls, all the macroeconomic numbers – then hit F1-control, and the answer would determine whether the country was acceptable."[14] The masses without the benefit of laptops are plugging other numbers into their heads – numbers of new jobs; housing sites and houses built; phone and electricity hookups; sewage systems installed; tap water and sanitary facilities available; garbage pickup; roads tarred, paved, and built; police stations in the area, ease of access to; speed of response and visibility of police, community infrastructure, sense of personal security, schools built, capacity, quality of teachers, availability of textbooks, health clinics in the area, accessibility to and quality of staffing; community centers constructed, accessibility to local councillors; efficiency and capacity of local government, and they, too, hit the F1-control that is in the recess of their brains, and the answers pop out: more times than not disconcerting answers they have lived to learn with.

"Participants across the board were opposed to having to use ID cards for voting – a mysterious process they were almost totally ignorant of, and intimidated by, and if voting was contingent on getting an ID card, then they would not vote."

When the process of voting and some of the benefits that could ensue from it were explained to participants, they indicated that they would vote for:
- Education, jobs, housing, peace (44)
- Democracy in South Africa (32)
- A better future for our children (29)
- Ending apartheid forever (15)
- Supporting their candidate and party (8)
- A New South Africa (5)
- Being able to stop the violence (2)

(*Why did violence rate so poorly? Were people so inured to violence that it no longer surfaced as an issue they felt voting could affect or did they believe that, voting or no voting, the violence would continue, that is, that the violence was not about voting? Especially since crime was one of the main, if not the main, preoc-*

cupation of participants – although it, too, did not surface as an issue, participants believed that voting would have an impact on it.)

The August 1993
HSRC Survey

- 77 per cent expected to participate in the April 1994 elections; 13 per cent did not. (The actual turnout was 90 per cent.)
- 55 per cent offered "the election will bring freedom" as their most important reason for participating; 18 per cent offered "getting rid of apartheid" as their reason for being prepared to do so.
- 49 per cent of South Africans discussed politics from "time to time" with friends/relatives/colleagues.
- 28 per cent believed that "freedom" would be the single most important benefit which would accrue to them personally as a result of the April 1994 election.
- 67 per cent believed that their standard of living would rise under the new government; 5 per cent thought it would fall.
- 56 per cent felt very unsafe or unsafe and 29 per cent felt very safe or safe.
- 35 per cent thought that the security force would be willing and able to provide protection to people in their immediate community in the time before and during the election; 15 per cent thought the security forces would be willing but unable; 19 per cent thought the security forces would be unable but willing, and 15 per cent that they would be both unwilling and unable. Thus, overall, 50 per cent thought the security forces would be willing, 34 per cent that they would be unwilling, 54 per cent that they would be able and 30 per cent that they would be unable.
- 51 per cent thought that there would be less violence in the runup to the election; 16 per cent that there would be more violence.
- 48 per cent thought that the Inkatha Freedom Party was most to blame for the violence, 10 per cent that the ANC was.
- 41 per cent thought that good government required a strong opposition, 30 per cent that it didn't.
- 44 per cent felt very close to the ANC, 8 per cent to the Inkatha Freedom Party, 6 per cent to the SACP, 5 per cent to the Pan Africanist Congress, 3 per cent to the Azanian People's Organization, 2 per cent to the National Party, and one per cent to the Democratic Party.

The results of this poll should be examined in the following context:

- Much of the uncertainty about the future was gone. A date for the election had been set; the parties were moving into electoral mode. The trauma following the assassination of Chris Hani had subsided; indeed, that event established Nelson Mandela as the *de facto* president of the country when he went on television to calm the nation and call for no retribution – in fact to urge blacks to take no actions that would damage or add to the deprivation of their own communities. Mandela reassured blacks; impressed whites. In terms of imagery, it was the first unmistakably tangible sign that the changing of the guard was under way, that the flow of power had moved in the direction of the ANC – and was irreversible.

- By August, arrangements for establishing the Transitional Executive Council (TEC) were well under way. The old order was dead; the new order experiencing the first pangs of birth.

In this light, some of the survey's findings stand out:

- The actual turnout for the election (89 per cent) was far higher than what the poll suggested it would be (77 per cent), indicating the efficacy of voter turnout programs and voters' sense of participation and involvement in the election as the actual date drew closer, and increasing excitement generated a momentum that in the end became unstoppable.
- For the vast majority of voters, the primary reason for voting was now associated with what had hitherto been their primary conceptions of democracy: 73 per cent were going to vote in order to end either apartheid or some oppression associated with apartheid, that is, the absence of freedom. Thus, voting was being associated with positive attributes, with the possibility of change in their lives.
- The makings of the contradiction that would prevail throughout the transition, and indeed will be a matter of intense debate during the 1999 campaign. While only 28 per cent believed that "freedom"– in whatever amorphous way that was defined – would be the single most important benefit that would accrue to them personally, the fact that 67 per cent believed that their standard of living would rise, and more important perhaps, that only 5 per cent thought it would fall, indicates that as the election grew nearer, people's interests were becoming more self-oriented; people were beginning to believe that the material things the government-in-waiting were promising would materialize and that they would be the beneficiaries. The people believed that there would be delivery on promises made.
- While 56 per cent felt very unsafe or unsafe and only 29 per cent felt very safe or safe, only 16 per cent thought that there would be more violence in the run-up to the election, while a majority (51 per cent) thought there would be less violence. Two observations: political violence or crime ranked highly among people's concerns prior to the 1994 election and did not suddenly emerge in the post-apartheid era; second, while the pundits were predicting all kinds of violence in the runup to the election, the average voter had an entirely different view of how things were going.

- Finally, the 44 per cent who felt "very close" to the ANC should be compared with the 35 per cent who felt the same way in September 1998.

(*Thus, if any major conclusion can be drawn from the 1992 focus group surveys and the 1993 Human Sciences Research Council survey, it would be that voters were beginning to pay a lot more attention to the impact a post-apartheid government would have on their standard of living, namely, the material things that would be available to them, and less to the benefits of freedom, although it should be stressed that the two are by no means exclusive, that, indeed, they are more likely to be intertwined Nevertheless, a "selfishness" factor had begun to manifest itself.*)

The November/December 1994 Focus Group Survey

These focus groups were conducted six months after that "miracle" election. A lingering sense of the euphoria the election engendered was still in the air, and blacks were what might best be described as being in a state of "waiting," although the sense of anticipation was slowly being eroded by a sense of impatience as to why it was taking so long for "their" government to deliver on the promises the ANC had so effusively made during the election campaign.

(*Given that "their" government had a lot more familiarity with the cell blocks of prisons than with the cabinet rooms of government, "their" government could be forgiven for asking for a little more time to learn the ropes, other than the hanging ones.*)

But the ANC itself had planted the seeds of disappointment and was now stuck with reaping the harvest of unmet expectations. Whites were beginning to feel a little more relaxed – no great upheavals had shattered their comfortable lives – but they, too, were still apprehensive; just because the government had not gotten around to changing the way they lived forever didn't mean it still wasn't its intention to do so. President Mandela's reassurances that whites were an integral part of and germane to the success of the new South Africa were being treated with the usual suspicion. In general, the mood of whites might also be described as one of waiting.

Again the focus group surveys were confined to nonwhites: respondents in nine groups were African, four were Coloured, and two were Indian. Eight of the groups comprised men, seven women. And groups were held in metropolitan, urban, rural, informal areas and hostels.

The FGS indicated the ambivalence of blacks. Overall, the majority of groups believed that little or no change had taken place since the election in April, and that what change had occurred was benefiting other groups, not theirs.

Coloured and Indian respondents felt that Africans were benefiting from the new order; rural Africans felt that urban Africans were benefiting at their expense.

"All the African respondents said that nondelivery on promises made before the election was causing anger and dissatisfaction with the government."

"It would have been better if we had not voted."

Indeed, once black responses were desegregated and considered on the basis of group affiliation, a darker landscape emerged, one of ambivalence and a selfish competitiveness for the resources that were there to distribute among them. Overall, most groups believed that little or no change had taken place since the election in April and that what change had occurred was benefiting other groups, not theirs. This was a recurring gripe, with little evocation of the need to either share or sacrifice in order to build the new nation. Coloured and Indian respondents felt that Africans were benefiting from the new order; rural Africans felt that urban Africans were benefiting at their expense. All assessments were made on a zero-sum calculus. Those who had seen change were optimistic about the future; those who hadn't were pessimistic.

(With all the emphasis on voter education and getting people out to vote, no one had, of course, paid any attention to educating people with regard to the realities of democracy and the conditions in which they lived, and how difficult it would be not only to master the sprawling bureaucracies with their fourteen departments for everything, but to consolidate them, integrate the former Transkei, Venda, Bophuthatswana, Ciskei [TVBC] states and the homelands, to rationale line functions, implement the golden handshakes that had been part of the World Trade Center agreement, bring in the new talent to run departments whose previous experience with running anything was solely confined to running from the authorities. With the unrelenting emphasis on teaching people to walk into a polling booth and do something they had never done before – cast a vote for one of the parties listed on the ballot sheet – no one had ever addressed them regarding the limits to the changes they might expect. And in this regard, no party was more irresponsible than the ANC. In setting its sights on total power at every level of government, it willfully misled the electorate, and the leadership who were well acquainted with the true state of things acquiesced in the lie, and in the act of asking the masses for their trust, they betrayed the masses from the very beginning, making the primary task of the new government – the building of one nation out of its divided fragments – so much more difficult. And all for what?

If voting meant getting the things they were denied under apartheid, then clearly they were not getting those things; therefore, voting made no difference. One reason for the rather quick onset of some disillusionment was the ANC's own fault: it had made the promises, it had raised expectations to an extraordinary level, and the stories that circulated around the time of the election – how some blacks were already picking out the houses in white urban areas they would move into after the ANC took over – were often more than merely apocryphal; thus if

*one and one made two, voting didn't, contrary to what they had been led to be-
lieve, bring jobs and houses.*

*Because their leaders had not trusted them to understand that undoing centu-
ries of oppression and its effects on every trajectory of their lives would take some
undoing before the "new order" might begin to produce what was within their own
restricted capacities to produce, the ANC leadership sold its people a bill of
goods.)*

Other under-the-surface resentments also emerged. Government was spending
too much time alleviating the fears of whites at the expense of the needs of the
African majority who had voted it into power. Indian and Coloured respondents
were worried about their financial and physical security under a government
mostly run by Africans. But even if blacks were disappointed, they thought things
would get better in the future when the government got more experience and got a
better grip on the reins of power. Experience would count.

Also, respondents were more realistic than blacks are often given credit for:
they were more than prepared to agree that the six-month period since the election
was too short a time to make assessments of change, that the government had
inherited formidable challenges it could not be expected to change overnight, that
elements of the "old order" would frustrate innovations to get things going, and
that unlike many of the elites that presumed to speak on their behalf, they drew
careful distinctions between what they wanted and what they thought they might
reasonably hope to get.

Although people were frustrated about the pace of change, they believed the
government should be given more time, and they were slowly beginning to see
change, limited but change nevertheless, emanate from the new structures. They
were still positive about transformation and satisfied with the government, although in the latter case it was a qualified satisfaction. These findings were confirmed, in large measure by focus group research conducted in November 1994
among urban and rural Africans by the Center for Policy Studies (CPS). In pre-
senting its findings, it emphasized that the fashionable belief among "many politicians, journalists, business people and academics," that the new government would
be unable to meet or manage popular aspirations, was unfounded.

> [The report] challenges the pessimism reigning in those quarters: it is not,
> however, optimism without qualification, for it finds that there are indeed
> expectations of change which the new democracy will have to meet.. There
> is definitely disappointment with the pace of change since the April election,
> but this has not produced widespread discontent with government. Rather,
> the findings suggest that the public is considerably more aware of the limits
> facing the new government, more realistic in its expectations than conven-
> tional wisdom holds. The people want to make the system work for them,
> not bring it down. They are also more disposed towards policies that are
> incremental, egalitarian, and involve popular contributions than is often

supposed. The results reveal a sense of priorities that places the concrete and immediate – jobs, houses, water – ahead of the symbolic or ideological issues like land.[15]

Research conducted by the Center for Policy Studies complemented in many respects the focus group research carried out by Community Agency for Social Inquiry.[16] On the question of education, for example, the CPS focus groups were no longer "accepting" of the grandiose visions the governing elites had dangled before their eyes – free education and access to white schools. In their own way they had come to the bottom-line conclusions that education in blacks might have a lot more to do with the behavior of students and teachers than with the more fancy appurtenances white schools were cluttered with and the plethora of extra-curricular activities available to them. And until and unless behaviors changed, little else was of much consequence.

The main preoccupation in the focus groups regarding the school system can be summed up in one word: discipline. After discipline, facilities and teacher qualifications are the most frequently mentioned concerns. Although it is recognised that students made an important contribution to the struggle,. against apartheid, all groups see scholars as being too polarised and out of control. These views were shared by people of all ages, including those under 35 who were personally involved in the anti-apartheid campaigns of the past. Even the participants in yesterday's struggles think it is time for the schools to calm down.

Teachers are often seen as contributing to the indiscipline by their own behavior; members complain that teachers sleep with students and are drunk at school. Another concern frequently voiced is the poor quality of instruction. Group members say this is due to teachers' limited competence in English, their poor training, and the large class sizes prevalent in African schools.[17]

(The reaction of Africans in particular is an indication of how high expectations had been. A mere six months into the new dispensation, and already "anger and dissatisfaction?" Was this because the ANC had been so successful in driving the message home to its constituencies that the act of voting itself would be a sufficient guarantee of their receiving all the things that they had been denied under apartheid? That the zeal with which votes were pursued superseded any sense of reality; that voters' anticipation of the changes that would materialize on the morning following the election had been honed to such an excess that when the thrill of victory retreated and they were faced with the same barren landscapes that had always been their lot in life, they felt not just let down, but somehow taken in? And to what extent must the ANC itself accept the responsibility for playing on the hopes of an electorate, deprived of hope for centuries, of creating expectations of change and transformation that would have required a degree of social engineering that would have been the envy of apartheid's architects? Objective analysts will be forced to the conclusion that the ANC itself must bear the largest share of the problems it created for itself in terms of people's disappointment,

disillusionment, and resentment since the ANC had been warned well before it assumed the reins of government that the coffers were bare, and that only austerity of the most severe kind would ward off economic collapse. Had not Derek Keys told Mandela in 1993 that the deficit, which then accounted for 9.3 per cent of GDP, was at its highest level ever and was unsustainable?

Keys's figures indicated that the government's finances had gone haywire. Salaries, pensions, and interest on the debt consumed almost everything, leaving an empty till for discretionary spending. His message: any additional government spending would lead to soaring inflation and spiraling debt.

The leadership of the ANC could have learned that President Nelson Mandela, the nation's most treasured asset, was himself part of the problem. Because he was so much admired the world over. Because he was held in such universal awe. Because he was regarded as the embodiment of all that is noble in the human condition. Because he exuded a moral stature in a world much in need of a moral compass. Because he never raised himself above ordinary people, the prisoner in him making impossible the pretense of the poseur. Because he spoke a language of compassion, of forgiveness for wrongs done, losses endured. Because he had an uncompromising and unyielding commitment to justice and human rights for all, irrespective of the causes they championed or the self-righteousness of their sometimes dubious causes. Because in a world that wrapped itself in hypocritical gestures, he spoke from the heart, never deviating from the truth no matter how bitter to swallow, and was himself living testimony to the heartache speaking from the heart can leave in its wake. Because he did not drench himself in the adulation poured on him by a world thirsting for heroes. Because the twenty-seven years of incarceration he lived through in order to secure the freedom of his people taught him to forgive his enemies. Because he harbored no bitterness for those who had robbed him of his life and freedom. Because he cherished freedom as the well- spring of all that ennobles our humanity, worth sacrificing life for, but more important, worth preserving life for. Because he enriched our humanity. And in his ordinariness became extraordinary.

But the tumultuous reception he received no matter where he went in the world, the honors, awards, acknowledgments, acclaim, approbation heaped on him, became associated in South Africa's mind not just with Mandela but with South Africa itself. It felt that his special standing in the world gave South Africa a special standing, that the encomiums lavished on him were encomiums being lavished on South Africa, that the captains of commerce and industry and heads of state who rushed to embrace him were embracing South Africa, that to bask in the reflection of his glory was to bask in the glory of the new South Africa. Thus the belief that the governments that came to South Africa or invited him to their capitals to pay homage and offer friendship were also paying homage and friend- ship to the nation he was forging; that they would out of the friendship so profligately offered provide the investment capital South Africa needed to rid itself of the legacies of apartheid, redress the injustices of the past, and jump-start the economic miracle that would surely follow the political miracle.

Mistaken judgments all. A colossal failure on the part of South Africa officials to distinguish between admiration for the man and a willingness to make the kinds of investment in South Africa that would either generate jobs, create the infra-structure, or lay the foundations for the structural transformations that would help the country make the difficult transition from authoritarianism to full democracy.

Not that Mandela himself was in the end under any illusions. In a revealing vignette in the Financial Times, *writer Philip Stephens captures the moment:*

> Back in the summer [of 1998] Nelson Mandela joined the 15 leaders of the European Union in Cardiff. His hosts were extravagant in their admiration. The South African president is accustomed to flattery. Mere politicians heap praise on this statesman in the hope of stealing a little of his magic. Yet their words have the hollowest of echoes. Mr Mandela knows it.

> As the compliments gushed forth on this particular occasion, one of those present whispered in Mr. Mandela's ear. Here was the moment to ask them to open their chequebooks, this observer said. The reply came with a wry smile and without rancour. It was all the more eloquent for that: 'They have no ink in their pens'.

"Those who had seen change were optimistic about the future; those who hadn't were pessimistic."

"Government was spending too much time alleviating the fears of whites at the expense of the needs of the African majority who had voted them into power."

"Indians and Coloureds were worried about their financial and physical security under a government mostly run by Africans. They were pessimistic about the future. Some felt insecure and scared. The fear of the unknown coupled with a rising fear of crime."

But even if Africans were disappointed, they thought things would get better in the future when the government got more experience and got a better grip on the reins of power. Experience would count. Also, respondents were ready to admit that the six-month period since the election was to short a period to make assessments of change.

(*Thus participants, although disappointed with the rate of change, were pre-pared to give the government more time – some said two years – to judge its efficacy, and also prepared to assume, or at least believe, that as the government got more experience it would get better. After six months, the government was still being given the benefit of the doubt.*)

"Participants had little knowledge or awareness of the RDP (Reconstruc-tion and Development Programme) or what it was about. The suggestion was that if people knew what it was about, they would likely be more optimistic about the future."

(*Considering the manner in which the RDP was launched, the across-the-board support it received from all parties in the Government of National Unity, the fact that its promotion and implementation were the exclusive responsibility of one minister, Jay Naidoo, the emphasis President Mandela put on it at his every speaking occasion, the enlistment of the business community and labour to hype its merits, the political gospel preached in the townships that the RDP was the key to the new South Africa, this finding is nothing short of breathtaking, should give every bureaucracy involved, no matter how peripherally, pause to examine how public policies are communicated to the public, and should be of special concern to the ANC that the cornerstone of its foundation upon which the future would be built was by and large a mystery to its constituents who were supposed to be active participants in its implementation. If in the end the RDP was allowed to wither on the vine, perhaps there was no vine there on which it could wither.*
All of which begs the question: Where was government feedback coming from? Who was evaluating it? And how could the rock upon which all other government policy was built become a pebble nonvisible to the eye?)

Even more bizarre, while the focus group research analysts could report that there was little or no awareness of what the RDP was, they could conclude, almost in the same breath:

"Respondents felt strongly that the community should play a strong role in finding solutions to their problems, but that the resources to play that role must come from the government."

"The eagerness to play a significant role was also reflected in respondents' comments that if they got jobs, they would be able to build houses, rather than wait for the government to provide them with a 'free house.' The community will and desire to be active players in their own development provides a bedrock of goodwill for the RDP at national and regional levels. This should be encouraged and built upon, but will not last without being nurtured."

"National government was seen as primarily responsible for change."

"Little awareness of the role and functions of provincial and local governments."

"Mandela was seen as the government by Africans."

That was the problem.

(The RDP withered on the vine. The Masakane *campaign to encourage town-ship residents to pay their arrears in rents and for services, which they had been encouraged not to do during the struggle days by the same liberation movement that was now desperately urging them to pay , after three or four years is still encountering difficulties. Is it because of the culture of entitlement? The habit of not even being able to remember when they last paid? Because they can't make ends meet if they pay? Don't have the money? And in some cases, see no delivery? By 1997, more than one-third of local municipalities were bankrupt, corruption and inefficiency were rife, people were more disillusioned, almost ready to throw in the towel. What killed the "spirit of the revolution" or was there ever a revolu-tion? See John Matisson's article in the Mail &Guardian for 6 November 1998:*

> One analyst who knows the ANC well argues that the interpretation of the ANC as a fundamentally revolutionary movement is wrong. "During the struggle, the ANC that journalists and outsiders saw tended to be the revolutionarie," said *Businessmap's* Jenny Cargill.

> "But we forget: the ANC was founded to unify tribal conflict and provide a forum for black intellectuals. It consistently nurtured tolerance and modera-tion." While it was a broad enough church to include the communist party, Mandela and Oliver Tambo, for example, were never Marxists or particu-larly rhetorical. Its character is pragmatic.

> What this analysis of the ANC means for the economics debate is that faced with the contradictions of the RDP, its highest concerns would be to balance the most powerful forces and avoid glaring risks.)

"Many African participants felt entitled to jobs on the basis of promises they feel were made to them during the election campaign."

(In the 1994 campaign, who fashioned the message, who handled marketing? Was the campaign really a subliminal replay of the Clinton 1992 campaign: It's the economy, stupid. Did "consultants" devise a campaign for the ANC that was inherently fraudulent in that the ANC had neither the resources nor the capacity to deliver on the promises so easily made? Did these advisers, in that sense, unwit-tingly or wittingly, create a climate conducive to a quick loss of faith in democracy as the instrument that would bring to people the things they were led to believe "their" government would bring? Was the drive to maximize the vote done at the price of creating the basis for a quick erosion of confidence in the newfangled thing called democracy?)

However it was not only the unemployed who complained. Employed respondents protested against poor working conditions, irregular hours, and unpaid overtime. Low wages in the heart of a recession were frequently mentioned. The absence of projects generated by the RDP was seen to be compounding the problem of unemployment.

Respondents who did not see visible changes in their area assume others are benefiting and became embittered.

All the "disadvantaged" groups were looking for benefits, even if they meant benefits at the expense of others. Hence, the underlying resentment that "others" were benefiting while they were not. Especially the hostility directed at Coloureds and Indians.

(The core of nation building is the creation of a sense of shared destiny, a common identity, a mutual sense of sacrifice in terms of there being obstacles to overcome, of shared values, of building together to create a future for the children, of a willingness to sacrifice on behalf of a common good, of a growing pride in each other's accomplishments, of confidence-building measures that reinforce the individual's belief in the other, of a national cohesiveness that emerges out of the understanding that nations are built, not erected overnight? If one analyses this focus group research for evidence of these developments, it is scant. What emerges is the powerful sense of entitlement. Me first, me last, me always. One can surmise on many levels, and often out of dubious lines of reasoning, but it just may be possible that blacks, having lived most of their lives either around selfish whites or having worked only for white "bosses" have been subconsciously imbued with some of their less desirable self-centred traits that put the satisfaction of self and the rewards of instant gratification of needs before every other consideration. Having been an appendage of whites for so long, is it not possible that blacks picked up part of their baggage? That the "role model" they were oppressed into emulating, which in many cases were the only "authority" models available, were the models presented by whites? Who, after all, were the frontiersmen of entitlement? Who usurped 87 per cent of a country for 13 per cent in the name of entitlement? Who turned privilege into a right?

(Nor was there a sense of cohesiveness among the disadvantaged – that they were all in it together and would need to sacrifice on behalf of one another. That their sacrifices now would earn dividends for their children. Had daily exposure to white consumerism – the ritzy stores at the Charlton, Rosebank, Sandton City, the proliferation of malls that cater to every need, built on Western layout "principles," adequately "arranged" to the ubiquity of Western consumerism, whether in clothes or music or pop culture; the barrage of consumer advertising to which they were exposed – billboards, newspapers, radio, television, simply turned them into ready-made consumers ripe for a new kind of exploitation?[18] In fact, two groups willing, indeed eager, to battle it out – white business and black consumers. Who are the power brokers of consumerism, the 3 per cent of blacks in the "middle class" or all whites, small in number, diminishing in number, and now accountable for the smaller proportion of consumer expenditure?)

At this point, crime had not yet raised its vicious head as an issue of major concern. Perhaps because in this period of the transition there was a hiatus of sorts:

political violence was way down, criminal violence had not yet filled the void. Perhaps people, so often the victims of political violence, had become used to seeing all violence in terms of politics, or that the sheer scale of the political violence had made them immune to the violence that engulfed them at other levels. In white areas, increasing urbanization in the wake of the abolition of all forms of population movement, the proliferation of squatter camps, and the breakdown in social controls made an increase in crime inevitable – a crime increase is a common phenomenon in countries undergoing rapid urbanization and transition, especially where the manacles of oppression are undone, in which there are huge disparities between rich and poor.

The focus of what people wanted, and their prioritization of their needs, appeared to have changed. Education, which had dominated the agenda in 1992 had slipped – indeed, in this focus group research it wasn't mentioned as being among respondents' top priorities. And it slipped again (as we shall see) in 1997 and 1998.

(Was this because education had become better and hence less of a priority in the sense that it was being adequately dealt with or an increase in me-tooism? Given Thabo Mbeki's lambasting of the South African Democratic Teachers Union in 1998, "Thanks to a form of behavior perhaps among a few of our educators, and especially teachers in our schools, the prestige of the profession is fast disappearing, to be replaced by contempt and derision for you, the professionals without whom the new society for which we yearn can never be born,"[19] and the plethora of problems reorganisation of education has encountered over the last four years,[20] the decline in the proportion passing matriculation, the problems of overcapacity and undercapacity, the endemic chaos in many of the schools in the townships, one must wonder why. Why has the future of children, only a few years previously the bandwagon for a new South Africa, become an albatross on the people's neck that in poll after poll it becomes an issue of lesser importance?)[21]

"Housing was mentioned as a concern by a number of respondents, particularly from informal settlements."

"The association of jobs, no matter how poorly paid, and housing – the attitude that if we had jobs we would be able to build houses ourselves and that there would be a decrease in crime and other social ailments."

(What did respondents mean by "house?" Had they any idea of what was involved in building a house or was this more an expression of a wish?)

"Affirmative action emerged as an area of contention among the different race groups."

"Africans thought there was a bias toward whites, Coloureds that there was a bias toward Africans. This country will never be the one everyone dreamed of."

"Xenophobia was on the increase – racism against Africans from elsewhere. Illegal immigrants, or even legal ones, were seen as being prepared to take jobs at lower wages than Africans, and taking limited resources away from South Africans."

"[Foreigners] will impregnate our sisters but will not marry them. We will soon have the added burden of feeding these children. They [the foreigners] are also responsible for spreading AIDS in the country."

(Considering what some of these countries went through to support the apartheid struggle, there is no feeling of reciprocal thanks involved here. See how Mozambique refugees are treated in Alexandra , and the more recent cases of immigrants on commuter trains being beaten to death. Allied to this is the fact that residents of many other countries in Africa don't like South Africans. Remember Derek Keys's remark that "if you have to be poor, South Africa isn't a bad country to be poor in.")

"For all of them, April 27, 1994, had become a symbol of the society South Africa could be. However, because of the negative post-election mood, South Africa is now looked back on nostalgically, as the one occasion when the new South Africa was with us."

"April 27 had entered the national consciousness as a moment of peace, democracy, and national unity. It was recalled with near spiritual feelings by respondents in all the focus groups, representing men and women, young and old, African, Coloured, and Indians, from cities, small towns, rural areas, and informal areas."

(Anomie had already set in. Anomie refers to a disconcerting condition in society where norms and values no longer control the behavior of people. Anomie is caused by the need to adjust to changing conditions and the difficulty people have without clear rules to guide them. Rules on how people ought to behave with each other break down, and people do not know what to expect from one another.

Sudden changes from a regulated to a deregulated society bring about the highest levels of anomie. People lose their sense of being subject to accepted and binding social norms and codes. Anomie feeds our sense of anguish and despair, our sense of purposelessness, as we struggle to find meaning in the new and seemingly bottomless cauldron of being into which we have been thrown, and as we free fall, we reach out for some anchor, some mooring to which we can attach ourselves and reconcile ourselves to a new paradigm of values. For many, anomie expresses itself in a consuming longing for the past , for the safety of a world of known and acknowledged values, for the security of knowing and accepting one's positionin the hierarchy of society.

South Africa is subsumed in anomie. With the demise of apartheid, the "rules" of forty years were consigned to the rubbish bin of history. What had been en-

trenched as dogma by the privileged was simply dismissed as the propaganda of venal men by the newly empowered. At many levels of society, the certainties that were the norm were eviscerated; the relationships between black and whites were transmogrified, sometimes even reversed; in the name of transformation the old order was eased out, sometimes with a harshness that caught many of its adherents off guard; the unsettling became the common; the uncertain the only certainty, the uneven and often contradictory signals from the new elite, as they too sought to reconcile irreconcilables, a frustrating exercise in trying to divine their intentions.

The country was moving in a new direction, and while whites were at the receiving end of much of the transformations simultaneously ploughing their way toward the light at the end of their respective tunnels, sometimes the tunnels themselves collapsed, and sometimes the tracks were derailed, and sometimes the light at the end of the tunnel was the light of another train approaching at the same break-neck speed.

With so many trains crowding the tracks, with engineers of varying experience and expertise in the driver's seat, some drivers hurling along at full steam, some chugging along at a rather leisurely pace, and some still at the station waiting for the stationmaster to raise the flag for departure, with all ostensibly heading in the same direction but with switching guards only sporadically at the switching points, collisions were unavoidable.

But inevitable: an inevitable part of the journey, of the process of change itself, leaving not only whites but blacks unsure of the present, apprehensive of the future, and uncertain as to where the country was heading. Roles had changed, but role-players had not adapted to the changing roles. Attitudes were questioned, but those who led the questioning were often themselves prisoners of the attitudes that underpinned their questioning. Values were put under a microscope, but sometimes the persons with the microscopes did not know how to use them, and sometimes they made incorrect diagnoses. White anomie has not shaped itself in a void; black anomie is as prevalent, though of a qualitatively different kind. Blacks and whites are struggling to find themselves and each other. And, as in all struggles, there were victims, some casualties of design, some casualties of accident, and some victims of an amnesia that obliterated from their memory banks the reasons for the struggle they had so invitingly embraced.)

Anomie continues to provide one of the most useful conceptual frameworks for understanding the transition in South Africa.

"In August 1993, all groups from informal areas, rural areas, and small towns complained of inadequate infrastructure in their areas. They were mainly concerned about the lack of water, electricity, sanitation, and recreation and medical facilities."

(See the July Institute for Democracy in South Africa [IDASA] 1998 poll, which no longer figured as issues of any significant extent; they were also the areas in

which the government had made the most progress: 2.7 million people of the 14 million who had no water in 1994 have water now; 70 per cent of 6 million houses that did not have electricity will be wired by election time.)

As regards crime and violence, there was some propensity to associate the coming of democracy with an increase in lawlessness. Most participants, however, attributed the increase in crime to lax punishment – crime paid. All wanted harsher penalties. Coloureds and Indians were prone to see crime in racial terms – there being a black government and crime as being committed by Africans.

(*Crime was becoming a symbol of racial divide among Africans/Coloureds/Indians.*)

Sexual abuse and rape were also seen as being on the increase.

Political violence was hardly mentioned at all.

(*Considering the state of the country in the years leading up to the 1994 election, this signifies a profound change.*)

"Contrary opinions were expressed regarding the issue of education. Some felt the system had become desegregated. Others felt whites were trying to frustrate attempts to integrate schools. Or that black educational standards were lower than whites', with the result that many African matriculants found themselves unemployable after finishing school while their white counterparts did not."

(*All matriculants take the same exams. The overall rate of passing has been falling since 1994. But despite this, some of the best results are achieved at the poorest schools. As elsewhere, the degree of parental involvement is the key.*)

Local Government
As regards local government, most participants were confused by what local government was. They were also confused that there were to be more elections. Were these a second general election? What knowledge they had came from their experiences with the apartheid local councils – seen as corrupt/part of old system. But participants also made the point that some civic leaders were also corrupt. Few knew of forthcoming local elections. One thing stood out: The illegitimate background to local elections would have to be overcome as part of the voter education program.

Overall, on the question of traditional leaders views were mixed – yes, traditional leaders should play a role, but few, if any, could put their fingers on what precisely that role should be.

There were three main reasons for voting: (1) change; (2) a better future; (3) to put blacks into power: only Africans said they voted to put blacks in government.

(Far less frequently mentioned reasons were for the rights and freedoms denied under apartheid. Increasingly, the focus was on delivery or the lack thereof — voters were going to vote for direct personal benefit rather than for any deepening of democracy.)

Since April 1994, respondents had become disillusioned. All had had high expectations of the immediate benefits that would accrue as a result of the election. Most felt their expectations had not been met.

(Did unfilled expectations make people less inclined to vote in the local elections?)

Their expectations: That there would have been an end to poverty, live immediately in a brick house, see changes by the "end of the week"/"by November."

"I was entertaining great hopes that everything would change quickly, according to the campaign promises."

Disillusionment: Respondents fell into two groups: those who felt betrayed; those who were prepared to give the government more time.

"Feelings of disillusionment seem to be strongest among respondents drawn from the poorer socio-economic areas. They are the ones in greatest need, and those who feel the backlash of white racism in the workplace. They are also those who were motivated to vote in order to get a black government. Those who had the highest expectations also had the most pressing needs. Some knew of the Reconstruction and Development Programme, but felt that it was benefiting others."

(The promises that were made in the 1994 election under the banner of the RDP were to "meet the basic needs of people — jobs, land, housing, water, electricity, telecommunications, transport, a clean and healthy environment, nutrition, health and social welfare." Its "achievable program" for the first five years would include programs to "redistribute a substantial amount of land to landless people, build over one million houses, provide clean water and sanitation to all, electrify 2.5 million new homes, and provide access to all to affordable health care and telecommunications." The ANC's campaign manifesto and political advertising included wording which created the illusion among people that "instant" change was going to happen. "Instant gratification": Who sold the ANC on this idea that the people could be sold anything? Why did the ANC make such extravagant promises when it was not necessary to do so? Did the medium become the message — an electorate never having had to deal with election promises, since neither elections nor promises existed in the past, mistook the promise for the deed in the belief that promises would not be made by "their party" unless they were going to be kept. Promises and delivery became synonymous for an electorate which had never heard those kinds of promises made before. It would appear that "freedom,"

"democracy," were seen almost exclusively in material terms of the delivery of goods and services – not the adoption of a code of values or a belief system. A free lunch in the offing.

What happened between 1992 and the elections? Were we seeing the aftermath of an election campaign structured on the basis of polling, and the polling messages were drummed in, so that people's conception of what the process was all about changed. They were told time and again what their needs were and that they would be fulfilled, once the ANC was in power. They were told by the ANC that if they voted for the party, they could expect brand-new houses and jobs. False expectations were created. But who was behind the creation of the false expectations? Who said to the ANC, "This is the way to do it. This is the way to get the largest possible slice of the vote," and if it took a little dissembling and flew in the face of every reality, so what? Derek Keys had briefed the ANC on the direction in which the economy was moving and the imminence of collapse. Who in the ANC said, "Let's deal with reality after we win." Given what ANC knew about the parlous state of the economy, where did it think the resources were coming from to fund these massive expenditures? Also interesting how many times "benefiting the other" cropped up, where the other did not stand for an individual but for another group. The precursor of a zero-sum mentality – others gaining at my expense.)

"The various RDP campaigns at national and regional levels urgently need to mount educational campaigns which both inform people about the RDP and involve them in the programme. These must target poorer socio-economic areas. The aim would be to inform people about the RDP and what it is trying to achieve while soliciting input from people who feel sidelined."

Other participants, especially women, felt less negative and were prepared to give the government more time. Other issues mentioned mostly by women: free child care; education; removal of white government; diminution of political violence; ability to brew and sell beer without fear of prosecution; feeling of citizenship.

Most felt that two years should be enough time for the government to begin delivering concrete benefits.

(It makes sense that women would be more disposed toward the government than men – the free child care, free medical care for pregnant women, education, all women's issues.)

People were confused as to why they had to vote again.

They did not understand for what they were going to vote, or for whom.

They did not know much about what local government did.

They believed it was too soon to vote again.

They understood that elections were about accountability, but believed it was too early to make judgments.

They had been told that they wouldn't have to vote again for five years.

Most respondents were concerned about the divisive, confusing, and potentially destructive impacts of different parties and groups at different levels.

"ANC supporters, especially younger blacks and township dwellers, were particularly concerned about these elections imposing 'apartheid' and undermining the government with divisions. Even after two hours, participants said these elections were confusing."

(*Association of new local government structures with the apartheid government's black councils?*)

They also expressed fears that the new local government structures would pit one area against another since they would divide people into smaller areas.

(*Again, the apartheid associations: of separateness; of being split up in order to dilute strength. But a lot had to do with ignorance. There were significant changes in attitudes once people were informed about the nature of local government. However, what were they being told? That local government would speed delivery? If so, then little wonder that people became a little more enthusiastic. That is, "respondents became excited about the idea of voting for local representatives who would act as a channel" for their complaints to reach the national Parliament and, as local people, would take responsibility for local services and concerns. "No wonder they became more excited. However, many of the candidates were simply foisted on the people, many of whom knew only a few of them, met fewer, and found their "voices' to be rather mute."*)

Many respondents felt that they should be given a list of candidates and that the candidates should earn their votes. They resented the "outsiders" suddenly appearing from nowhere, and introducing themselves as candidates for local office. Many had never met them or had any idea who their local councillors were.

Young men in rural areas were most likely to say that the role of traditional leaders in local government should be confined to solving family disputes and resolving social problems in the community.

Having to register to vote posed a problem. Some absolutely refused to do it. Indeed, many were angry at the suggestion that they would have to register: giving details about their families, their addresses, and so forth, was anathema to most.

(Again, the residual fears of the past; the association of registration of any type with pass laws, and others.)

"Although a degree of cynicism existed regarding the 'rewards' of voting, it had not yet reached a level where people would disenfranchise themselves because of it."

"The problem with local government elections was not 'voting' – once it was explained to them what local government was about, most were enthusiastic, but only about what they were voting for."

Two strategies were put forward: (1) Promote elections as the next step in democracy – "finish the job;" (2) educate voters with regard to what local government is about and have voters participate in choosing that level of government.

The focus group recommended the second on the grounds that South Africans were tiring of symbolic progress; they wanted tangible improvements for their families. The message for local government could focus on getting those results.

(If the message did, it may backfire against the ANC in the 1999 elections. While promises of great things to come are always an attractive way to get a simple message out, they may begin to lose their appeal if the promised delivery never occurs. This, more than anything, turns people off and leaves them more cynical.)

Many people talked about the "distance" of the national government: every group expressed a sense of distance and a lack of voice.

People felt emotional about the national government's forgetting them. They liked the idea of personalizing government and felt that councillors drawn from their districts would be more like the residents and more responsive to their needs, that local elections would speed up and localize change.

(If the case being made here is for democracies getting off the ground, a constituency rather than a party list system may be preferable. If you want to give people a sense of belonging to government or to part of what is going on, especially when they are not going to feel the impact of the "revolution" for a long time, and in the short run things are likely to get tougher rather than better.)

People viewed local elections as a way to involve "ordinary" people in politics, people who are more community-oriented and less political.

"We'll vote for people who will listen to our problems."

Few thought they would use their vote to express a protest at things not done or to air to their grievances.

Although people were frustrated about the pace of change, they believed that government should be given more time, and they were slowly
beginning to see change emanate from the new structures. They were still
positive about transformation.

Again and again the mantra: "If Mandela says I must vote, I will vote."

*(It will be interesting to see whether the same tactic works in the 1999
election – the old "win one for the Gipper" routine. What augurs well for the ANC
in this regard is the finding in the 1999 Helen Suzman Foundation survey that
"South African political culture is characterized by an extremely strong emphasis
on leadership, especially among Coloureds, Africans, and white Afrikaners.
Among African ANC voters, no less than 31 per cent strongly agree and 43 per
cent agree somewhat with the statement ,"I will stand by my political party and its
leader even if I disagree with many of its policies".)*

*(Also very notable: in all the focus group surveys, there wasn't a single mention
of provincial government! Why?)*

The June/July 1996
HSRC Omnibus Survey

Political Trends

- In May 1994, 76 per cent of respondents indicated their general satisfaction
  with political developments; this response had dropped to 45 per cent in July
  1996, a drop of more than 30 per cent.
- There was also a decline in general satisfaction with economic developments. In May 1994, 51 per cent of respondents were positive; in July 1996
  this had dropped to 34 per cent. For the first time since the April 1994
  election, more than half the respondents said they were dissatisfied with the
  general economic situation.

These trends may have been influenced by a variety of factors, the following being
among the most important.
- The euphoria and widespread feeling of optimism that followed the 1994
  election slowly began to dissipate in the face of the enormous problems with
  which the country found itself confronted: by the lack of experience and
  capacity that bedeviled the early years; by the recognition first on the part of
  government that transformation would take years if not decades to accomplish, that you simply don't declare that things will change and change
  follows; by structural and behavioral residuals that precluded change; by the
  unwillingness or inability of the people themselves to face up to what change

entailed and that change required sacrifices on the part of the oppressed as well a their former oppressors; by the fact that South Africa gained its sovereignty precisely at a point where concepts of national sovereignty were becoming passé, by the fact that in a global society every country was no longer free to determine its economic and social policies without due regard to the external constraints of the outside; by the failure of fixed foreign investment to materialize on a scale that had almost been taken for granted. The collapse of the Government of National Unity also undermined the feeling that all South Africans were working toward the same objectives, the first small pinches of affirmative action convincing whites that there was no future for them in the new South Africa, the lack of tangible progress on any number of economic and social fronts convincing many blacks that nothing much was going to change in the new South Africa and that their living conditions and economic circumstances were not about to undergo miraculous turnabouts. The rand had begun its slow, inexorable slide contributing to the general malaise that while things were not quite falling apart, they were definitely not coming together. Violence in KwaZulu-Natal was still occurring with a sufficiently periodic frequency that left a lingering question mark over the future of the province. And, of course, the escalation in the level of crime, the public's increasing preoccupation with its own safety, became a general barometer of government's effectiveness, begging the question that if the government could not protect its citizenry from what appeared to be brazenly contemptuous acts of both horrendous and petty acts of crime, it was failing to carry out the most fundamental act of government: the provision of stability and order.

- But if one were to interpret this overlapping and often contradictory jetsam of the outcome of the multiple and random reactions to the new order as a sign of hopelessness, one would be mistaken. Parallel with the drop in satisfaction in both the political and economic arenas was the pervasiveness of high hopes for the future. Over 85 per cent of respondents expected their standard of living to improve noticeably within the next five years, 62 per cent before the general election in 1999. Given the limitations that the economy faces, these expectations will be very difficult indeed, in view of the economic crisis that crisscrossed the globe in 1998–1999 and its continuing fallouts, in reality impossible to achieve.
- But there are still other variables, more psychological than concrete, that add to the complexities of rationalizing attitudes in South Africa. (See the Stellenbosch poll cited below regarding blacks' and whites' different attitudes about the future – the positive attitudes among blacks, the negative attitudes among whites.) Two nations live according to different hopes, aspirations, and norms.

Disparity

(*If the white view of inequality is that white affluence relative to blacks is not due
to white exploitation of blacks, which has contributed to the relative and absolute
poverty of blacks, then Mbeki's delineation of two nations, one white and well-off,
the other black and poor, is lost on whites and is one more instance of the refusal
on the part of whites to acknowledge the damage that apartheid did, especially in
confining the education of blacks to a level which ensured that they could not rise
above a certain functional level, of serving as the human fuel for the white industrial machines and as the underground excavators of the mineral wealth that
enriched the white fraternity. If whites cannot bring themselves to see, and acknowledge, that they exploited blacks in the past, and especially under apartheid,
then the future for improved race relations is bleak, and an increasingly resentful
black elite will seek retribution through the means whites fear most, redistribution
through taxation. How can one speak of nation building when the people who are
supposedly the rudimentary core of the nation engage each other with such silent
enmity?*

*Mkebi once raised the German example: the West Germans were so ardent for
all Germans to be reunited under one flag and the enfolding arms of one nation
that they were prepared to pay a "unity tax," a 7.5 per cent surcharge on personal
income tax that made possible a transfer of $586 billion in public funds from West
to East to eliminate some of the huge imbalances in income levels that existed
between the two. Even the mention of some similar mechanism to correct apart-
heid-induced imbalances in South Africa sends whites scampering to their fear
stations.*[22]

*On their own behalf, whites point to the progress that has been made in the last
decade in narrowing income differentials. According to the 1995 Central Statistics
Survey (CSS) of household income and expenditure in the twelve main urban
areas, the Gini coefficient decreased from 0.63 in 1990 to 0.55 in 1995. In these
areas, over the same period, the ratio of white to black household income dropped
from 5.85 to 1 to 2.35 to 1. Black household incomes grew by 140 per cent in real
terms while those for whites dropped by 3.4 per cent.*

It is not clear from the research cited in Finance Week *whether their data refer
to household income per household or household incomes in the aggregate.
Research suggests that the income ratio between unemployed and employed blacks
is 29 to 1 [$230 per month compared with $8 per month]. This is the biggest
income differential that exists in South Africa and stands in contrast to the 3.4: to
differential between employed whites and blacks in manufacturing.*[23]

In its analysis of the CSS data, Finance Week *concludes that "Mbeki's claim
that [South Africa] is two nations may be true. But they are not black and white;
they are the employed and the unemployed." But* Finance Week *is indulging itself
in a chimera, since, at most, 3 per cent of the white workforce is unemployed, the
real comparison is between black and white employed and black unemployed, for*

97 per cent of the unemployed are black.[24] (Or on further disaggregation: in 1996 more than 22 per cent of South African households were earning less than $85 a month. A total of 31 per cent of African households were earning less than $85 a month compared with 3 per cent of Coloureds, Indians, and white households.[25] The United Nations Human Development Report indicates that the poorest 40 per cent of households in South Africa (almost entirely African) earned only 9 per cent of the country's income and the richest 20 per cent (almost entirely white) earned 19 times more than the poorest 20 per cent.[26]

Again, the point is worth repeating: there is a growing black middle class which, in terms of numbers alone, is roughly equal to the country's white population; the disparities between white wage earners and black wage earners is decreasing; the number of blacks in senior management positions is increasing dramatically; the Employment Equity Act will have a fundamental effect on the composition of the labor force; and the number of unemployed is increasing – as companies downsize in response to the opening up of markets and the liberalization of trade, they attempt to become more competitive in a global economy that has little time or sympathy for the fact that they are tentatively making their way out of the protectionist policies in which they wrapped themselves in the past, shed labor in favor of capital either because of capital's superior productivity or because labor legislation intended to correct the imbalances of the past proving too restrictive, making investment in labor a less cost-efficient or a more risk-intensive proposition.

Employment in the formal sector will, according to most surveys, will in the next two years at least, and these estimates don't take into account the 500,000-plus school leavers who enter the job market each year.[27]

A World Bank report suggests that wage increases which exceed the rate of inflation often result in job losses. It quotes some examples: a 10 per cent increase in real wages for workers may lead to a 7 per cent loss in jobs, although this may vary from sector to sector. The bank also found that more than half the job losses occur about two and a half years after increases are implemented.[28] Since 1995, real wages have risen every year, and for the first three quarters of 1997, settlements averaged a real 2 per cent. Hence, according to this analysis, more workers than ever could find themselves on the street by 2000, hardly the most auspicious start to the millennium.

Economists, for the most part, argue that wage pressures are the key to investment decisions by private companies. A further consideration that adds to the cost of hiring labor is the degree of difficulty a company faces in times of economic hardship when it has to resort to worker layoffs. The more inflexible the labor market in this regard, especially if specific procedures have to be followed in accordance with a country's labor laws, the more jaundiced the prospects for foreign direct investment. South Africa's labor laws are, in its own words, "labor friendly."[29]

But when the plethora of data is put aside, the abiding question remains: Given the democratic changes in South Africa, has there been a real and meaningful redistribution of power in favor of the poor?

In the introduction to Creating Action Space, *co-editor Conrad Barberton boldly sets out the dimensions and context of the problem:*

> The fact is that poor people the world over face similar challenges, namely, how to democratize governance at all levels, and how to change the distribution of economic power to ensure that resources are not monopolised by a small, rich elite, but used to meet all people's needs equally.

> The struggle to establish a more just socio-political and socio-economic distribution of power is ongoing, and is likely to sharpen as the majority of the world's population continues to get poorer and the gap between rich and poor increases.

> Poor people's lack of control over resources and institutions of governance limits their capacity to influence the events and circumstances that govern their existence.

> To change this, to give the poor greater control over their lives, means challenging the status quo: struggling to empower the poor economically and politically. This means challenging present economic power relationships by seeking to change the way both the stock and flow of resources are divided between rich and poor. It also means challenging the political power of elite groups that dominate the institutions of governance at all levels – locally, nationally and internationally.

> The struggle against apartheid in South Africa bears many similarities to the struggles of poor people elsewhere in the world. The struggle was about realising political justice and realising socio-economic justice in that it challenged the institutions and social structures that perpetuated political, social and economic inequity between people and groups.

> In South Africa,, the colonial and apartheid regime used "democratic" institutions, the rule of law and the state bureaucracy to sanction and facilitate the exploitation and impoverishment of millions of people, to increase the profits of foreign and domestic companies, and to enrich a small minority. Obtaining the right to vote was seen as an important step to wrestling control of these institutions in order to remould them to serve the interests of the majority of South Africans. This is borne out by the origins of the ANC, the Freedom Charter, the activities of the United Democratic Front and Mass Democratic Movement and the struggles of the trade unions, civics, and other mass organizations.

> Over many, many years, and at great cost, ordinary people organised to oppose the Land Acts, the group Areas Act, Bantu education, the pass laws, and migrant labour system, separate amenities, discrimination in the workplace, etc. Policies such as these had a direct impact on the majority's

socio-economic rights. Through them the majority of South Africans were denied the right to a life of dignity, and millions of people were made poor.

The right to vote was an end in itself, as well as a means to an end. South Africa's first democratic election on 27–28 April 1994 was a tremendous victory over political injustice. Millions of people voted for the first time and elected "their" government. However, it was also the realization of an important first step in the far more difficult and important process of realising socio-economic justice.

In the period immediately following the election, ordinary people, buoyed by election promises and the vision of the Reconstruction and Development Programme (RDP), really had a sense that it was possible to realise significant improvements in their living standards. There was widespread activity around the country as communities spontaneously set-up RDP forums which the new government said were needed to facilitate development initiatives in their areas. People were active and involved, looking forward to playing their part in the envisaged "people-driven development" process.

Ordinary people felt a sense of ownership and excitement at the prospect of "their" government governing. They had given the government a mandate to implement the RDP. It was an idea, a word that was on everyone's lips and they responded eagerly to the call to participate in their own development. There was a sense of anticipation that now that, at last, attacking poverty and deprivation was indeed the first priority of the government.

The national RDP Office and the Minister Without Portfolio were the most tangible symbols of this new direction It seemed as though nothing would stop the transformation of the government into an institution that really sought to serve the needs of the people.

However, it soon became apparent that the untransformed bureaucracy and inexperienced government did not have the capacity to respond to the enthusiasm for change on the ground. Delay followed delay, complicated business plans that had been painstakingly drawn up by RDP forums went nowhere in most cases, and eventually the national RDP Office, which was supposed to drive the change process, was closed down and its funding shifted back to the Department of Finance.

The old elite interests (in association with the new elite interests) began to make themselves felt. International financial institutions and domestic business interests began to put pressure on the government to abandon the "idealism" of the RDP and start living in the "real" world. The politics of power and political opportunism began to make its effects known. People who perceived the struggle to be over began to put their own interests above those of the community. The outcome of these trends has been a definite narrowing of possibilities.

The scope to challenge the power of established interest groups was further limited by the abandonment of the national RDP Office, the enactment of the new Constitution, and the adoption of Growth, Employment and Redistribution (GEAR). The interests of property owners have been entrenched. Economic policy is supposedly "non-negotiable." The stream has entered a course of stone. Some erosion can still occur, but to effect any kind of change in direction is going to be very difficult.

Increasingly parliamentary procedures designed to foster participatory policy-making are being by-passed. The free flow of progressive ideas and options for change is increasingly stifled. And what it is being replaced with is a high-handed technocratic, "expert" consultant-driven approach that simply assumes what people want or need (and will get), with little or no consultation or participation by the people who will be affected.

Whereas a few years ago there was great optimism about realising far reaching change in almost all spheres, now only incremental and limited change seems all the government seems willing and able to do, given the nature of the political and economic compromises that have been made to date. The tremendous effort placed into creating structures over the last three years is now bearing the fruit of increasing control, rather than increased participation (as was the intention). The vision of a people-centred development process has been largely lost.

As a result the mood on the ground is gradually becoming more adversarial, more impatient with the slow delivery of the most basic needs (water, sanitation, housing), the government's failure to support community development initiatives and the continued day-to-day experience of unemployment and poverty. There is a growing perception that not enough has changed in the way the government does things.

More significantly, government policy has shifted from the "people-centred" development approach of the RDP to the adoption of the Growth, Employment and Redistribution (GEAR) strategy which, in essence , is a private sector driven growth strategy. It is ironic that this new growth policy's success is dependent on the goodwill and investment of the very groups that benefited from the policies of the apartheid regime.[30]

A survey conducted by the Bureau for Economic Research [BER] at Stellenbosch University indicated that consumer confidence in the third quarter of 1998 fell sharply, reversing all gains made to the three weeks to June as a result of the increase in interest rates and continued volatility in the markets.

The decline in confidence, however, was decidedly asymmetrical. Black consumer confidence remained largely unchanged, while white consumer confidence dropped significantly.

White consumer confidence dropped 25 index points, the largest fall since the fourth quarter of 1985, when the prime rate also increased to 25 per cent and the rand depreciated 50 per cent against the dollar in the aftermath of P. W. Botha's Rubicon speech. In contrast, black consumer confidence remained unaffected by volatility in the markets and increasing interest rates.[31]([According to the report]

"Black consumers expect a continued improvement in the economic performance and their financial position over the next twelve months. The majority also re-garded the present as the right time to buy durable goods like household furniture and equipment." [Again, in contrast] "a sizable majority of white consumers expect the economy's performance and their own financial position to deteriorate over the next year. The number expecting a deterioration in the economy increased from 37 per cent in the second quarter to 59 per cent in the third."

Explaining the divergence in consumer confidence, the BER said it was prob-ably due to "the difference in the impact that high interest rates had on high and low income earnings." The survey results indicated that there was a sharp drop in the confidence of higher income households – predominantly white – while those of lower income households – predominantly black – remained stable. Thus, the report concludes:

> A larger share of the expenditure of high income households goes towards paying monthly mortgage repayments.

> The hike in the mortgage rate by 3.5 percentage points in July, therefore, severely dented the discretionary disposable income of high income house-holds.

> The financial market instability since the middle of May might also have heightened uncertainty amongst higher income earners and blacks who have recently moved into the higher income groups will also be similarly affected.

> In contrast, the increase in interest rates, had no direct effect on low income households, as the majority do not make use of formal financial services.[32]

Evidence of the meaninglessness of the banking system in the lives of most black South Africans was presented by the Alliance for Micro-Enterprise Develop-ment Practitioners at the annual conference of the South African National Nongovernmental Organization Coalition in September 1998. Only 37 per cent of South Africans, the alliance reported, had access to banking and financial services, reinforcing the BER's conclusion that rising interest rates don't have much of a direct impact on most black South Africans. Consider also that 19 million South Africans, representing almost 50 per cent of the population, are "poor" in the sense that their incomes fall below the critical "poverty line" – defined in terms of basic consumption needs. In addition, the Gini coefficient, which measures the inequal-ity of income distribution, is the second highest in the world.[33] Consider also the behavior of the rate of inflation. In August, the rise in interest rates was largely responsible for pushing the rate up to 7.6 per cent from 6.6 per cent in July.[34] But while the core rate – the indicator the Reserve Bank uses for monetary policy purposes which excludes mortgages rates, certain fresh and frozen foods, and value-added tax – also rose to 7.6 per cent in August, increasing from a 7.2 per cent level in July.

From July to August, the overall consumer price index [CPI] rose 1.1 per cent. Housing costs contributed 0.8 per cent, transport contributed 0.2 per cent, due mainly to an increase of 11c per litre in the petrol price. Food prices, however, helped to keep a lid on the rise in inflation, with a month to month fall of 0.2 per cent. Household consumables also declined in price. In October, the price of petrol is expected to decrease by at least 10c per litre.

(What do these data, taken in aggregate, say? On the one hand the obvious: that there are two economies: one for the better-off and one for the less fortunate. They also strongly suggest that the economy for the more affluent is far more vulnerable to market forces, whether in the form of the impact of higher interest they must pay on their mortgages, the higher prices they must pay for the imported goods they are accustomed to buying, the value of their assets, whether in pension funds or stocks and shares, in the face of capital flight, currency depreciation, and global volatility. These are considerations which are far from the minds of the 50 per cent below the poverty line and the economy of the informal sector – the only part of the economy that is growing. Here, conditions are close to the ground; the basics for survival are the preoccupation of day-to-day living, how to procure them the consuming concern. What they need to survive is least vulnerable to market fluctuations, whether in the and or in interest rates. What they need above all are jobs, which will not materialize without economic growth, which will not materialize without lower interest rates.

Thus, by lowering interest rates, the Reserve Bank would open the way to job creation, alleviate not only the unacceptable levels of unemployment but also reduce that component of crime attributable to people's needs to acquire the means for survival one way or another, ease the pressure on homeowners, give a boost to the construction industry, which is already sinking in the quicksand of increasing uncertainty and lack of confidence about the future.[35] Allow the rand to find its own level in the market and make no interventions. Undoubtedly, imports would rise sharply in price, but this would be compensated for by a lower volume of imports and a higher level of exports, thus improving the country's balance of payments and adding to its foreign reserves, and if the price to be paid is higher inflation, even double-digit inflation, that may be the inevitable trade-off that has to be made for dealing with the country's overriding problem, unemployment, identified by blacks and whites alike as being the most important issue facing the country.[36] Even the venerable Milton Friedman, who was awarded a Nobel Prize for his contribution to determining the overriding role monetary policy played in regulating the economy and his emphasis on interest rates, and more important, on the money supply, as the key variables in policy decision making, comes out on the side of letting the rand find its own level in the market, free of Reserve Bank interference, and fine-tuning the money supply to bring interest rates down:

My view for emerging smaller countries [he argues] is that either of two exchange rate arrangements make sense. They should have either a fixed exchange rate. Or they should have a truly floating exchange rate.

I would certainly advise your central bank governor simply to follow monetary policies appropriate to the domestic economy and let the exchange rate go wherever it wants to go. "No country [he concludes] with a truly floating exchange rate has had an international financial crisis.[37]

Perhaps the factor that escapes many analysts of politics in South Africa is that it makes no difference how the government performs. No matter how abysmal its performance come election day, Africans are going to vote for the ANC, and while the Coloured vote may be up for grabs, no white party has much of a chance of expanding its vote beyond its diminishing base. Negative sentiment towards opposition parties far outweighs negative sentiment towards the ANC. Besides, Africans have a propriety disposition towards the ANC. Political preferences of ANC supporters run in one direction only, a phenomenon not dissimilar from political behavior in other countries in a post-colonization phase. It is "their" party. To a degree it's like family. Family members have a right to criticize each other in a way that "outsiders" don't. When "outsiders" turn on the family, even to express the concerns that family members have been complaining about, the family closes ranks. It is, for all intents and purposes, a closed shop. Moreover, as the Truth and Reconciliation Commission [TRC] so vividly illustrated, whites do not remember the past. It is something blacks do not fail to remember.)

A few polls illustrate the point: In the July 1996 HSRC poll, support levels for the political parties, the HSRC compared support levels for the parties in May 1994 and July 1996:

Table 1

Party	May 1994 %	July 1996 %
ANC	63	53
NP	9	18
IFP	4	7
Right-wing	3	3
DP	1	1
PAC	1	2

[According to the HSRC analysts]:

The support lost by the ANC has not resulted in a gain for other parties and could have shifted to the "uncertain" or "refuse to answer" categories. This may be an early indication that dissatisfied ANC supporters may decide not to vote rather than vote against the ANC. Overall, the support for the parties has changed little or not at all since the general election. There is no indication their criticism of the government has seriously affected the support of the ANC or increased that of opposition parties.

On a related question, whether respondents had considered voting for another party in the next election, 72 per cent said no while only 14 per cent said yes. In fact, on further analysis, the survey data indicated that whatever voting shift might occur among the 14 per cent might not benefit the minority parties. On the contrary, the majority party could gain from the minorities.

Finally, the rigidity of support was reflected in a series of questions on how "close" or "distant" respondents felt towards the parties. The most striking aspect of the responses was that in all cases except the ANC, 58 per cent or more of the respondents felt "distant" towards the other parties.

One indicator of the extent of the political malaise that has set in can be found in the results of the *Opinion '99* survey conducted in September 1998 on voter attitudes and intentions, and how they have changed since the halcyon days of 1994.

From mid-1994 through mid-1997, surveys regularly showed that between 61 per cent and 64 per cent of potential voters would vote for the ANC if an election were held "today." In September 1998 that figure had dropped to 51 per cent, and only 35 per cent said they identified with the ANC. The reason for the rather dramatic turnaround is that, in 1994, 76 per cent of the people believed that the country was headed in the right direction (and given the promises of the new government, who wouldn't have?), that optimism had slowly declined in the following years and became more precipitous since 1996, dropping to 43 per cent in the third quarter of 1998 – the first time the optimistic/pessimistic trend lines crossed – while 44 per cent thought the country was going in the wrong direction.[38] Other surveys have tracked a steady decrease in the proportion of people saying the national economy has been improving, as well as in the proportion that believes it will improve in the next year. The drop in optimistic expectations has been especially noticeable among blacks.[39] A mere 18 per cent think the government is doing a good job with the economy. And only 12 per cent think the government is doing a good job creating jobs.

But if the people have become more disillusioned about the prospects for a brighter future and their expectations regarding what the ANC will or can deliver on the promises made back in 1994, no other political party has been able to turn that disillusionment into political support. Even while surveys show that there has been real, and substantial, declines in confirmed ANC support, the intention to vote for any opposition party remains at 28 per cent, exactly where it stood in late 1994. Thus the good news for the ANC: while fewer and fewer voters feel a connection to the party, they are not deserting it for other parties – only 9 per cent of the electorate identify with any opposition party) – there is no transfer of allegiance but rather a gathering and increasing pool of undecided voters. More than one voter in five was unable to "identify" with a political party. More than half the electorate does not feel "close" to any political party.[40]

(Given the deep cleavages that continue to exist across the racial divide, the chances of African voters crossing that divide to vote for the National Party or even the Democratic Party are remote. On election day they will either return to the fold or stay at home. The IFP has become for all practical purposes a provincial that may be hard pushed to retain the plurality it commanded in KwaZulu-Natal in 1994. The likelihood is that the ANC and the IFP will form a voluntary coalition after the 1999 election, thus giving the ANC the free hand it is looking for in exchange for a deputy presidency or a like honour for Chief Buthelezi. In this sense, the ANC has little reason to be apprehensive about the outcome of the next election – there is simply no credible alternative in waiting. And perhaps, in the longer run, this vacuum poses the gravest threat to South Africa's gradually slipping into the ways of a one-party state. Certainly, the Opinion '99 survey should provide the opposition parties with the stimulus for some soul-searching. Or perhaps the explanation for the intended voter is simple: non-African parties are a sidebar in the political arena.

The belief among white political parties that they can somehow attract African voters is just further evidence that they still don't get it: don't get the magnitude of the injustice apartheid did to blacks; don't grasp the profound impression their being unable or unwilling to get it has on the black psyche; don't get the extent of the damage they inflicted on blacks and the inevitable consequences of that damage; don't get that even their solicitation of black votes is an insult to blacks since it negates their past experiences, almost brushes aside the oppression the white state ruthlessly imposed in their name, even if not always with their full knowledge, as an insufficient reason not to consider voting for them in the new dispensation; that attempting to lure blacks into supporting white parties is an insult to blacks, especially in the absence of an unqualified apology on the part of whites for apartheid and some gesture of genuine remorse and willingness to pay the price of undoing the legacy of apartheid wrongs.)

The November/December 1996
Focus Group Surveys

These focus group surveys (FGS) consisted of eighteen groups, at least one of which came from each of the nine provinces. Participants, community leaders and activists, included prominent locals who had a strong influence on opinion in their communities.

The focus group research states:

"Across race and party lines, the mood of South African community leaders is one of ambivalence. Community leaders participating expressed frustration with the rate of change, disappointment in broken promises, nervousness about the future, but that was combined with a fundamental, if not all that firmly rooted belief that the country was moving in the right direction, and the understanding that change takes time. While they were struggling to address severe problems in their communities – unemployment, housing, crime, and health care delivery, they did see some progress, and the advent of democracy continues to be a powerful and emotional force."

(The memory of the first election still elicits strong emotional reaction. That election had entered the realm of myth – the JFK assassination syndrome; it had become the defining moment of democracy, not an event that signaled the beginning of the long, hard struggle to create and propagate democratic norms and values but the culminating apogee of democracy itself. The April 1994 election had assumed a mystical reverence; it had represented the apex of the struggle, not the beginning, the one shining moment when "hope and history met," when everything seemed possible, the sky was the limit; one had only to wish and the wish would come true.

It may be unfair to attribute the high expectations blacks had of the changes that would follow the election of "their" government – expectations which had been relentlessly fostered by the internal opposition to apartheid, especially with the advent of the UDF in 1983. The emphasis was always on tearing things down, destroying apartheid structures, abolishing apartheid laws. People were given no understanding of the meaning of freedom other than its being the opposite of apartheid; but there was no effort to make the masses understand that their "own" rule would bring with it immense obligations, that they would have to sacrifice in order to build a new South Africa, that South Africa was a poor country, that poverty was pervasive, that while they were not as poor as their neighbors, the poverty was nevertheless real and would not be eliminated overnight, that even taking a lot from whites wouldn't go very far when they tried to spread it around, because despite the ostentatiousness of whites, they were few in number and blacks were many, that the mythical belief that if only the white government was disposed of, everyone could live as comfortably as whites.

All of which reinforced a culture of dependency and learned helplessness with a culture that perceived change in terms of the changes that whites had to make but ignored those which blacks would have to make Everything was perceived in terms of a one-sided equation. For all the calls to "let my people go," few had much idea where to take them, and when the ideological underpinnings of socialism fell apart, they found themselves more or less coerced into free-market thinking, again without much thought to where that would lead them. Hence the half-hearted commitment to GEAR. On the one hand, international institutions must see them as playing according to the book plays of the "Washington consensus;" on the other, the game somehow wasn't turning out the way the playbook had forecast, and the effort to trim ideological sails yet give the impression to the masses that the Freedom Charter remained the touchstone of the movement, the Bible, Gospel, and Road Map to the Future all rolled onto one. The effort to square so many circles absorbed the intellectual energies of a fractious elite, producing more muddled thinking than clarity of vision.

One more thing: the constant harping on apartheid as the obstacle to black progress or self-initiative was conducive to blacks' believing this to be the case; hence no effort was called for since it would only be stymied by apartheid. Their actions reinforced their own passivity, and one fed on the other. It would be interesting to get a map of the geographic spread of resistance and the pattern of arrests. Was resistance really an urban phenomenon? To what extent, if at all, was there rural participation?)

"The Constitution had already achieved enormous legitimacy and permanence as a document that should not be easily altered. The most frequent criticism of the Constitution was that it granted too many rights and is to blame for rising crime and social disintegration."

(At the same time, they saw the Constitution as "an expression of common principles and a protection of their rights. And one would think that if the "too many rights" were to blame for "rising crime and social disintegration," they would be in favor of amending it to get rid of these "too many rights.")

Another seeming contradiction: a number of community leaders expressed concern that the Constitution was not well understood by the people; they were concerned by the lack of democratic education and wanted better civic training.

(The contradiction is that we're discussing what this "elite" believe on the one hand, and what they believe the masses understand. Question: If these are the civic and community leaders, why aren't they doing more to educate the "masses" re: the Constitution and other subjects? If they don't do it, who do they expect will?)

Thus the focus group says the following.

"The Constitution has achieved enormous legitimacy and permanence, that as a document it should not be easily changed, and that community leaders feel a great sense of ownership and pride in the Constitution, it is also clear to these community leaders that the Constitution is not well understood by most of the people for whom it serves as the supreme law, and that in this sense allegiance is amorphous rather than absolute, something people take pride in, perhaps because it is theirs, rather than being committed to, and hence the need for civic education at the grassroots level to familiarize people with the principles of the Constitution, how those principles apply to their everyday lives, and how their increased knowledge of the Constitution will advance democracy and in the [end] must lead to a better life for all."

"Community leaders have a fairly clear view of what they expect from national and local government. From national government they expect planning, direction, and allocation of resources. From local government they expect implementation. Provincial government, however, remains ill defined. Community leaders have strong views of their local governments, which they expect to be in close touch with the grass roots and to deliver visible results. South African community leaders are increasingly looking for real results and accountability as they move from the revolution to a functional democracy. Particularly at the local level, not only must government listen, it must respond and deliver. When local government succeeds, it is widely praised; where it fails it is harshly criticized."

"Community leaders are much more mixed in their assessment of national government. On the one hand, most credit national government with doing a reasonably good job in setting national policy. On the other, they criticize the national government for failing to provide the necessary resources to implement policy."

"Government corruption is viewed as a serious problem, but most do not view it as the most serious problem they face. Indeed, discussions about corruption emerged spontaneously in only six of the eighteen focus groups. In each of these groups, the issues raised by participants were either corruption at the provincial level or in police departments. Corruption at the national level, while viewed as serious, was not a topic that emerged on its own. One Johannesburg leader summarized the general attitude, 'While corruption should be looked on with a critical eye,' he said, 'we should not concentrate on it.'

"However, once the topic was raised, most participants expressed great unhappiness with the level of corruption. It disappoints them because they expected better; they see it as hypocritical from a government that has pledged equality and democracy; they worry about 'going the way' of other African nations; they are angry about the waste of resources; and they are frustrated that it makes it harder to govern. They are cynical about politicians who were once part of the revolution but have already become corrupted."

"At the same time, they put the question in two perspectives: One, that while significant government exists in the new South Africa, it is probably no worse than it was under the old regime. The difference, most agree, it that corruption is visible now, whereas before it was hidden. Thus, the difference between the two lay in the new transparency. There was a propensity to believe that the fact that people were becoming more aware of corruption was an indication not that there was more of it than in the 'old days,' but that government had become much more transparent about it and prepared to expose it to public scrutiny. The government's willingness to be accountable and transparent stood it in good stead."

"Community leaders point to two reasons why South Africa is moving in the right direction: the advent of democracy and civil liberties, and signs of genuine, albeit insufficient progress in areas like housing and education. There is an increasing understanding among blacks that the expectations they had in 1994, that the opportunity to elect 'their government' would bring about a sea change in their economic and social circumstances, were unfounded. There is much disappointment that promises have not been kept; much disappointment that change has been too slow, and much doubt and uncertainty regarding the future. Perhaps the mood is best captured by a black leader in Cape Town who ruefully observed, 'We had high expectations but all of a sudden we're doubtful. We don't know if we are coming or going.'

"What is most conspicuous in the 1996 focus group surveys is the emergence of crime as a major, if not the major, issue. Leaders complain vociferously that criminals are cuddled; that criminals have too many rights, and almost unanimously they want the death penalty to be reinstated."

(*Crime is a unique issue for two reasons. First, it is an issue that leaders clearly believe is not moving in the right direction, rather that the situation is worsening; and second, unlike other issues, it is seen as a constitutional issue – and is one of the few sources of criticism of the Constitution. To most community leaders, the Constitution is soft on crime. The most harsh criticism scathingly voiced: The Constitution does not protect the innocent but the criminal," or "I think our Constitution has many flaws that need to be rectified. You find a murderer, after killing someone, claiming he has the right to sleep in a bed and watch TV. Our Constitution tries to accommodate everyone, even wrong ones."*)

"What is also significant with regard to the response of participants is their failure to identify corruption, but more importantly, their singular failure to identify unemployment as a major source of concern in their communities, or even to make tenuous connections with dire economic conditions and increasing crime."

"Most community leaders believe that political parties are a necessary and important part of the Constitution."

Three reasons were cited most often:

- They give people a voice in the political process and provide for diversity of expression.

- They represent freedom of expression and association.

- And particularly in black townships, leaders were prone to say that political parties were instrumental in problem solving and delivery of services.

Some leaders (almost all African) saw political parties as a legitimate provider of jobs and as providing the goods for the broader community.

But no one questioned that the ANC would be the dominant political party for a long time to come – and few saw this as an undesirable thing, or as being in any way unfair or illegitimate. On the contrary, there is a prevailing if not overwhelming belief that ANC dominance is justifiable in a time of transition; that it provides for stability and minimizes the ravages of political faction-fighting, gives government officials the time to acquire the experience that will allow them to perform more effectively. While community leaders from parties other than those aligned with the ANC also conceded the inevitability of ANC dominance, they also expressed frustration that their voices are not heard, never mind needed:

"Big parties don't worry about small parties. They don't listen to them. They disregard and degrade them."

The October 1998
Focus Group Study

This study, carried out in five of the nine provinces, consisted of twenty-three focus groups representing a spread across gender, age, socio-economic status, level of urbanization, and previous participation in voting. Eight of the groups were either exclusively or predominantly first-time voters.

Two broad trends characterize the South African electorate at this stage.

"On the one hand, voters protest the insufficient level of change to their lives. On the other, they have settled into the business of elections and democratic representation. They often have highly critical assessments of government, but cherish the notions of elections and the electoral power afforded to them."

"Voters protest the fact that 'so little has changed in their lives.' Yet all participants in these groups, especially black South Africans, acknowledge the value of human rights, human dignity, and political power. These are the victories they hope to consolidate. Elections and voting are the means through which they envisage this consolidation will happen."

"On the material and social service front, not all participants have experienced significant change to their lives. Most have experienced some change, yet these changes often fall short of expectations. Most voters still have hope that things are to change for them as well."

(Does this mean that they think more has changed for other people than for them? See also the consistency here; both the HSRC poll and the Stellenbosch poll identify the hope of people for a better future, even though the circumstances of their lives would not appear to warrant such hope.)

The vision of 1994 of a better life for all remains fresh in the minds of these voters. The biggest stumbling block is the creation of jobs.

(This is the first focus group study that specifically identifies jobs as the issue.)
Urban voters are highly affected by the interaction between unemployment and crime; rural voters are concerned with the breakdown of previous relationships of authority and perceived lessened chances of "ever finding a job."

Unemployment and its effects on society color virtually all views of these focus group participants. It represents the ultimate litmus test of much of government's actions; it helps define the purpose of elections.
(How?)

There is evidence of subsiding euphoria and growing realism in the expectations of what elections can achieve. Yet elections remain for most of these voters a symbol of hope. The 1994 election symbolized liberation and victory. The associated voting power for the typical South African voter means that they continue to wield the power to continue changing a stubbornly changing system. There is an ongoing commitment to the ANC. The two overriding beliefs among these voters are that the ANC government "needs more time" and that "1999 has to give government a second chance."

Voters in the focus group study believe that competition among political parties mainly is a means of "ensuring better performance by the government." They are adamant, however, that democracy does not depend on them switching their votes in order to ensure stronger opposition parties. Democracy is seen as "the right to vote for the party of your choice."

In the opinion of the majority, votes for several of the current opposition parties might cause a return to the past. (See the HSRC 1996 survey where almost one-third of respondents did not believe that changing the party in government was a prerequisite for democratic governance.)

(The past means different things to blacks and whites. Whites, given their reactions to the TRC, their mean-spiritedness in insisting that since gross violations of human rights were committed by both sides this somehow "neutralizes" their culpability, their continual denial of any collective responsibility for the past, their rejection of the meaning of restorative justice, seem incapable of being able to grasp the sheer scale of the injury they inflicted on blacks. It's as if their imaginations cannot expand to accept what was done in their names. The naive belief of their leaders that the "new" generation represented by the New National Party can somehow distance itself from the sins of their fathers to the point where black voters will vote for them, without their having to earn that trust on their bended knees, speaks for itself and practically ensures that they will never wield real political power because they refuse to acknowledge the nature of their predicament and the fact that it is of their own making.)

"For this generation of black voters, the possibility of retrogressive change should they switch political parties continues to haunt them. Therefore, the motivation to vote comes because of their fear of any backsliding, of there being no wayward miscalculation that would result in them finding themselves entrapped in a situation analogous to the past. That too will motivate them not to boycott the election or abstain from voting. The liberation party will continue to receive their support, despite the modesty of the gains it has brought to their personal lives. Not to vote for the ANC is to invite regression."

The association between "race" and "opposition politics" is one of the factors that contribute to a high level of motivation to vote. Support for an opposition party, almost invariably in the minds of [black] voters, remains related to support for a "white political party" with a strong association in turn with the former governing party.

"Those voters who say they will not vote are mostly motivated by a sense of disappointment and moderate alienation. They were in a clear minority. For the most part, voters, despite not seeing 'full delivery' believe 'it is important to continue voting.' Even if they just vote to guarantee the right to criticize afterwards."

"The biggest obstacle to voter turnout appears to be voter registration. Even in October 1998, when the focus group study was carried out, many voters did not understand that if they did not register, they could not vote. Voters believe that the electoral process will be efficiently run, that balloting will be secret, that there will not be violence or intimidation, but they also believe that the optimal system was the one used in 1994 – no registration and the choice of voting location."

"The major need for voter education relates to first-time voters to stimulate the motivation of the voting act. More experienced, as well as first-time voters, have a need for reassurance voter education. They wish to be reminded of the steps in the voting process, especially if these are different than they were in 1994. They prefer visual rather than verbal presentations. They also prefer minimal word usage and clear photographic or drawing presentations."

"Voters have a high regard for the [Independent Electoral Council]. This comes from the spillover effect of the 'miracle' of 1994. IEC is assumed to be able to deliver another miracle."

In contrast to the findings of public opinion polls throughout 1998 [Markinor/IDASA/SABC, Markdata], which consistently found that a large proportion of the South African electorate remained politically uncommitted or uncertain whether they would actually vote in 1999, and concluded that voters were more likely to abstain from voting in 1999 in contrast to 1994, the October 1998 [study] found that underneath the surface of the "disappointed and disillusioned" South African voter was one "of sophisticated political judgment with a high level of commitment to electoral participation." Furthermore, these South African voters were determined to use the power to vote to control individual politicians and to ensure that their best interests are being served.

Regarding the Mood of the Electorate

"Things are both better and worse."

"There was widespread recognition that the government had made inroads and that many people had been beneficiaries. Problems remained. But the memories of an infinitely worse and very racial past predominated participants' thinking."

(Perhaps much of the research was carried out in October 1998 in the days immediately preceding the release of the Truth and Reconciliation Commission report. The media already had begun to publish extracts of the report, and its impending release may have jarred participants' memories.)

Voters know that they want more and deserve more. They are prepared to apply their muscle to try to get what they need. Voting and elections have become ingrained in their "political psyches."

(Yet in the CASE study on local elections people were confused as to why they had to vote again.)

When participants convert to discussions of specifics, their own communities and their political and human rights positions, few voices accumulate around the "no change" poll of the debate.

(This, too, represents a change from where people were at in August–September 1994: Then when respondents pointed to change, it always took place in someone else's backyard.)

Participants stress that they criticize because they expect better. Even the worst affected have reports of some, even if minimal, changes and expressions of continuing hope. Even those who insisted that "nothing had changed" entertained discussions about experiencing more freedom, receiving respect as human beings, having knowledge of some change happening to other people, and of least being listened to when they complain.

(Throughout all these focus groups, perhaps the most recurrent mantra is not that things are not going sufficiently right or that delivery is slow or even nonexistent but that they continue to have hope, even when they have little that points to why they should. But if you think about it for a moment, you will realize that they have to have hope, for without hope the future would merely loom as a formless litany of miseries, one piled on another, no end to the nightmare of living at subsubsistence level, with no promise of freedom on the horizon, no possible reward for sacrifice, no Mandela, no liberation; that it all had turned out to be a charade. Given that at the moment they have no one to turn to other than the ANC, there is a certain desperation to their need to keep hope. They have not yet developed to the point of having "alternatives," hence the necessity to keep the faith at all costs and the need for the rhetoric of revolution, for enemies, for Third Forces, for the ever-present saboteurs who dream of the old days of domination. In an ironic twist, they cannot fully free themselves until they free themselves of the ANC, that is, until they develop alternatives to the ANC to which they can turn if the ANC cannot fulfill their hopes, to alternatives that offer the fulfillment of hopes the ANC is unable to fulfill. Thus, if the masses' hopes are not met, the ANC will split, creating the alternatives that will allow themselves to express full freedom of choice. Today, they do not have that choice; nor will they have it in 1999.)

"White participants in the focus groups were divided in their views of the new South Africa. Most felt that despite severe changes to their lives, many positives had been added. Few would like to return to 'life pre-1994.' They note the 'turning of the tables' in which 'anything we complain about is construed as a racial issue.' Some grudgingly accept and find fault with the new order."

"Of all the participants in these groups, Coloured working-class participants felt most unempowered. There were few expressions of positive feedback over the last years and few expressions of hope for the future."

"Again, foremost in the minds of all participants is "the curse of lack of jobs.' It is the one issue that consistently threatens to overwhelm the sense of progress and achievement since 1994."

"Some have a sense that however bad the past, at least one had a chance of finding a job."

(In this sense, unemployment had superseded crime as the problem participants were most concerned with. In the Opinion '99 *survey carried out at about the same time as this focus group research, 73 per cent of respondents rated unemployment as the most serious problem in the country; 64 per cent rated crime as the most serious problem. Since another 18 per cent rated "managing the economy" as their most serious concern, in overall terms, some 91 per cent of respondents were concerned about the economy in on e way or another.)*

(See earlier remarks on the economy. South Africa was going through its worst economic crisis in years, being buffeted on all sides by the dominolike impact of the Asian financial crisis. The rand depreciated on a daily basis; workers were being retrenched; markets disappearing; and the free flow of capital was wreaking havoc in the marketplace. Globalization is here to stay, Thabo Mbeki informed the citizenry. The crisis South Africa faces was not of its own making; rather it was a case of South Africa's being caught in the fallout following the collapse of the Asian markets. "The stark reality," Mbeki told the NAM summit in Durban in August 1998,"is that the power to influence markets lies exclusively in the hands of those who dominate those markets, which we, even collectively, do not.")[41]

National government receives the most credit, yet is heavily criticized. Many of the criticisms about national government centred on the lack of visibility of MPs. Positive perceptions are most often linked to the persona of Nelson Mandela, that is, Mandela equals the government. A distinction is made between Parliament and the government.

Assessment of provincial government is most severe. These governments are seen in many cases "as the most corrupt of them all," as not really having anything meaningful to do, or at best invisible to the ordinary citizen.

(These assessments on the part of the public help to make the case for the ANC's revamping of its processes for selecting the premier of a parliament. If the provincial governments fail so miserably to make the grade, the premier must to a large extent bear a considerable part of the blame.)

Group participants have divergent experiences of local government. In some cases local councillors are seen as people who really make a differ-ence, in the majority of cases, participants see councillors as mostly absent, absorbed in a new life of luxury, given to nepotism. Local government is often described as nonexistent. Others stress incapacity, alienation, the misuse of funds, and corruption. Among the most typical responses: 'The problem with local councillors is that they do their work on a part-time basis'; 'They cater to their own needs'; 'They are doing nothing for us'.

"More important, irrespective of the sphere of government, voters often feel neglected and forgotten. They want to learn more about what government has done in the post-1994 era. They want to see their elected representatives and ascertain what they have been doing. The focus study group analysts conclude that the 'rhetoric of forgotten promises' is being used to taunt the politicians into dialogue with local communities, and in so doing 'force' their representatives into doing a better job."

(These findings indicate that there is a lot of anger among blacks with the ANC. After four years they have little idea of what functions different levels of government perform, what relationships different branches have with one another, which branch is responsible for what service. Their comments with regard to provincial government are of special concern and add more justification to the ANC's decision to have premiers appointed by the NWC. But what leverage do blacks have? If the comments cited in the focus group surveys are accurate, it is rather a sad commentary on the degree to which MPs keep in touch with their "constituents" and the fault lines of the party proportional representation system. Again, if people want choices, the alliance will have to split.)

Many severe criticisms of the new order were made. Crime, poverty, no respect for human life, fraud and corruption were among the more recurrent themes.

Corruption, fraud, and disintegration of public service were issues that were much more likely to receive mention from whites and Indians. Nepotism and partial caring for needs was the African angle on the same problem.

White voices often were the harshest in the judgments of public service in the country. "Inability," "inefficiency," and "incompetence" were most often the words used in their description of post-1994 South Africa.

(Again we are faced with the inability of whites to understand the world which they had occupied for forty years and the world they were entering. Under the old order, there were fourteen departments of everything. Only one set of those departments was allocated solely to white service needs. The amounts spent on these departments were six to nine times higher than expenditures for service delivery to other population groups. Hence whites lived in an exclusive and privileged world where the servicing of their needs was the main priority of government. Now they enter a post-apartheid world. All these departments, including those of the TVBC

states and the homelands, had to be amalgamated into one public service with one department servicing everyone in a particular service area. Besides the huge logistical problems this task involved, there was also the equally formidable task of a redistribution of resources, the application of the principle of equity, and the rationalization of the hundreds of bureaucratic entities that had proliferated over the years with no accountability or control mechanisms in place to weed out the unnecessary, the duplications, and the patronage. Whites steadfastly refuse to come to grips with the way their own systems of governance worked in the past and are therefore incapable of understanding how things work now. Their context for understanding is all skewed.)

National, provincial, and local government are not always clearly distinguished from each other.

Participants have clear but often very abstract notions of what national government does; they are most clear about local government, and most fuzzy about provincial government.

"They criticize, but their criticisms are tinged with an understanding that the demands on government are enormous, that government needs more time, and that inexperience in office often contributes to mistakes being made."

"Despite their disappointments that democracy did not deliver more faster, the voters continue in their dreams for a 'better life.' They commonly agree that a second chance should be given to the existing government to accomplish the better life that they are still dreaming about. There is hardly any perception that government is not trying. The catch phrase is that government should be trying even harder."

"A number of voices emphasized that the ANC as government has not had all the power it needs to implement required change. Voters look forward to the time when the ANC will become the majority party in the real sense, because then there will no longer be delivery problems."

(What do they mean when they say they want the ANC to have a "majority in the real sense"? Do they mean that the ANC needs more than two-thirds of the vote? Will this make them receptive to the ANC's call for that kind of mandate? What leads them to believe that with a larger mandate – the ANC already has a majority of 63 per cent – "there will no longer be delivery problems."? Surely, voters are setting themselves up for further disappointment if they believe so, and more disillusionment if the ANC lead them to believe so.)

In South Africa, as elsewhere, the masses themselves are the problem.

{When disappointment turns to disillusionment, populist solutions become an antidote for despair. Thus, in August 1998, the ANC National Executive Council decided to separate the posts of provincial leader from that of provincial premier. Whereas in the 1994 elections the two positions were synonymous, the head of the party's ticket in a province automatically assuming the unions in provinces in which the ANC held a majority, the 1998 ruling delinked the two.

Henceforth, the NEC would appoint premiers who might or might not be head of the party's ticket in the province or might not even be a member of the ticket itself. In explaining its actions, the ANC said it had a responsibility to "ensure unity within its ranks," and "appoint people on the basis of leadership qualities." [42] *In three provinces – Free State, Gauteng, and Northern Province – the ANC had run into problems when branches refused to go along with the national leadership's preferred candidates for one or the other posts.*

Not unexpectedly, the ANC's decision elicited the usual chorus of condemnation from the opposition parties, with the usual accusations of "democratic centralism" emanating from the usual sources." [43] *Anyone with faith in the democratic system will be worried by the plan," the Mercury editorialized, "as it appears indicative of the ruling ANC to centralize power wherever possible."* [44] *It allowed, however, that "looking at the move in the most objective way possible, it could be said that the decision will allow the party's national executive committee to prevent obviously unsuitable people being chosen for the premierships, no matter how 'popular' they might be." Nevertheless, it concluded that the ANC executive was "obviously keen to put its own men and women into the powerful premier positions and may be willing to meddle with the democratic process to achieve that," and that "the members of the provincial legislatures represent the will of the electorate and should be left to democratically elect the premiers."*

However, a far different view was taken by one much respected political commentator:

> The ANC [he argued] will be doing the correct and logical thing when it hand picks premiers for the provinces it wins in next year's elections.
>
> This should be extended to other key positions in the provinces and town councils to stymie the political careerists who use populism to sway restless and gullible masses.
>
> What also gives credence to the decision that premiers be appointed is the elections mayhem in the provinces. The results of the elections in the Free State may be a victory for democracy, but they are a disaster for the country. [45]
>
> In the run-up to the national and local elections, black political parties did not have the necessary brain-power, or just suitable bodies in abundance. All comers with names in the black community were accepted, even white political organizations welcomed any black face and appointed them to national, provincial, and local positions. Now we are paying the price.

How can we explain a situation in which a mayor stabs another person to death over a woman? Then we have a mayor who is caught in a diamond trap. We have a MEC for Health whose only qualification is that he was a former male nurse.

The democratic process takes its course when we elect MPs, members of provincial legislatures, and town councillors. From then on the party takes over. It must give us officials with the appropriate skills and motivation if the ruling party is to give us a future we can be proud of.[46]

The issues raised here are fundamental: Do you tamper with "democracy" in order to save democracy? Is freedom unfettered, bound only by the provisions of the Constitution, or must degrees of freedom be calculated with capacity for responsibility and accountability. If accountability is alien to the masses, indeed, if they have been constantly extolled to be neither accountable nor responsible in the name of attaining freedom, how is one to expect an instant metamorphosis where accountability and responsibility become the barometers of freedom itself?

Furthermore, in what can best be regarded as a well-meaning attempt to ensure the quality of provincial premiers, the ANC is perhaps creating a situation that will exacerbate provincial tensions by creating two poles of power in provinces it controls in which the provincial leadership will continually snipe at the legislative leadership in the pursuit of "personal agendas underscored by greed and the lust for power" – the very "sins" the ANC decision was designed to excoriate in the first place. Nor can one simply eliminate "the lust for power" by executive decree. One of the by-products of any system of governance, whether totalitarianism or democratic, is this so-called lust for power, a generic predisposition of the human condition, one that has not proven particularly amenable to attempts to stamp it out over the course of human history in the name of utopias that in the end destroy what they had intended to defend.)

Indeed, the people's concepts of power, the principles that underpin it, and the conditions under which it is exercised were the subject of a study conducted by the Helen Suzman Foundation.[47]

The Two-Thirds-Majority Issue
Using Markdata's Omnibus Survey carried out on June 1–19, 1998, the Suzman Foundation probed attitudes on a possible ANC two-thirds majority in the 1999 elections, a target set by the ANC's secretary-general, Kgalema Monlanthe, who spoke of using the unilateral power of constitutional amendment, which such a majority would bestow, to bring such independent bodies as the Reserve Bank, the auditor-general, the provincial attorneys general, and the judiciary under tighter political control.

(When Monlanthe's ambitions for the party provoked a political backlash, both President Mandela and Deputy President Mbeki distanced themselves from his remarks, pledging that the ANC did not want to alter the Constitution in any

fundamental way. Neither, however, discounted the ANC's wish to make some "technical" amendments to the Constitution, and neither disavowed the notion of a two-thirds majority. The ANC now speaks in terms of an "overwhelming majority" as if it did not already enjoy one.

But within months, with the economy being battered by the backlash of the Asian crisis and amid signs that support for the ANC was slipping in some provinces, Mandela himself renewed the call on his people to give the ANC the two-thirds majority it now avidly sought. "We have decided we want a two-thirds majority in this country," he declared. "If we get another 62 per cent, we will have failed. We will be fighting this election in a different context to 1994." [48] *This was the same Mandela who admitted he was relieved that the ANC did not receive a two-thirds majority in 1994, that he had fretted about one party having the power to write a constitution to its own liking. Obviously, having the power to rewrite parts of the Constitution not to its liking didn't fall under the same rubric.*

One other way the ANC might achieve a working two-thirds majority would be to form some kind of post-election coalition with the IFP and the PAC. However, when respondents were asked whether it would be good or bad for the ANC to obtain such a majority, only 49 per cent of voters thought it would be good and 45 per cent were opposed, compared with the almost 63 per cent of the vote that the party won in the 1994 elections. Huge majorities of whites, Coloureds, and Indians were opposed, while 28 per cent of Africans were also opposed. Among ANC voters, 12 per cent, representing some 1.5 million voters, expressed reservations about the ANC's having a majority of this size. Support for the idea of a two-thirds majority came primarily from the youngest, the least educated, the unemployed, and urban squatters, indicating a divide between the haves and the have-nots that is increasingly the fulcrum of South African politics.

In the opposition-ruled provinces of KwaZulu-Natal and the Western Cape, support for an ANC two-thirds majority collapsed to just 15 per cent and 25 per cent, respectively, and in the ANC-controlled Northern Cape, support fell to 26 per cent, a result the survey analysts interpreted as a sign that the province was about to defect from the ANC.

Another question pointed out that a two-thirds-majority vote for the ANC would give it unilateral power to change the Constitution. The number of voters who believed this would be bad jumped to 60 per cent, and the number believing it to be good dropped to 29 per cent. Even African voters were sceptical, 53 per cent opposing and 37 per cent continuing to support a two-thirds majority for the ANC. Nor were ANC voters overenthusiastic about the idea – 51 per cent favored such an outcome, but a solid 39 per cent did not. Support for a two-thirds majority collapsed in the provinces that had been the staunchest supporters of the ANC in 1994. In the Northern Province, where the ANC won 93 per cent of the vote in 1994, support for a nationwide two-thirds majority dropped to 42 per cent when the constitutional implications were pointed out, and in the Eastern Cape, where the ANC had amassed 84 per cent of the vote in 1994, it fell to 30 per cent. Among those who did not want the ANC to have a two-thirds majority, 27 per cent said "a strong opposition is vital" and a further 11 per cent cited their fears of a one-party state. Ironically, Africans – 31 per cent – were most likely to state their belief in the need for a strong opposition, contrary to the stereotypical conceptions of Africans' supposed penchant for one-party states. Moreover, while only 39 per cent of ANC voters were opposed to the idea of the party having the unilateral power to change the Constitution, 51 per cent expressed nervousness about the possible results of such an outcome.

In short, the foundation's analysts concluded that at least half of ANC voters distrusted their own party's intentions if the party was given too much power.

When the question was put in the form of respondents believing that the ANC might get a two-thirds majority, only 60 per cent of African voters said they would be more likely to vote for the ANC, in contrast to the 85 per cent who actually did in 1994, and the racial minorities, previously ANC voters, would desert it in huge numbers.

A final question on the matter of black unity revealed an almost even divide. While 48 per cent were in favor of black unity, 45 per cent were opposed. Most opposed were Coloureds, Asians, and whites, but 63 per cent of Africans liked the idea. With regard to party breakdown, 24 per cent of ANC voters rejected the idea as did 44 per cent of IFP voters, 38 per cent supporting the idea; the UDM split 50 per cent to 49 per cent in favor, and PAC voters were most enthusiastic about the idea, 54 per cent being for it and 32 per cent against.

But if pollsters and pundits were reading all kinds of dark portents into the study's findings, the ANC was close to dismissive. What party, it argued, would prepare for an election not wanting to maximize its vote? And who ever heard of a party begging its supporters to vote for the opposition so that Parliament would enjoy the dubious benefits of a strong opposition, especially when the opposition parties were more concerned with protecting the privileges their constituencies had accumulated in the past on the backs of the disenfranchised rather than with promoting equality and equity for the newly enfranchised? Was it to ask its supporters to stay at home on election day, thus re-disenfranchising themselves, so that their former oppressors could further muddy the waters and employ endless delaying tactics in order to forestall the economic and social changes that were germane to genuine transformation?)

The position of the elites, for the most part predominantly if not exclusively white, is summed up in a 1998 editorial in *Leadership* entitled, "The Two-Thirds Majority: Lead Us Not Into Temptation".[53] The editorial stated that:

> President Mandela declares that the party has no intention of changing the Constitution but that will not be his decision; he will have retired to elder statesmanship. Other ministers, anxious not to frighten the horses, have lamely reiterated his position. Still others in the party, from its secretary-general downward, have made their intention quite plain: to use the two-

thirds majority to change the Constitution. Who is correct, the president or the party? We think the party.

Moreover, if the ANC is thwarted in its own name, then its secret weapon is the Inkatha Freedom Party. Sipho Mzimela is already manoeuvering to give the ANC its wish by other means, by pressing for a race coalition whose effect could be to give the ruling party its constitutional majority through the absorption of a chunk of its opposition. Presumably the IFP and its supporters have taken note.

The Africanist, indeed racist, pitch of Mzimela's call illuminates the hull of the argument that the ANC will put to the electorate. It will argue that aspects of the Constitution, and the intransigence of those privileged under apartheid, have undercut the government's efforts to transform institutions and extend socio-economic rights, thus shielding the privileged and withholding fulfillment of the party's 1994 election promises. It will argue that only a two-thirds majority can unlock the social and economic advancement it could not deliver these past four years. This is tantamount to a witgevaar platform – "Give us this mandate to break white power for good and all" – its object: capturing the Constitution for the party.

This is the electorate's prerogative to give the government a blank check; people get the governments they deserve. But the people should be aware that a government in control of the Constitution which empowers it may assume dimensions in which abuse of its original mandate is almost inevitable. The last South African (minority) electorate to hand its government a blank check ended up being led into civil war. Along the way, that government arrogated to itself draconian powers which it used to run the country for its own account, suppress dissent, and murder its opponents. South Africa is not alone in this history. Ruling parties whose parliamentary majorities place them beyond the restraints of constitutional government condemn their countries to the multiple tyrannies of mediocrity, institutional sclerosis, nonaccountability, corruption, and impoverishment. The governments of Zimbabwe, Kenya, and Nigeria are good examples of the same phenomenon.

While the Mandela government deserves some sympathy for its inability to overcome the legacy of apartheid, a two-thirds majority for the Mbeki government will not be the silver bullet whicht dispatches that legacy, as the ANC knows well enough. Its ability to fiddle with the Constitution after 1999 will only make it easier to pass unsound laws. Imagine, in that case, the reaction of capital here and abroad to the diminution of property rights or the kneecapping of the judiciary. The ANC should therefore resist at all cost empty electoral rhetoric which, were its object to come to pass, would be shown up for just that – well within the term of the next government and at considerable cost to the party's credibility and the country's stability. In the meantime, the ANC will have pulled the Constitution down into the political arena it is meant to regulate and corrupted the ideal for which South Africans fought so hard and paid so heavily.

The Constitution was founded on the principle of compromise. We agree that some compromise is needed, but to subject the Constitution to Parliament would be to subvert that founding principle, con the electorate, undercut confidence, and introduce a coercive, corrosive, and deadening majoritarianism that would achieve the opposite of what was intended. The ANC has enough power to govern well without doing that. Its leaders and its allies should think carefully before leading us into this temptation.

Regarding Life in the Community

"When people talk about their communities, 'their dreams and patience sometimes begin to wear thin.' Almost all groups relate experiences of reconstruction and change since 1994, although often accompanied by tales of decay and disintegration. 'These positive experiences sometimes are also fragmentary and dwarfed by greater need.' Some participants struggled to come up with much that they liked or appreciated in their communities."

" While participants 'concede' [word and quotation marks chosen by the FGS analysts] that the changes for the better that have happened are fine, they also make it clear that they need and expect much more."

"Especially galling is their perception that now that there are some services available, they do not have the jobs to pay for them. In many communities there is still an absence of running water, electricity, and a small number of toilets have to serve a whole informal settlement. Physical hardship is amplified by unemployment; the absence of job prospects results in increases in crime and social decay. The elder people had little hope for their children or for the youth in their communities. The young wanted to taste the 'good life' or had trouble finding 'good' role models they could identify with."

(All has not utterly changed; indeed, at the community level, there appears to be little positive change that residents can identify with. Life goes on, untouched by the great issues being debated in Cape Town and the endless flow of policy instruments emanating from Pretoria.

Church leaders call for a national conference to address what they refer to as the despair permeating many segments of South African society.[49] They speak of the collapse of the moral fabric.[50] Police Commissioner George Fivaz attributes the disregard for the law and the prevalence of rampant crime to "the absence of norms and values."[51] Deputy President Thabo Mbeki believes there should be some kind of "moral summit."[52] "Something has gone terribly wrong," says Judge Lucy Mailula. "It seems there has been a collapse of moral fibre. Maybe the new freedom is being interpreted in the wrong way."[53]

All were struggling to put their fingers on the same thing: anomie.

Addressing the Anti-Corruption Summit Conference on 10 November 1998, Mbeki offered one explanation of South Africa's moral predicament:

> In anomie [he said] we see the erosion of authority structures and the collapse of the moral order, thus breeding social upheaval, while in alienation we experience powerlessness and futility in the midst of an impinging national framework of values and norms.
>
> The collapse of the old order and ushering in of the new one necessitates a reorientation of a nation's world view. Those who do not immediately benefit from the transition will see its futility for themselves and seek to question its legitimacy by resisting its fringe or "soft" assumptions such as morals, norms, and values.
>
> In this situation, patterns of behavior would gradually take root, leading inevitably to a corrosion of a good national character and a moral identity crisis.
>
> In such an environment public officials will find themselves quite vulnerable, especially when they observe that perpetrators of the old order continue to enjoy the benefits of the new, long after the latter came into being.)

Elections

"Election 1994 continues to mean liberation, freedom, and dignity to the bulk of South African voters. Even if the post-1994 epoch is displaying cavities, this experience of democracy far outshines the preceding oppressive system."

"The participants were people who revere in their experience of elections and their power as individual voters. But they were burdened by severe unemployment, and this experience to threaten life in the new democracy."

"It is with regard to the immediate economic situation (with implications for worsening crime) that participants sometimes retract into 'life was better before'."

When participants are asked what images spring into their minds when they hear the word *elections*, a "rich and overwhelmingly positive tapestry" sprung to mind. Change, democracy, freedom, new government, a government for all people, a way of bettering our lives, to forgive and forget, to unite were some of the images. But above all, one word, *expectations*, stood out.

Among black voters, the 1994 elections remain intertwined with the end of white oppression. The rationality of voters' current assessments of elections extends into the recognition that this victory still needs to be consolidated and that the party of the majority's trust, the ANC, needs to be supported to continue the pursuit of "the better life." Hence a considerable part of electoral sentiment is motivated by considerations of "stopping whites from returning to power." The 1999 election, they argue, will bring them one step closer to the better life. In a general kind of way, hope and elections have become equated with finding employment.

"Despite their disappointments, and without 1999 election promises from political parties, the human nature of these voters compel them already to link the 1999 elections to hope for change in their lives. It is the only instrument at their disposal, the only way in which they can reach out to government structures and resources."

(This, in a kernel, is it. Entering the June 1999 elections, blacks have no option but to hope that somehow the ANC can get its act together after the next election. Despite all their disappointments, they are willing to give the ANC the benefit of the doubt. After all, what alternatives do they have? The ANC is not about to split. The opposition parties are seen as ineffectual, leftovers of the past, proponents of white privilege, obstacles to change, part of the problem insofar as they obstruct transformation, whites, namely, irrevocably associated with the past who would, if they had their way, reintroduce many of the "trimmings" of the past. Hence the tenor of Mandela's speech in Mafikeng, of Mbeki's "Two Nations" address, of refuge in the African Renaissance. Without hope there is only despair.)

Two major considerations account for the South African voter's dedication to the act of voting. There is a strong sense of the individual voter's power of efficacy, of the power of the individual voters to make an impact or to be listened to. Second, the typical voter is driven by the need to see the job of political and social liberation completed.

("Need" here should be interpreted in the broader sense – it almost amounts to a compelling necessity. Otherwise the struggle for liberation will have been one big lie.

Thus, the "typical" voter who emerges from this argues that the ANC, flaws and all, needs continuous support in order to make the dream of a better life become fulfilled. The voter's motivation is both technical and emotive. The ANC remains linked with liberation and the associated rights and dignities. The ANC is also seen as the party closest to the interests of the average voter. On a technical level, the typical voter sees that the ANC is trying, has made a head start in the process of change, and insufficient as that progress might be, there is no sense in abstaining or considering a change in party – besides, to whom does one change? There is virtually no passive sense of voting "because of duty to vote.")

- More time is needed.

- Four versus forty years: The ANC can't be expected to dismantle in four years what it took the NP forty years to put in place.

- Agreement that corruption has taken a toll.

- 1999 as a 'second chance election' for the ANC. Given the two realities of disappointment with the ANC's performance and the belief that opposition parties do not really have the average black voter's interests in mind, abstention is to be avoided. Voters are determined to hold the ANC government to the promises they perceived it to have made in 1994, given that they do not see another credible contender for power.

Disappointments with politicians and their often low ability to deliver with greater speed only minimally detract from voters' belief in voting.

Embedded in the belief in elections as a tool for change is both the belief in pressurizing the governing party to make true on "promises" and the recognition that elections are the tool to change government if so desired.

Multiparty Democracy

"Voters welcome the participation of opposition parties, especially if they seem to pose a threat to the ANC and are therefore likely to make the ANC try harder. They want to make the ANC work for their votes. They do not want their loyalty taken for granted. But because the ANC now has experience in government, voters see the improved prospect of an ANC government making a difference in their lives. Current opposition parties are not trusted. Voters do not buy the argument that the evolution of multiparty depends on voting for the opposition – opposition parties should have every right to exist and be free to make their cases to the electorate, but democracy means being free to be able to vote for whom you want to."

"Besides, attitudes to opposition parties are influenced by where they stood in relation to apartheid. Forces of the former order need to be stopped from returning to power."

Opinion '99

Opinion '99, a consortium of news-gathering and polling services – the SABC, Markinor, and IDASA – began in September 1998 to carry out a series of public opinion surveys intended to "track" the course of public opinion as South Africa began to prepare itself for its second general election, now scheduled to take place on 2 June 1999. The election promises, like the first election, to be a momentous occasion, marking the departure of President Nelson Mandela from politics, the advent of his chosen successor, Deputy President Thabo Mbeki, to the helm of the state, the beginning of the post-Mandela era in politics, and a referendum on the ANC's performance in government. That the ANC will win is taken for granted. It will be judged not by the fact that it has won, but by the margin of its victory.

Party Support and Voting intention

In the introduction to the first *Opinion '99* poll, based on interviews conducted in September 1998, the poll found:

> Since 1994, political analysts have expressed concerns about the prospects of an electorate tightly locked into various political parties, leaving little room for persuasion, voter fluidity and electoral change. Moreover, since one party, the ANC, had the lion's share of that support, analysts have openly wondered about the prospects of South Africa developing into a "dominant party" system offering little prospect of real multi-party competition.

The results from the first *Opinion '99* survey suggest that these concerns about the political system might need to be framed in a new light.

- "Voter identification" with political parties is the lowest since 1994. More than one-half the electorate does not feel "close" to any political party.
- While voter identification with the ANC stands at slightly over one-third of the electorate, less than one in ten identifies with any opposition party.
- These trends in voter identification with political parties are making an impact on people's likely voting behavior. Potential support for the ANC is also at the lowest level since the new South Africa came into being. Yet with the exception of the Democratic Party, there have been no real gains among any of the opposition parties. Rather, one in five voters do not know whom they will vote for.
- The actual result of the election will depend a great deal on the level of turnout on Election Day. With a "low" turnout election, the prospects of an ANC two-thirds majority are real. The prospects of the opposition parties, however, improve with increasing levels of turnout.

(In fact, what the survey is saying is that even though electoral support for the ANC may be at an all-time low, other parties are losing support at an even more rapid rate. As a result, the ANC could end up with at least a two-thirds majority in the new assembly.)

A few data illustrate the extent of the opposition parties' precarious standing. The following table shows a selected pattern of voting intentions:

Table 2

	September– October 1994 %	November 1995 %	July 1998 %	September 1998 %
ANC	61	64	57	51
NP	16	14	9	10
DP	1	2	6	7
IFP	5	3	5	4
PAC	2	2	2	2
UDM	2	3	1	1
ACDP	1	1	1	1
AZAPO	1	1	1	1
CP	1	1	1	1
Others	I	I	I	I
Don't know/ Undisclosed	12	8	14	21

As regards turnout and voting, the ANC would receive 64 per cent of the vote in the event of a low turnout (55 per cent of eligible voters); 60 per cent in the event of a moderate turnout (75 per cent of eligible voters); and 56 per cent in the event of a high turnout. Only in the last case does it appear that an opposition party would break into double digits – the National Party registers at 10 per cent.

As regards the ANC's drop from 57 per cent to 51 per cent in the three months from July to September 1998, one has only to recall that during this period the economy was almost in a free fall, and analysts were forecasting more trouble ahead rather than bridges over troubled waters.

In large measure, this survey confirms the findings of the focus group research we have reviewed. One sees this more clearly by examining the attitudes of the electorate toward opposition parties.

Opposition Parties

Opinion'99 found that opposition parties have a largely poor, and to a lesser extent unknown, image among the electorate:

- Few people saw any of the opposition parties as ready to govern the country. While two-thirds of the electorate felt that the African National Congress would do a good job running the national government, the next closest parties to were the National Party (28 per cent) and the Democratic Party (21 per cent).

- Indeed, significant proportions thought opposition parties would do a poor job running the government – 61 per cent in the case of the Inkatha Freedom Party, 55 per cent in the case of the NP, 45 per cent in the case of the Freedom Front (FF), 42 per cent in the case of the Pan Africanist Congress (PAC), 34 per cent in the case of the DP, and 30 per cent in the case of the United Democratic Movement (UDM).
- Low proportions of eligible voters think that, in general, the opposition parties have done a good job.
- Most of the specific actions undertaken by opposition parties over the past few years have failed to improve their image.
- Most people saw the opposition parties as exclusive, representative of only one specific group.
- As a consequence, opposition parties are not seen as believable, or trustworthy.
- Finally, large portions of the electorate were unfamiliar with many of the actions of the opposition over the past few years and unable to offer opinions about many of the attributes of the opposition, most specifically the Democratic Party, Pan Africanist Congress, Freedom Front, and United Democratic Movement.

Thus, even if the results demonstrate that people are increasingly critical of government and ANC performance, they do not perceive that there is any credible or legitimate alternative. This helps explain why the opposition fails to pick up substantial support when the ANC loses ground, resulting rather in growing numbers of "undecided" voters (now at 21 per cent).

From one perspective, these findings constitute a fairly damning indictment of the opposition parties and their strategies and performance over the past four years.

Opposition parties would probably argue that these perceptions (either negative or unknown) are to be expected, given the nature and amount of exposure they receive from the print and broadcast media.

(Given the ANC's attitude towards the media as a "tool" of the old order, this perspective on the part of the opposition parties would probably be met with cynical mirth by the ANC!)

Indeed, significant proportions think opposition parties would do a poor job governing the country: IFP, 61 per cent; NP, 55 per cent; FF, 45 per cent; PAC, 42 per cent; DP, 34 per cent; and UDM, 30 per cent.

Thus, while the NP and IFP both have relatively definite and negative images among the entire electorate, the UDM, DP, FF, and PAC at least have the potential for improved images among the large propositions of voters who do not yet have a firm image of the parties. The UDM, for instance, did not have the opportunity to be judged on its performance in Parliament.

The major reason the voters do not view the opposition as able to govern the country is because:

- They do not like what these parties have been doing;

- They do not see them as inclusive and representative parties;
- They do not feel they are believable or trustworthy.

Another major reason is that significant proportions of the public do not feel that they know enough about many opposition parties to form an opinion. Few people feel that the opposition parties have been doing good jobs as political parties. Only the ANC receives a strong favorable rating (69 per cent).

Majorities or large pluralities felt that many opposition parties had actually been doing a poor job in carrying out their functions: NP (58 per cent), FF (40 per cent), and PAC (40 per cent).

The ANC actions *Opinion '99* asked about resulted in improved images among the broader electorate. A significant proportion of people could not give answers on the ANC's stance on GEAR, and on how it handled criticism of GEAR. In contrast, all the NP actions *Opinion '99* asked about had a net negative impact on broader perceptions of the party. About one-fifth could not offer any opinion on NP activities.

(Therefore, when President Mandela lashed out at the opposition parties at the ANC's 50th Congress at Mafikeng in December 1997, he was playing into the hearts and minds of blacks all over South Africa, finding resonance with their beliefs, often non-expressed but nevertheless deeply held in the hidden recesses of their minds.)

Trust in Electoral Institutions
Elections must not only be free and fair, they must also be seen to be free and fair by an overwhelming majority of the electorate. Without such perceptions on a widespread scale, the legitimacy of the election, and thus the government produced by such an election, might be called into question.

To the extent that South Africa can achieve this, its electoral system will produce governments with widespread legitimacy, and it will have taken a major step towards consolidating democracy.

According to the *Opinion '99* survey:
- The widespread legitimacy of this election cannot be taken for granted and needs to be fostered.
- More than just one-half the electorate believe they can trust the IEC, and slightly less than half say they will be able to trust their local presiding voting officials. Over two-thirds say the 1994 election was conducted unfairly.
- Significant minorities distrust the IEC (one-quarter) and their local officials (one-third). More than one in ten feel that the 1994 elections were conducted unfairly.
- Levels of distrust in electoral institutions were especially high among specific groups. In terms of race, white and Indian voters have more negative views. Geographically, respondents in KwaZulu-Natal have quite negative

attitudes (Western Cape, Mpumalanga, and Gauteng also constitute potential problem areas). In terms of party support, Freedom Front and Democratic Party supporters have very negative views of the country's voting institutions.

Overall, 52 per cent say they will be able to trust the IEC to do what is right when managing the election process just about always or most of the time; 46 per cent believe they will be able to trust their local presiding voting officials to do what is right when administering the process. When asked about their perceptions of the 1994 elections, a majority (68 per cent) believed that the 1994 elections had been conducted fairly.

However, just over a quarter (27 per cent) say that they can trust the IEC only some of the time (21 per cent) or never (6 per cent). Local voting officials received a lower measure of trust with 34 per cent of respondents indicating that they cannot trust them, 14 per cent feel that the 1994 elections were not concluded fairly.

Voter Participation

A significant proportion of people (20 per cent) did not possess the correct documents necessary to vote.

Four in ten voters did not know they had to register and did not accept the reason given for registering. However, most people (80 per cent) seemed ready to register.

The desire to vote in the 1999 election appeared to be very high and did not appear to have suffered as much of a drop-off as has been experienced in a post-liberation phase.

(Again, this corroborates the findings of the focus group surveys – there is no unwillingness to vote. Ironically, we seem to be adopting Western standards of how people should behave. Since our experience in the West, namely, the barometric judges of what is democratic or not is that voter turnout falls as democracy consolidates itself – although there are no studies or we are carefully concealing them – as to the size of the turnouts in the early days of the franchise in the West [go back to elections in the UK] and since we systemically disenfranchised women. Even into the middle part of the century, we continually find ourselves applying standards of order to behavior that we have accepted for ourselves only after decades of debate into standards that must be immediately accepted by other people.)

The requirement that all voters have bar-coded identity documents in order to register to vote in the 1999 election has certainly been controversial. The debate has centred around the Department of Home Affairs' capacity to deliver these documents to all those who do not as of yet have them and to avoid disenfranchising any willing voters. A large part of the arguments revolve around estimates of how many people still do not have the right documents. On one side, Home Affairs has estimated that approximately 2.5 million voters needed to get these documents and was confident of providing them by the required date.

On the other side, the IEC, based on a survey undertaken by the HSRC, estimated that between 5.3 and 5.9 million documents would have to be provided, a number far too large to be processed in the given amount of time.

Our first *Opinion '99* survey examined this question by asking people which sorts of identity documents they possessed, and by attempting to verify this information wherever possible. Fieldwork was conducted in September and as of that date 78 per cent of the overall sample said they had the necessary bar-coded identity documents (we were able to visually verify 97 per cent of these, or 76 per cent of the entire electorate). This is the same as the HSRC finding of 76 per cent with the correct documents.

If one takes the number of those who say they have the bar-coded document as the operative figure, this means that 22 per cent did not, as of the fieldwork dates, have the correct documents. Even using the most recent revised estimates of the 1996 Census provided by the Statistics SA, which placed the over-eighteen population slightly lower, 24,800,000 eligible voters, the number of undocumented voters would still lie between 5,208,000 and 5,704,000.

There are some important partisan implications. Higher proportions of likely ANC voters (82 per cent) and IFP voters (84 per cent) have the correct documents than PAC (73 per cent), UDM (72 per cent), NP (71 per cent), or DP voters (65 per cent); 76 per cent of undecided voters have the correct documents.

Regardless of who actually possesses the actual documents, another relevant question concerns the extent to which people will actually bother to register. Half the sample says they are "very likely" to register (49 per cent) and another 29 per cent are likely. This leaves a small but significant minority (13 per cent) who say they are unlikely to register (another 8 per cent do not know).

Large differences can be seen between racial groups, with much larger numbers of whites (86 per cent) and blacks (78 per cent) likely to register than coloured (70 per cent) or Indian (65 per cent) respondents. While likely DP voters were less likely to possess the correct documents, they are most likely to register (94 per cent); 93 per cent of likely PAC voters say it is they expect to register, as well as 89 per cent ANC, 86 per cent UDM, and 86 per cent FF voters. The proportions are somewhat lower for NP voters (82 per cent) and much lower for IFP voters (73 per cent), reflecting the problems reported above in KwaZulu-Natal. Likely registration drops even further among the growing number of undecided voters (41 per cent), reflecting the importance of a partisan role in mobilizing people into the political process.

A major problem confronting the registration effort is that many eligible voters simply do not seem to realize that they will not be able to vote if they do not register. Overall, just one-quarter of all voters (23 per cent) believe that everyone will be able to vote regardless of whether they have registered or not. Another 19 per cent are unsure. Only 58 per cent were able to choose the correct answer: that people will have to be registered in order to vote.

By way of comparison, voter awareness of the necessity of registration is far lower than it was before the 1995 local government elections, when 85 per cent knew they had to register to vote.

Economic Evaluations

Perceptions about the overall direction of the country, the economy, and government performance in managing the economy are the key factors that voters take into account when reasoning which party best represents their interests and the interests of the country. These factors may become increasingly relevant for the government as it enters into an election campaign, especially in view of the battering of the currency and the rise in interest rates over the past six months, as well as the continuing high levels of unemployment.

Overall, the *Opinion '99* survey found the following:

- The range of indicators demonstrates a definite loss of economic optimism amongst the South African public.
- The percentage of South Africans saying that the country is headed in the right direction has decreased consistently since mid-1995.
- Evaluations of the national economy were at the lowest levels since 1994.
- While people still have more optimism about the future than they do about present conditions, optimistic expectations are also falling.
- Evaluations of the government's management of the economy are mixed, with very negative ratings of its overall handling of the economy and job creation. Evaluations are fairly positive in the areas of housing, income redistribution, and foreign investment.
- Evaluations of the economy vary across different race groups. Black South Africans are the most optimistic about future national economic conditions.

The percentage of people who feel that the country is headed in the right direction is at the lowest we have seen in the new South Africa, dropping by 33 percentage points since the heady days following the country's first election. Forty-three per cent now feel that the country is headed in the right direction, while 44 per cent feel that it is headed in the wrong direction.

South Africans' evaluations of the national economy seem to be following the same general trend of increasing pessimism. In 1994, just under one-half of the electorate (46 per cent) said that the economy had improved over the previous twelve months. By September 1998, that figure stood at only one-quarter (25 per cent). In 1997, one-quarter of the electorate (27 per cent) said that they were satisfied with the present economic situation of the economy. The proportion dropped to 17 per cent in September 1998.

Concerning the government's overall management of the economy, only 22 per cent of South Africans say it is managing the economy very well or fairly well. (This is the first time *Opinion '99* asked this question).

With regard to job creation, the figures are even lower, with only 12 per cent saying the government is doing a good job. While government performance on this dimension has never been received very well, positive evaluations have dropped sharply over the past few years, compared with a high of 36 per cent in 1996 and 1997.

The government receives more positive evaluations in terms of housing construction. On this dimension, 53 per cent say government is doing a good job, the highest rating it has received thus far, up from a low of 32 per cent in 1996.

On larger issues of redistribution, 45 per cent say the government is doing a good job narrowing the income gap between different race groups.

Differences in economic satisfaction across population groups are visible, with white and Indian respondents the most pessimistic and Africans the most optimistic. However, economic evaluations are declining amongst South Africans of all population groups.

While blacks still feel, on balance, that things are going in the right direction, that number had fallen to 53 per cent, compared with the very high levels in 1994 and 1995. Whites, Coloureds, and Indians are more pessimistic and have become increasingly more pessimistic. Moreover, while blacks remain far more optimistic about the future of the economy than other South Africans, their expectations have moderated in the past year.

Supporters of different parties have divergent views of the direction of the country. Those who identify with the ANC remain fairly optimistic; UDM and PAC identifiers are relatively optimistic and other party identifiers fairly pessimistic.

Government Evaluations

The first *Opinion '99* survey established that while the ANC holds a commanding lead in the electoral stakes for next year's general election, its measured support stands at one of the lowest levels in recent years, in terms of partisan identification as well as voting intentions.

To make sense of this apparent dilemma, one must conduct a close examination of how people evaluate the performance of the government in running the country over the past four years, as well as how they see the opposition

Opinion '99 found the following.

- For the first time since 1994, more eligible voters think the country is moving in the wrong rather than the right direction. Most voters hold the government responsible for the overall direction of the country. But among the majority of the electorate, black voters, those who think things are going in the wrong direction are more likely to find factors besides the government partially, or even more, responsible for the overall direction of the country.
- Evaluations of government performance still remain strong, especially for President Mandela and Deputy President Mbeki, but less so for the government as a whole.
- Evaluations of specific government performance in various areas vary sharply depending on the issue.

- On those issues that the public sees as the most important problems facing the country, government performance is rated especially negative.

As reported in "Economic Evaluations," another *Opinion ' 99* survey conducted in September found that only 43 per cent think the country is headed in the right direction, 44 per cent say things are going in the wrong direction, and 13 per cent are not sure. This is a sharp drop of 33 per cent points since the heady days following the country's first election. But these evaluations are even sharply lower than they were just two days previously.

In South Africa, there has been a great deal of debate about the extent to which the new ANC government could claim credit, or be blamed, for whatever achievement or setbacks the country has confronted since 1994. When respondents asked voters who was responsible for the overall direction of the country, 59 per cent said that the government is either totally responsible (47 per cent) or mainly responsible (12 per cent) for the way things have been going, 12 per cent feel that other factors besides the government are mostly responsible (8 per cent) or wholly (4 per cent) responsible.

Looked at in another way, 44 per cent feel that at least other factors besides the government are responsible for the overall recent direction of the country, compared with 47 per cent who lay all blame or reward at the door of the government. Of those black voters who say things are going in the right direction, 55 per cent give full responsibility to the government, However, increasingly large numbers of black voters are saying the country is moving in the wrong direction. But before opposition parties get too excited, they should take note that only 37 per cent of this group say it is solely the government's fault, and 49 per cent assign at least some responsibility to factors other than the government.

On the other hand, 12 per cent of white voters think the country is headed in the right direction, but there is no joy for the ANC among the group. Only 16 per cent of these people give full credit to the government, the rest assigning some or most reward to factors other than the government.

Opinion '99 continues.

> The fact that so many people can see some other factors that are responsible for the overall direction of the country besides the government, may help explain why the government still commands fairly positive job performance ratings, even though as many people now say the country is headed in the wrong direction as say it is headed in the right direction.

The stature of President Mandela is still exceptionally strong and widespread. This is very important for the 1999 election, since evidence from elections in other countries suggests that the performance of an incumbent party running for re-election is strongly related to evaluations of the president or the prime minister.

And while both Mandela and Mbeki fare much better in public approval than the government as whole, a majority (58 per cent) still feel that the government is doing its job "very" or "fairly" well.

- On most of the problems that people identity as the important ones facing the country today, the government got rather poor evaluations.

To the extent that it has one, this could be the government's central political problem heading into the next election. There are several issues on which it clearly wants to claim credit for impressive achievements and on which it receives strong public approval (water and electricity delivery and, to a lesser extent, health care). Yet these issues do not receive and never have received substantial priority from the electorate.

It is important to note that this is not because they are satisfied with government performance so that the issue is no longer a pressing one. Rather, these issues have never received high levels of public priority at any time since 1994. This is not because people prioritize things as problems only when the government is addressing them badly. In the past, the government has received relatively strong approval on several high-priority problems even though people rate them as important national problems (education and housing, for example).

However, two other points need to be kept in mind.
- Even if they do not rate high in the public consciousness as public problems, the sheer visibility of many Reconstruction and Development Programme basic delivery problems, specifically in the areas of water and electricity delivery, may have a strong, positive "demonstration effect" in that they at least create a widespread impression that the government is doing some things very well, and hold out the hope that it will also achieve similar results in other areas once it turns its full attention to them.
- Second, opposition parties have failed to offer a credible alternative across these issues (see "The Opposition"). So even if most people think that the government is not doing particularly well on some important areas, the vast majority of voters do not see any other party that they would trust to do any better.

On the issue that people cite as the worst problem, job creation, cited by 73 per cent of the electorate, only 12 per cent think the government is handling it "very well" or "fairly well." While government performance on this dimension has never been received very well, positive evaluations have dropped sharply over the past few years, compared with a high of 36 per cent in 1996 and 1997.

On crime prevention, selected by 64 per cent, only 18 per cent give the government positive marks, a sharp drop in contrast to the 45 per cent positive rating of May 1996.

The government got better marks on education, selected as an important problem by 24 per cent, 47 per cent say it has addressed the educational needs of all South Africans "very well" or "fairly well." Yet this is a marked decline from the 69 per cent who gave positive ratings as recently as November 1997. Fifty-three per cent gave favorable ratings to government handling of housing, a problem cited by 22 per cent. It is important to note that the survey analysis observes that public evaluations of government performance on housing have risen steadily over the past few years from a low 32 per cent in November 1996.

On overall management of the economy, it receives positive ratings from only 22 per cent. A higher 36 per cent say it is doing a good job controlling inflation, 45 per cent approve of its performance in narrowing income inequalities, and a much larger 66 per cent give the government high marks on encouraging foreign investment.

On the sixth most frequently cited national problem, health care, selected by 13 per cent, the government receives strong approval, with 57 per cent saying it handled this "very well" or "fairly well." Yet this represents a sharp drop from the 73 per cent who approved of government performance in June 1997.

On the seventh rated problem, corruption, selected by 6 per cent, only 26 per cent say the government is handling this problem well. On the related issue of maintaining transparency and accountability, only 31 per cent say it is doing a good job.

Fully 67 per cent say the government is doing a good job with regard to water provision, yet only 5 per cent cite this as an important problem; 62 per cent say it has done a good job in ending political violence, a problem cited by 8 per cent; 6 per cent say it has done a good job in nation building yet hardly any people mention this as a problem.

Quite clearly, the ANC has claimed credit for what it sees as historic and unparalleled achievement in terms of basic service delivery, especially primary health care, electricity, and water.It has also tried to deflect attention away from continuing problems in crime, housing, and education, often blaming them on the legacy of apartheid.

The Issues

Since 1994, South Africans have consistently identified four problem that they want government to address:

- job creation (chosen by 67 per cent in 1994, by 74 per cent in 1995, 68 per cent in 1997, and 73 per cent in 1998);
- crime (chosen by 6 per cent in 1994, by 32 per cent in 1995, 58 per cent in 1997, by 64 per cent in 1998);
- housing (chosen by 41 per cent in 1994, by 54 per cent in 1995, by 44 per cent in 1997, by 22 per cent in 1998); and
- education (chosen by 34 per cent in 1994, by 20 per cent in 1995, 20 per cent in 1997, and 24 per cent in 1998).

With the increase in concern over crime, the proportioning mentioning "violence" or "political violence" dropped from 56 per cent in 1994 to 8 per cent in 1998.

The number citing problems of "inequality," "discrimination," or equal rights" dropped from 23 per cent in 1994 to 3 per cent in 1997.

Yet paradoxically, the issues which most often surface as the "flavor of the month" in the media are cited by few people as being the issues they urgently want government to address. Thus:

- immigration (3 per cent in 1995, 1 per cent in 1997); land (cited by one per cent or fewer in three national surveys since 1994);

- food (one per cent or less in every survey);
- water (reached its highest level of concern in 1997);
- wages (4 per cent in every survey since 1994);
- corruption (6 per cent in 1997 and in 1998);
- the economy (6 per cent in 1997, 18 per cent in 1998); and
- health care (10 per cent in 1997, 13 per cent in 1998).

(Where is AIDS? It doesn't even register on the scale of concerns, despite the fact that HIV is spreading at the rate of 1600 infections per day – the fastest growing number in sub-Saharan Africa. Was AIDS even specifically mentioned in the scale of issues or was it left to the respondent to refer to the disease freely?)

The October 1998
Suzman Foundation Poll

In October 1998, the Helen Suzman Foundation commissioned Mark Data to carry out a national opinion survey based on a representative sample of 2,232 voters. An additional survey of 800 voters in December 1998 was drawn only from the minorities living in the Western Cape, KwaZulu-Natal, and Gauteng.

South African political culture is characterized by an extremely strong emphasis on leadership: "United Democratic Movement of Bantu Holomisa and Roelf Meyer." Voters can understand that question but have often not heard of the UDM.

In 1994, all the party leaders except one were more popular than their parties: F.W.de Klerk was far more popular than the New National Party (NNP), Mandela was more popular than the ANC, Buthelezi more popular than the IFP, and so on. Only the Democratic Party was more popular than its leader Zach De Beer, which probably contributed significantly to the party's poor showing in 1994.

Just how strong the cult of leadership is may be seen by the answers the poll got to the question "How far do you agree with the statement: 'I will stand by my political party and its leader even if I disagree with many of its policies'? "

The appeal of strong leadership is particularly marked among Coloureds, Africans, and white Afrikaners. The more middle class a group the less likely it is to be overwhelmingly leadership oriented. Among African ANC voters no less than 31 per cent strongly agree with the proposition and 43 per cent agree somewhat; only 25 per cent disagree to any extent at all. Among Coloureds, NNP supporters are more likely to feel this than the ANC voters NNP supporting Coloureds are more working class than ANC supporting Coloureds.

Issues often varied with race and economic situation in particular. Crime mattered most to people who were in jobs. Among those either suffering or fearing unemployment, job creation was an overriding preoccupation. Whereas English-speaking whites are obsessed by crime, Africans are far less so and are much more concerned with job creation. The fear of an ANC two-thirds majority mobilizes considerable numbers of

189

Afrikans, Coloureds, and English-speaking whites against it, but the idea of obtaining such a majority awakes no answering response among Africans. Thus, the more the ANC wants a two-thirds majority, the less it should mention it.

Table 3

In making up your mind how to vote, what are the most important issues you will consider?

	Africans	Coloured	Asian	White Afrikans	English
Creating more jobs	66	39	33	18	16
Dealing with crime	9	21	46	39	58
Improving education	6	4	12	3	3
Improving health facilities and other services	3	1	2	2	3
Building more houses	3	1	1	2	1
Helping the ANC get a 2/3 majority	2	2	1	0	0
Stopping the ANC from getting a 2/3 majority	1	13	1	21	13
Improving the standard of living	6	15	5	5	3

All surveys, whether within countries or among them, indicate that the majority of people are concerned about the same things, such as:

- *Respondents' replies usually resonate a sense of disillusionment or a common sense of purpose. In fact, it encourages the latter, going to war with each other. Rather than common misery breeding a common bond, it indicates the opposite, between countries and among them. Rather than poverty bringing people together, it pulls them apart. Rather than an awareness of inequality starting to awaken people, it induces a slumber of sorts, a slumber that becomes nightmarish, dreams that dream dreams of hostility. Once marginally taken care of, the expectation is always to be taken care of; never having been taken care of, the expectation is that one should be taken care of – the dance of the River Dance in rivulets, dried up in streams of tears and rage.*
- *the common noise is because of the voice of an accepted dominance, not authoritarian but the product of an ingrained passivity. In South Africa, the passivity has won. Exiles thought of themselves as "revolutionaries," internal people thought of themselves as people fighting for "individual and human rights." Struggle assumed different meanings in the face of a com-*

mon enemy. And it is that, of course, to repeat myself again and again, which keeps the alliance together.

- *The strongest argument for keeping the alliance in South Africa is that, for a fixed period in time, there must be stability. Without stability, the general appearance of disorder would become the prism of perception, presaging the end of the South African dream.*

Questions and Considerations

- *What do people expect from democracy and the ANC? How do you differentiate between them?*
- *They want their needs met? How do they define their needs – in terms of their material concerns being met, or in terms of abstractions like "justice," "dignity," and the like?*
- *People fight against injustice; they don't necessarily fight for justice. There appears to be an incredible sense of justice unserved. But there is a difference reflected. What I get is justly deserved. What others get is unjustly deserved. In transitions there is an incredible amount of "me-tooism."*
- *Senses of justice are not abstracts of philosophy, but the daily means of asserting oneself.*
- *All concepts from politics, for that matter, are local, and in that sense concepts of governance work their way from the top to the bottom.*
- *Want has taken precedence over need.*
- *Not having dealt with the psychological impact of the past, South Africa still has no coherent sense of identity.*
- *The ANC promised a nonracial society: it is not a nonracial society but a multiracial one. The longer it take to understand this, the longer it will take South Africa to heal.*
- *Blacks have very little choice, choice in the real sense of the term, of being able to choose between real alternatives, not artificial ones. The ANC has let them down, but this does not mean that they are about to abandon it. A crude analogy: the abused wife and why she doesn't simply leave her husband. She has nowhere else to go. All alternatives are worse. There is also the question of learned helplessness: under apartheid, the lives of blacks were regulated and controlled to an unbelievable extent; under the new dispensation they have to let go of these behaviors; they have to get over their dependency on government, of government's being responsible for doing things for them, of a lack of senses of accountability and responsibility, of taking things into their own hands, becoming masters of their own fates.*
- *One must draw distinctions between what people say and what they might believe; between what people wish to believe and what they actually believe;*

between what they profess not to be angry about and what they are angry about; between anger and disillusionment; between hope and despair; between hope based on a genuine sense of optimism and hope based on desperation.

- *Despair is the starting point. Work backwards.*
- *The sadness about "new" freedom is that there is no freedom at all. The freedom to be able to speak your mind breaks down in the face of the nonfreedoms: no work, no sense of ownership, no sense of having a better life. Like most revolutions that were not fought purely on military grounds, most blacks in South Africa were not involved in the struggle; indeed, more blacks may have fought on the side of the state than fought on the side of the struggle. What does this say not only for focus groups but people's past and future?*
- *There was never a "national uprising." Township violence was sporadic and for the most part confined to specific locations. How do people contrast what went on under the security forces, township gangs, and what goes on today?*
- *Hope and despair: all the ANC still has to do is to push the "apartheid" buttons. How easy it is. And how effective. Keep the memories of apartheid alive. The more you do so, the more you preclude fragmentation.*
- *The guiding principle for any liberation movement is to keep itself together. The lesson: when there is one movement, it is not about to "unliberate itself" by splitting: keep the face of the enemy alive. See Mandela's speech to the 50th Congress .*
- *When a little has to be spread over a large number, the incremental change seems marginal; at the same time the loss to the many is minimal. For most there is little gain; for the few there is little pain.*
- *Balancing inequities is impossible when the inequities are so huge, and using indices of a per capita nature are misleading because they fail to take account of absolute disparities.*
- *Some things you can't change unless you impose an authoritarianism that is inimical to the principles that undermine your rule of law.*
- *Governments are increasingly subject to external constraint. The more emerging the country, the greater the impact of these constraints.*
- *Populations in emerging countries don't understand constraints. They have been raised on the expectations of the consumer market.*
- *For emerging democracies, the capacity to meet these expectations and to bridge them to capacity is virtually impossible. OK?*
- *In the short run, or perhaps even the longer run, there is a divergence between what the country can deliver and can afford and the expectations of the populations.*
- *What drives expectations? Television and information technology. The "flowable" commodities of consumerism, free movement of capital, the global village, the street market.*

- *In the absence of alternatives, people make certain inevitable choices since they have nowhere else to turn to.*
- *In the focus group surveys, people consistently contradict themselves, but they rarely, if ever, condemn the ANC (condemn as distinct from criticizing the ANC).*
- *It is not that they do not harbor fears; rather it's the difference between what they reveal and what they don't. They are still wary of the past.*
- *Indeed, why, after forty years' oppression, the threat of arbitrary arrest, interrogation, and so on, should they suddenly open up to pollsters and the like? Why should these people be trusted? So, in one sense, all our data are "contaminated."*

Afterthoughts

In a recent column, "No Repeat of Our Glorious 1994," one of South Africa's most prominent political commentators, Kaiser Nyatsumba wrote:

> Many will take memories of those special days to their graves. There they were, on 27 and 28 April 1994, maids standing with their madams, labourers standing with their masters, all eager to cast a vote in our democratic national elections. Those were probably the most cathartic days in the history of this country. South Africa is again facing an election in a matter of months. Although we will not be a typically "normal" country for a few more years, our politics have nevertheless begun to lose their "special" image. There may well be many in politics today who believe they are there to serve the nation, but by and large many others are there to make a living. To them, politics is an occupation like any other, and some will lie and cheat to remain in office to reap the benefits of being in parliaments or government.

A second observation came from Albie Sachs, onetime activist and presently a member of the country's Constitutional Court, "We were able to achieve a miracle, but we can't achieve the achievable."

When the Truth and Reconciliation Commission, which was supposed to open the floodgates to the horrors of apartheid past and by some mysterious alchemy achieve reconciliation in South Africa, released its final report at the end of October 1998, it was damned by all political parties. Its full repercussions are only beginning to sink in. Truth it did reveal; but it is an incomplete truth. Justice remains very much in the balance. Reconciliation is a far cry.

Ironically, the attempt of the ANC to block publication of the report diverted attention from its more serious findings concerning the modus operandi of apartheid itself and the commission's unequivocal emphasis on the culpability of successive National Party governments and its all-too-willing surrogates in every sector of South African society.

For President Mandela, the responses the report elicited, especially from the ANC, must have been especially disappointing. He devoted the better part of his presidency to trying to bring about reconciliation between blacks and whites, often to the point where he was criticized by some blacks for paying more attention to ameliorating the fears of whites than with ameliorating the inequities blacks had suffered.

But President Mandela wanted to put in place the foundation stones for a nation, not to settle scores or seek retribution. The TRC has not brought about reconciliation in the here and now. Reconciliation is a process, not an instantaneous epiphany. It is not a once-over, an ending to something, a closing of the books. Rather, it is the beginning of something new, the opening of a new book that can only add additional pages out of a process that begins with catharsis, engenders anger, invites recrimination, leads to reflection, genuflects to the need for acknowledgment, provides the road map for the way to healing, again a painful exploration and reconciliation, again not a final closing of the wounds, but a mutual tending to one another's wounds.

When he retires from office in June 1999, Mandela will leave a South Africa full of contradictions, with enormous social and political challenges to overcome, a South Africa still in the process of transformation, a South Africa not yet out of the woods, not yet one in which democracy has fully taken root, although the vine is ripening.

If one were to finger the greatest failure of the Mandela years, it would perhaps come down to something very simple: the African National Congress simply underestimated the task it faced. Indeed, the nature and dimensions of the task itself, requiring that it transform itself almost overnight from liberation movement to government, were overwhelming, and the ANC, not surprisingly, was unable to deliver on the promises it had made to the people. And it learned, too, that the learning curve is steep. As a result many blacks became disappointed with the government, and in time that disappointment has turned to some disillusionment.

According to recent surveys, this is not going to result in African voters voting for another party in the 1999 elections. There is in effect no other party. Voters, if they wish to register their disapproval, will express their disillusionment by staying at home, resulting in a lower voter turnout. The drop in voter turnout will be the significant indicator of blacks' dissatisfaction with government, not the percentage of the vote the ANC receives.

Even though it has enjoyed an overwhelming majority in Parliament, the ANC is supersensitive to criticism, seeing it as racially motivated and a thinly veiled insinuation that blacks simply aren't up to the task of governing. This hypersensitivity in turn has bred hubris – a propensity to dismiss all criticism, justified or not, an axiomatic response that everything that has gone wrong is somehow linked to the "legacy of apartheid," and that whites who draw attention to such things are apartheid fellow travelers in drag.

Indeed, so convincing did this morally unanswerable response become for every failure that the government succumbed to its own propaganda. In such circumstances there was no need for accountability. The ANC merely trots out the apartheid mantra and tells the opposition to go stuff it.

Because Parliament is so firmly under the thumb of the ANC, government is immune from criticism from ANC MPs. There are, of course, free-spirited and open debates, and ongoing clashes of personalities; some of the most policy-directed exchanges come from ANC portfolio committees whose ANC members frequently cross swords with other ANC members and express whatever opinions they want to. But there is no faulting of the ANC. Never hand ammunition to the apartheid opposition. The fact that all members of the opposition have abandoned any form of apartheid or ceased to be advocates on its behalf is irrelevant.

If ANC members find fault with government actions, they must channel their criticisms through party structures – behind closed doors. Public criticism is equated with "behavior bringing the party into disrepute" and the critic is subject to "disciplinary measures."

Although not by any measure a one-party state, South Africa is, and will remain for the foreseeable future, a one-party dominant democracy. Nor is this necessarily a bad thing during a period of transition when the government is called on to engineer fundamental and radical reform at all levels of society in order to undo the apartheid arrangements, attitudes, structures, and social/public/cultural hierarchies that permeated the country's fabric.

But whatever disillusionment blacks may feel, it never extends to Mandela himself. He is above reproach. Even in matters that properly fall within his domain, if things don't work out the way blacks expect them to, they criticize the government, but never Mandela. Blacks make a very clear distinction between Mandela and the government. Whites do not. Indeed, it often seems they go to the opposite extreme: everything that is found wanting in government – and among whites the litany is almost endless – they put at the doorstep of Mandela.

Though he is revered abroad, whites – perhaps more accurately, older whites – have never warmed to Mandela. They may respect him, have a grudging admiration for the way in which he has destigmatized South Africa in the international arena; they may take pride, perhaps, in the acclaim with which he is received in other countries to the degree that the acclaim reflects favorably on South Africa; they may even have grown fond of him as he edges toward retirement, but there is nothing about him that would impel them to refer to him as *Madiba*, or even affectionately as the "old man."

And for all his efforts to assuage their fears, to assure them that their remaining in South Africa is crucial to the country's future, that they too are as African as their black country brethren, they have responded to his courting with wariness. The day he querulously disparaged the increasing number of whites emigrating as not being real South Africans willing to stand their ground, as being "on the chicken run," and echoed Thabo Mbeki's "good riddance, they felt that he had dropped the facade, and that for once he was revealing his true feelings – and by extension the true feelings of blacks – towards whites. Which, if one considers that their most consuming fear a few years earlier had been that once blacks "took over" they would turn on whites and treat them in the same way whites had treated blacks for decades, might be regarded as a giant leap forward.

Four questions arise:
- What is the Mandela legacy?
- What is the state of the nation Mbeki will inherit?
- What is the state of the psyche of the country?
- What must Mbeki do to address the manifold problems the country faces, not all of which are of its own making and not all of which can be dealt with by the actions of a sovereign nation when globalization has curtailed free-dom of unilateral action on the part of sovereign nations, and, more impor-tant, its efficacy; when sovereign nations, especially the smaller and less powerful ones, are in many respects spectators at rather than participants in the global chess game?

And finally, what context must be used to evaluate South Africa's successes or failures in the future? This is hardly the place to examine these questions in detail, but to present the broad parameters of the kinds of questions that should engage us as we get a better understanding of the kinds of travails which societies emerging into the sunlight of democracy have to put to themselves.

There is little confidence in the political system on the part of the opposition parties. Elections for president and the National Assembly will be held in June 1999. No one is holding his or her breath, least of all the opposition parties. Elections are also due to take place in South Africa in 1999. The bad news for the ANC is that it appears to be losing support, hardly surprising given the levels of unemployment and crime and the spillover effects of the Asian crisis on the economy. The good news for the ANC is that as fast as it is losing support, all opposition parties are losing support at an even more alarming rate. For the ANC it is a win-win situation. To consolidate its African base, old enemies, the ANC and the IFP, are talking a voluntary coalition with a deputy presidency or a like honor for Chief Mangosuthu Buthelezi, head of the IFP and for years during the struggle the ANC's personification of collaboration with the apartheid regime. When the TRC found that Chief Buthelezi was indeed a state collaborator and behind hit squads that targeted the ANC in the 1980s and 1990s, the ANC pooh-poohed the commission's findings and went ahead with its plans for a grand alliance. F.W. De Klerk, of course, is gone, pilloried in the end by his own people for having sold them out. The National Party, now renamed the New National Party, has imploded, and the diminishing white vote has nowhere to go, except perhaps, like much else in white South Africa, to the oblivion of political irrelevance. The New National Party and the Democratic Party, a party of white liberals, went to court charging that the government's requirement that voters could not vote unless they were in possession of a bar-coded Identity Document disenfranchised millions of blacks. The Constitutional Court ruled in favour of the government's position – not barcoded ID, no vote. But then again, in the fiercely competetive corridors of power words like "loyalty" and adherence to "party discipline" and "bringing the party into disrepute" are buzzwords for imminent exclusion leads most of those who aspire to power to keep not only the stiff upper lip but to keep their mouths tightly shut. Orthodontists are in short supply.

But despite the disparities the focus groups and surveys I have drawn upon to illustrate the political landscape of South Africa, president-in-waiting Thabo Mbeki has one strong, perhaps the only, variable that really counts which would allow him to speed up the process of transformation.

According to the last HSRC survey poll conducted in December 1998, sympathy for non-alternatives to democracy falls below 10 per cent for all racial categories and below 15 per cent for all provinces. There is "an unconditional preference for democracy in South Africa"; only 7 per cent said that "only an authoritarian government or dictatorship might be preferable to democracy." Support for democracy on the other hand has increased 74 per cent since February 1988. The fact that support for democracy, despite South Africa's having slipped into a depression, is a very positive sign, as it indicates that many South Africans are prepared to accept democracy as a system of government even when times are tough.

Furthermore, according to the HSRC survey, support for democracy among South Africans is high in comparison with most other countries that have experienced political transitions since the 1980s. Among the figures that are available only Uruguay – South American with a long but interrupted history of constitutional government – leads South Africa.

Notes

1. Greta Steyn "Export performance 'disappointing'" faxed by NDI on 2 November 1998
2. See Deputy President Thabo Mbeki's speech to Parliament, 3 June 1998.
3. For one example, see the report in the *Star* 5 June 1998: Detectives uncovered a 16 member car syndicate, which included five policemen, after a year long operation dubbed "Operation Clean Deal." After the arrest of the gang, police recovered stolen and hijacked luxury cars valued at more than R5 million. Indeed, in Gauteng, many police are under investigation for being involved in some form of illegal activity. The police force is so depleted that most of those under investigation, and even some of those against whom charges will be brought are allowed to remain on active duty.
4. CODESA - Convention for a Democratic South Africa. Nineteen parties attended. It ran from December 1991 until May 1992. Resumed in March 1993 with 26 parties present. In November 1993 an agreement was reached among all parties to the talks, opening the way for the elections in April 1994 and "one man one vote".

5. On the 29 September 1992, several ANC supporters demonstrating in Bisho, against the homeland of Ciskei, were killed and a large number wounded. This heightened tensions and moved the incorporation of the homelands up the political agenda.

6. CODESA 11 - (see footnote 4) The negotiations resumed at Kempton Park, Johannesburg in 1993. After the Record of Understanding was reached between the ANC and NP, in September 1992, negotiations resumed once more in March 1993 and were known as known as CODESA II or otherwise known as the Kempton Park Negotiations.

7. A massacre on 17 June 1992, Boipetong, in which 46 people were killed and hundreds injured. The TRC thought that the massacre was engineered by the IFP, in collaboration with the South African Police, but the TRC came to no definitive conclusion.

8. Leipzig Model - The "People's" battle in Leipzig, Germany in 1989, broke the back of Communist rule in East Germany, led to the collapse of the ruling regime, and the historical dismantling of the Berlin Wall, paving the way for the unification of Germany, and the collapse of Communisism as we know it in all of Eastern Europe and the former Soviet Union.

9. Patti Waldmeir - *Anatomy of a Miracle: The End of Apartheid and the Birth of the New South Africa.* New York, W.Norton, 1997.

10. Interview with Derek Keys, former Minister of Finance for South Africa.

11. "The Report of the Truth and Reconciliation Commission," TRC, Cape Town, 1998.

12. *ibid.*, vol. 1, chap. 4, 8–9.

13. Opinion '99, Institute for Democracy in South Africa (IDASA), 1999.

14. Quoted in Matisonn, *Mail and Guardian*, 6 November 1998.

15. Craig Charney: Voices of a New Democracy: African Expectations in the New South Africa. *Transition Series.* Research Report. 1995, Centre for Policy Studies, Johannesburg.

16. Focus group research conducted on behalf of the NDI (see Appendix A)

17. See John Kane-Berman's *The Silent Revolution.* South African Institute for Race Relations, Johannesburg, 1996.

18. Speech by Deputy President Thabo Mbeki at the South African Democratic Teacher's Union Congress (SADTU), September 1998.

19. *ibid.*

20. *ibid.*

21. The Helen Suzman Foundation Poll Reports, Johannesburg, 1999.

22. Speech by Thabo Mbeki on Reconciliation and Nation-Building, at the opening of debate in the National Assembly: National Assembly, Cape Town, 29 May 1998.

23. See John Kane-Berman. *ibid.*

24. According to the Central Statistical Services reports, 87.2 percent of the unemployed were Africans, 8.2 percent were Coloureds, 1.4 percent were Indians, and 3.4 percent were white. Data cited in *Pulse: Assessing South Africa's Transition*, IDASA, 1998.

25. South Africa Institute of Race Relations (SAIRR), *South Africa 1996/1997* (Johannesburg: SAIRR, 1997).

26. World Bank, *World Development Report 1997: The State in a Changing World* (New York: World Bank, 1997).

27. Lunsche, Sven, "Government carries joblessness albatross into 1999 election," *Business Times*, 12 April 1998. Total employment in the formal manufacturing, construction, electricity, and mining and quarrying sectors decreased by 106,000, or 4.5 per cent between November 1996 and November 1997. See Central Statistical Service # P0242.1, March 1998.

28. World Bank, see note 26.

29. *ibid.*

30. *Creating Action Space: The Challenge of Poverty and Democracy in South Africa,* Cape Town, Institute for Democracy in South Africa, 1998.
31. The Bureau for Economic Research (BER) is located at Stellenbosch University. *Business Day,* 14 September 1998.
32. Philip Black, "Task Facing SA Is Too Big for Government Alone," *Business Day,* 22 September 1998.
33. *Business Day,* 23 September 1998, quoting Statistics SA.
34. *Business Day,* 23 September 1998.
35. "Milton Friedman on the Crisis." *Financial Mail* interview with Milton Friedman, 4 September 1998.
36. *ibid.*
37. *ibid.*
38. Robert Mattes, "The ANC and the Seven Dwarfs," *Daily Mail and Guardian,* 9 December 1998.
39. *ibid.*
40. *Opinion ' 99.* Cape Town, IDASA, 1999.
41. *Star,* 1 September 1998.
42. *Business Day,* 17 August 1998.
43. The National Party: "This weakens the autonomy and independence of the provinces and adds to the ANC's centrist dominance over matters best dealt with at the provincial level." The DP: The attempt by the ANC NEC to select premiers at the national level showed a contempt for the democratic process in the provinces." *Star,* 8 August 1998. The ANC: "The expertise required to run the provincial structures of the ANC is not necessarily the same qualities required for the running of a provincial government. The decision will enable the ANC to choose the best candidate for the position [of premier]." Smuts Ngonyama, ANC head of presidency. *Business Day,* 28 August 1998.
44. *Mercury,* 19 August 1998.
45. In August 1998, Ace Magashule, the former Free State MEC and longtime rival of Patrick "Terror" Lekota, who had been elected premier of the Free State in 1994, were both removed from office by the ANC NEC when their bitter rivalry threatened to tear the ANC in the province apart. Lekota was appointed to the chairmanship of NCOP and was elected chairman of the ANC in December 1997. Magashule, meanwhile, was consigned to the political wilderness. However, he was elected provincial chairman of the ANC in the Free State in August 1998. Dr. Ivy Matsepe-Cassaburri, who had been appointed premier by the NEC in place of Lekota, did not even make it past the nomination list stage. At the time analysts said that she would hold on to her position only because of the support she enjoyed from President Mandela and Deputy President Mbeki and from several other senior party members. *Saturday Star,* 29 August 1998. This has proved to be the case.
46. *Business Week,* 27 August 1998.
47. R.W Johnson. Helen Suzman Foundation. Press Statement 27 August, Cape Town, 1998.
48. President Mandela launching the ANC's Gauteng voter registration campaign. Faxed by NDI on 2 November 1998.
49. *Citizen,* 5 August 1998.
50. Interview with Commissioner George Fivas, 20 July 1998.
51. Speech by Deputy President Thabo Mbeki in the National Assembly, 3 June 1998.
52. *Cape Times,* 7 September 1998.
53. *Leadership* Vol. 17 Number 2, 1998. "The Two-Thirds Majority: Lead Us Not Into Temptation."

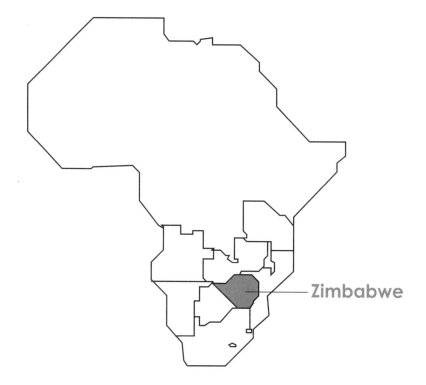

Zimbabwe

Zimbabwe's Electoral Experience

Towards Election 2000 and Beyond

Masipula Sithole

For the better part of the 1980s, Zimbabwe's political leadership and the ruling Zimbabwe African National Union-Patriotic Front (ZANU[PF]) party aggressively advocated for the now moribund Marxist-Leninist ideology and the anachronistic notion of a one-party state. This tended to reinforce, particularly among outsiders, the mistaken perception that Zimbabwe was, until the 1990s, a one-party state. Neither before nor after independence in 1980 has Zimbabwe ever been a one-party state. However, it has been a *de facto* one-party state, a tendency that predates the independence era.[1] The tendency towards *de jure* one-party governance is a post-independence development, but it was never actualized

Zimbabwe has always existed as a multiparty state; it has held general elections at regular five-year intervals since the independence general elections of 1980, and has held two presidential elections at six-year intervals since the 1990 presidential election. Although Zimbabwe has never foreclosed multiparty electoral opportunities, it has constrained them by maintaining and perpetuating a one-party-state political psychology for the first 11 years of independence.

To date, including the 1979 "internal settlement" election, Zimbabwe has had five general elections: the first in 1979, the second in 1980, the third in 1985, the fourth in 1990, and the fifth in 1995. The two presidential elections took place in 1990 and 1996. Although different parties have contested in these elections, the ruling ZANU(PF) has held electoral hegemony since the independence election of 1980. While voter turnout was very high in the 1980s elections, there has been a sharp decline in the 1990s. This decline has been evident not only in parliamentary and presidential elections, but also in local government elections.

This article borrows heavily, but with major modifications, from an article Dr Masiupla Sithole published with John Makumbe, "Elections in Zimbabwe: The ZANU(PF) Hegemony and the Incipient Decline," African Journal of Political Science 2, no. 1 (1998). *Dr Sithole is Professor of Political Science at the University of Zimbabwe in Harare. His research and writings have addressed political parties, democratization, elections and ethnicity in southern Africa.*

Since the 1987 incorporation of Patriotic Front-Zimbabwe African People's Union (PF-ZAPU) into the ruling ZANU(PF) party, and the scrapping, in the same year, of the 20 seats reserved for the white electorate, the remaining opposition parties have been very weak. Under the circumstances independent candidates have arisen to challenge the electoral hegemony of ZANU(PF), though they have met with limited success. However, as we approach the years 2000 and 2002, when Zimbabwe is scheduled to hold its sixth general and third presidential elections, respectively, ZANU(PF)'s hold on the Zimbabwe electorate is on the decline.

This article seeks to detail Zimbabwe's electoral experience since majority rule and to suggest possible scenarios for the general and presidential elections in 2000 and 2002. Given the decline of the ruling party's grip on the Zimbabwe electorate, what are the chances of a strong opposition's emerging in this country? What is the opposition saying about electoral politics, and what are the ruling party's and the government's responses? In other words, what are the chances that future elections will be contested on an even playing field? To examine these questions, I start first with Zimbabwe's electoral system.

The Electoral System

The majority of black Zimbabweans were enfranchised by the Zimbabwe-Rhodesia "internal settlement" Constitution, which produced the short-lived Muzorewa government of 1979. Thus, for the black majority, electoral politics essentially began in 1979. The electoral system used for this election was proportional representation (PR) based on the party list system. According to this method, seats in the National Assembly were allocated in proportion to the number of votes each contesting party won in each of the country's eight provinces. This was the first time in the electoral history of Zimbabwe that proportional representation was used. A threshold limit of 5 per cent was used for allocating seats in each province. This PR system, again used for the 1980 independence general election, was abandoned in the 1985 election, which brought back the single member district (SMD) or first-past-the-post, winner-takes-all system used during the colonial era. This electoral system has been used in all subsequent elections.

Several reasons were given for introducing the PR system for both the internal settlement and the independence elections. The major reason was the security situation that prevailed in the country at the time. It should be remembered that by 1979 the Rhodesian security forces and nationalist guerrillas were still fighting over territories in most parts of the country. This made the delimitation of constituencies as required by the single member district electoral system difficult and hazardous. Moreover, delimitation would be time-consuming for a people impatient to exercise the vote for which they had waited and fought for many years. Another reason given for PR, advanced particularly by white Rhodesian politicians, was that PR is more reflective of democratic representation. They conveniently argued that in a plural society such as Zimbabwe, the PR system prevented one group from having a monopoly of power in either the national legislature or the cabinet.[2]

However, mainstream nationalists were sceptical of PR; they saw it as a device by white politicians to prevent a clear electoral victory by African nationalists by enabling whites to form a coalition government with moderate and malleable African personalities and parties.[3] By and large, the nationalists, particularly those of the Patriotic Front led by Robert Mugabe and Joshua Nkomo, accepted PR only as a temporary and emergency measure. Their preference for the first-past-the-post electoral system was made known during the 1979 Lancaster Conference. It was their intention to rewrite the Electoral Act in order to reintroduce the constituency-based SMD system if they won the independence elections.[4]

Many political scientists, particularly those who have studied Africa in the 1990s, have argued that the PR system is not only more democratic than the SMD system, but that it is also an effective mechanism for managing and accommodating ethnic and other cleavages in plural societies.[5] Jonathan Moyo has argued strongly in favour of the PR system for societies which, like Zimbabwe, are in the process of developing a democratic culture.[6]

The Electoral Experience

The temptation is always to start from the 1980 independence election, but electoral politics for the vast majority of Zimbabweans started with the so-called internal settlement election of 1979, when the franchise was extended to the majority of the African people. Moreover, many major features of Zimbabwean electoral politics are traceable to this election. For instance, besides universal adult suffrage, such institutions and mechanisms as a bicameral parliament, reserved white seats for a specified period, the election supervisory commission, the election directorate, the practice of inviting international election monitors, voter education, polling procedures, the use of "indelible" ink, et cetera, employed in subsequent elections were all introduced in the 1979 election. In fact, it can be argued that the Constitution of Zimbabwe as agreed to at the Lancaster House Conference at the end of 1979 was but a replica of the 1978 internal settlement Constitution of Zimbabwe-Rhodesia.[7]

The 1979 Election
Five political parties contested the election of 1979 under the PR party list system using the threshold of 5 per cent in the eight provinces. The total common roll poll was 1,852,772 of an estimated voting population of 2.9 million. Thus, 64.45 per cent of potential voters cast their vote. Bishop Abel Muzorewa's United African National Council (UANC) won a clear majority, capturing 51 of the 72 common

roll seats; ZANU (N. Sithole) came second with 12 seats; and the United National Federal Party (UNFP), led by Chief Kaisa Ndiweni, came third with nine seats, won mainly in the two Matebeleland provinces, his home area. The total national strength of each party that took part in the 1979 elections is shown in Table 1.

Table 1

Zimbabwe-Rhodesia:
Results of the 1979 Election

Party	Valid Votes	Per centage of Valid Votes	Seats Won
UANC (Muzorewa)	1,212,639	68	51
ZANU (Sithole)	262,928	15	12
UNFP (Ndiweni)	194,446	11	9
ZUPO (Chirau)	114,570	6	—
NDU (Chiota)	1,870	1	—
Total	1,786,453	100	72

Estimated voting population: 2,900,000.
Total poll: 1,852,772 (64 per cent of voting population).
Spoilt papers: 66,319 (4 per cent of votes cast).

Source: Masipula Sithole, "The General Elections: 1979–1985," in *Zimbabwe: The Political Economy of Transition 1980–1985,* edited by Ibbo Mandaza (Dakar: CODESRIA, 1986), 79.

Robert Mugabe's ZANU(PF) and Joshua Nkomo's PF-ZAPU, together repre-senting the mainstream nationalist movement, then staging a guerrilla war from exile, did not take part in the election. This boycott cast a huge shadow of doubt as to the legitimacy of the election, thereby necessitating the "all-party" Lancaster House Constitutional Conference towards the end of 1979, at which a constitution for an independent Zimbabwe was agreed upon.

The 1980 Independence Election
Similarly, the independence election of 1980 was conducted under the proportional representation system for reasons of security and expediency. Again, a 5 per cent threshold was used in allocating seats in the eight provinces. A total of nine parties contested these elections held over a period of three exciting days, 27–29 March 1980. However, only three parties, Mugabe's ZANU(PF), Nkomo's PF-ZAPU, and Muzorewa's UANC, won any seats. ZANU(PF), winning 57 of the 80 common roll seats and capturing 63 per cent of the popular vote, emerged as the clear winner. Nkomo's PF-ZAPU, taking 24 per cent of the popular vote, came second, winning 20 seats. Muzorewa's UANC came third with 8 per cent of the popular vote, capturing the remaining three seats.

In losing, the other six parties together polled 5 per cent of the popular vote. The number of valid votes totalled 2,649,529. No party boycotted the election this time. Notwithstanding the possibility of electorate contamination, for example, by swelling the numbers with cross-border recruits from Mozambique to support ZANU(PF), from Zambia and Botswana to support PF-ZAPU, and from apartheid South Africa to support the internal settlement parties, as well as other electoral fraud, the 90 per cent independence poll would remain an all-time high. Table 2 below shows the results of the 1980 independence election.

Table 2

Zimbabwe: Results of the 1980 Election

Party	Valid Votes	Per centage of Valid Votes	Seats Won
ZANU(PF) (Mugabe)	1,668,992	63	57
PF-ZAPU (Nkomo)	638,879	24	20
UANC (Muzorewa)	219,307	8	3
ZANU (Sithole)	53,343	2	—
ZDP (Chikerema)	28,181	1	—
NFZ (Mandaza)	18,794	1	—
NDU (Chiota)	15,056	1	—
UNFP (Ndiweni)	5,796	0	—
UPAM	1,181	0	—
TOTAL	2,649,529	100	80

Estimated voting population: 3,000,000.
Total poll: 2,702,275 (90 per cent of voter population).
Spoilt papers: 52,746 (2 per cent of votes cast).

Source: Masipula Sithole, "The General Elections: 1979–1985," in *Zimbabwe: The Political Economy of Transition 1980–1985*, edited by Ibbo Mandaza (Dakar: CODESRIA, 1986), 83.

The 1985 Election
The first post-independence election was held in 1985. This election, following the anticipated amendment to the Electoral Act, was now held using the single-member-district or winner-takes-all electoral system. A total of six political parties contested these elections. The same voting pattern as that of the 1980 election was repeated, except that Muzorewa now lost his three seats to Mugabe's party, which won 64 seats, but in turn lost one seat to Sithole's party in the eastern Chipinge district, the home of the latter's ethnic Ndau. Nkomo's PF-ZAPU won every single constituency in Matebeleland where the Delimitation Commission had allocated 15 seats. PF-ZAPU lost the five seats it had won in the 1980 party list poll. These were

mainly in the Midlands province, where the Shona-Ndebele mix is substantial, and where, in turn, the 1985 constituencies had presumably been gerrymandered.[8]

Of a total 2,893,285 valid votes cast, 77.20 per cent went to Mugabe's ZANU(PF), 19.30 per cent to Nkomo's PF-ZAPU, while 1.25 per cent went to Sithole's ZANU faction. However, Muzorewa's UANC polled 2.24 per cent, almost double that of Sithole's party, but did not secure a single seat. Sithole was the beneficiary of the SMD electoral system. Again, no party boycotted this election although Sithole had gone into voluntary exile, leaving a surrogate candidate.[9] Table 3 shows the results of the 1985 parliamentary election.

Table 3

Zimbabwe: Results of the 1985 Election

Party	Valid Votes	Per centage of Valid Votes	Seats Won
ZANU(PF) (Mugabe)	2,233,320	77	64
PF-ZAPU (Nkomo)	558,771	19	15
ZANU (Sithole)	36,054	1	1
UANC (Muzorewa)	64,764	2	—
NDU (Chiota)	295	0	—
NFZ (Mandaza)	81	0	—
TOTAL	2,893,285	100	80

Registered voters: 3,500,000.
Total poll: 2,972,146 (85 per cent of voting population).
Spoilt papers: 78,861 (3 per cent of votes cast).

Source: Masipula Sithole, "The General Elections: 1979–1985," in *Zimbabwe: The Political Economy of Transition 1980–1985*, edited by Ibbo Mandaza (Dakar: CODESRIA, 1986), 90.

The 1990 Election

The 1990 general election took place after the 1987 unity accord between ZANU(PF) and PF-ZAPU, traditionally the main opponent parties in Zimbabwe's African politics. Five political parties contested the 1990 election, but a new opposition party, the Zimbabwe Unity Movement (ZUM) led by Edgar Tekere, was the main opposition. It was formed in 1989 amidst speculation that Zimbabwe would declare a one-party state after the 1990 election. ZUM had widespread national appeal, the first opposition party to achieve it since independence. Although it was thoroughly defeated (2 seats to the united ZANU(PF)'s 117 of the 120 contestable seats) in an election again held under the winner-takes-all constituency-based SMD system, ZUM won 18 per cent of the national popular vote. Had the election been held with the proportional representation system, ZUM would have won at least 20 seats.[10]

The results of the 1990 election still reflected ethnic preference in the sense that the united party, ZANU(PF), had the common sense not to put up Shona candidates in Ndebele constituencies, and vice versa. Moreover, notwithstanding ZUM's national appeal, its two seats were won in the Manicaland, the home province of its leader, Edgar Tekere, where ZUM polled the highest. Again, the Chipinge constituency went to Sithole's surrogate, with Sithole himself still in exile.

An important point to note about the 1990 election is the decline in voter turnout. From 85 per cent in the 1985 election, the turnout had dropped to 47 per cent in 1990, a significant 38 per cent drop. This phenomenon would be repeated in subsequent elections, both parliamentary and presidential, as well as in local government elections, particularly in urban areas.[11] Another significant feature of the 1990 election was the rather high per centage of spoilt votes, 6 per cent of the total poll. In the 1979 election, the spoilt vote was 4 per cent; in 1980, 2 per cent; in 1985, 3 per cent. The 6 per cent recorded in 1990 represented a 50 per cent increase of spoilt votes from the 1980 elections. This pattern would rise from 6 per cent in 1990 to an all-time high of 8 per cent in the 1995 election. (See Tables 1–5.)

Table 4

Zimbabwe: Results of the 1990 Election

Party	Valid Votes	Per centage of Valid Votes	Seats Won
ZANU(PF) (Mugabe)	1,690,071	81	117
ZUM (Tekere)	369,031	18	2
ZANU (Sithole)	19,448	1	1
UANC (Muzorewa)	9,667	1	—
Independents (7)	9,478	0.5	—
NDU	498	0	—
Total	2,098,193	100	120

Registered voters: 4,800,000.
Total poll: 2,232,529 (47 per cent of voting population).
Spoilt papers: 134,336 (6 per cent of votes cast).

Source: Computed from data in Jonathan Moyo, *Voting for Democracy: Electoral Politics in Zimbabwe* (Harare: University of Zimbabwe Publications, 1992), 166–181.

The 1995 Election

The 1995 general election was the first to be boycotted since the independence election of 1980. However, six political parties entered, with only two parties and one independent candidate winning seats. ZANU(PF) again won by an overwhelming majority. It captured 117 seats and 76 per cent of the valid votes cast in a national poll of 1,482,807. This represented a voter turnout of 57 per cent of an estimated 2.6 million registered voters in a population of nearly 5 million potential voters, so that about half the voting population did not exercise their franchise.[12] The results of the 1995 elections appear in Table 5.

Table 5

Zimbabwe: Results of the 1990 Election

Party	Valid Votes	Per centage of Valid Votes	Seats Won
ZANU(PF) (Mugabe)	1,126,822	76	117
ZANU (Ndonga) (Sithole)	93,546	6	2
FPZ (Dumbutshena)	88,223	6	—
Independents (29)	62,085	4	1
Zimbabwe Aristocrats	147	0	—
Total	1,370,823	92	120

Registered voters: 2,600,000.
Total poll: 1,482,807(57 per cent of voting population).
Spoilt papers: 111,984 (8 per cent of votes cast).

Source: Computed from election results published in *The Herald,* 11 April 1995.

With Sithole back from exile, his Zimbzbwe African National Union (ZANU [Ndonga]) won two seats, capturing 93,546 voters or 6 per cent of the total valid poll. Although Dumbutshena's Forum Party of Zimbabwe (FPZ) polled 88,223 or 6 per cent of the valid votes, it did not win a seat. ZANU(Ndonga) was again the beneficiary of a constituency-based SMD electoral system. Moreover, the two constituencies, Chiping North and Chiping South, had the largest concentration of Sithole's ethnic Ndau, who constitute about 330,000 or 3 per cent of the country's nearly 11 million people. The then FPZ leader, Enoc Dumbutshena, like Mugabe, is a Zezuru; invariably his party must share the ethnic Zezuru vote with ZANU(PF) in regions with a large concentration of Zezurus. The Zezuru constitute about 18 per cent of the African population. Although the national capital Harare is multiethnic, it is largely Zezuru.[13] Dumbutshena contested Florence Chitauro of ZANU(PF) in the Harare Central constituency and won 3,858 or 29 per cent of the vote to Chitauro's 9,417 or 71 per cent, while Sithole won 15,400 or 76 per cent of the vote to ZANU(PF)'s Edgar Musikavanhu, who polled 4,722 or 24 per cent of the vote in the Chipinge South constituency.

A significant development in the 1995 parliamentary election is the number of independent candidates. There had been none in the previous three elections, but 12 candidates stood in the 1990 election. In the 1995 election, the number of independent candidates rose to 29, one of them winning against a ZANU(PF) candidate, to the chagrin of both the party and Mugabe.[14] The proliferation of independent candidates is also apparent in municipal elections in which some of the independents have won in city council and mayoral elections, defeating ruling ZANU(PF) candidates.[15]

Voter turnout continued to decline, and the per centage of spoilt votes rose from the 6 per cent recorded for the 1990 election to 8 per cent in 1995. One would have expected that at least by 1990, the voting population, because of their participation in four previous elections, would have been used to the nuances of casting a ballot paper properly. It would appear that the more the electorate votes, the less they know how to cast a valid vote. It is, however, a possibility that spoilt votes could represent protest votes.[16]

The 1990 Presidential Election

In 1987, Zimbabwe amended its Constitution and introduced an executive president who would be elected directly by the people every six years, starting in 1990. Previously, Zimbabwe had a titular president who was elected by an electoral college comprising Parliament and the Senate. Both the titular president and the Senate were disbanded in 1987. In 1990 Parliament was expanded from 100 to 150 members, 120 of whom were chosen directly by the electorate, with the remaining 30 to be appointed by the president. The office of prime minister, who previously had executive powers, was abolished. These powers were now invested in the executive president who, as head of state, also had ceremonial duties.

Accordingly, Zimbabwe held its first presidential election ever in 1990. There were two candidates in this election, ZANU(PF)'s Robert Mugabe and ZUM's Edgar Tekere. As in the 1990 parliamentary election (held jointly with the presidential election) 54 per cent of the registered voters cast their vote. Mugabe won 83 per cent of the valid votes, leaving Tekere with 17 per cent, yet another crushing victory for ZANU(PF) and Mugabe. Table 6 contains the election results of the 1990 presidential election.

Table 6

Zimbabwe: Results of the 1990 Presidential Election

Candidate	Party	Valid Votes	Per centage of Valid Votes
R.G. Mugabe	ZANU(PF)	2,026,976	83
Tekere	ZUM	413,840	17
Total		2,440,816	100

Registered voters: 4,800,000.
Total poll: 2,587,204 (54 per cent of voting population).
Spoilt papers: 146,388 (6 per cent of votes cast).

Source: Computed from data in Jonathan Moyo, *Voting for Democracy: Electoral Politics in Zimbabwe* (Harare: University of Zimbabwe Publications, 1992), 182.

The 1996 Presidential Election
Although there were now more than a dozen political parties in the Zimbabwe political landscape, only two put up candidates to challenge ZANU(PF)'s Robert Mugabe. Most of the other opposition parties announced that they were boycotting the election, which they claimed was being held on an uneven playing field. Those who registered their participation – Muzorewa of the newly formed United Parties (UP) and Sithole of ZANU(Ndonga) – withdrew belatedly, citing similar reasons. The election still went ahead as scheduled with both Muzorewa and Sithole on the ballot.[17] Mugabe retained the presidency, winning 1,404,501 or 93 per cent of the valid votes in a poor voter turnout of 32 per cent of an estimated voting population of 5 million. Muzorewa attracted 72,600 votes or 5 per cent, while Sithole came third with 36,960 or 2 per cent. Table 7 shows the results of the 1996 presidential elections.

Table 7

Zimbabwe: Results of the 1996 Presidential Election

Candidate	Party	Valid Votes	Per centage of Valid Votes
R.G. Mugabe	ZANU(PF)	1,404,501	93
E.T. Muzorewa	UP	72,600	5
N. Sithole	ZANU (Ndonga)	36,960	2
Total		1,514,061	100

Registered voters: 4,900,000.
Total poll: 1,557,552 (32 per cent of voting population).
Spoilt papers: 43,491 (3 per cent of votes cast).

Source: Computed from election results published in *The Herald,* 20 March 1996. The results from four provinces were not published and are therefore not included in the computation.

Note: Numerous efforts to get the unpublished results from the Registrar-General's office were to no avail. Moreover, the voters rolls for this election were reported to be in shambles. See also endnote 12.

Explaining ZANU(PF) Dominance

It is clear from the above analysis and tables that ZANU(PF) has dominated the Zimbabwean electoral landscape since the 1980 independence election, whether contesting subsequent elections alone as a single party in 1980 and 1985 or together with PF-ZAPU as a united party in 1990 and 1995 and using either the PR or the SMD voting system. The question is: What explains ZANU(PF)'s electoral hegemony and the weak performance of opposition parties?

Many authoritative accounts have been written on the fate of the opposition in Zimbabwe's one-party dominant regime. These have been critical of the ruling ZANU(PF) regime's attitude and behaviour towards opposition parties since independence. The use of state institutions, especially the Central Intelligence Organization (CIO), police, army, and the media – daily newspapers, radio, and television – have been cited.

Also, until mid-1992, the ruling party was financed from public funds through the now nominally defunct Ministry of Political Affairs, which received approximately Z$50 million every year and operated from a multistorey, multimillion-dollar headquarters in Harare, the nation's capital. No other party had access to these funds. As a result of growing criticism, this ministry was abolished, but the financing of the ruling party continued under the self-serving Political Parties (Finance) Act of 1994, which allowed only parties with at least 15 seats in Parliament to be entitled to public funds.

However, following a High Court ruling in 1997, a bottom threshold of 5 per cent was set so that parties would be entitled to public funding in proportion to their per centage of votes. This would take effect in subsequent elections. Until then, the ruling party would not only continue to monopolize public funding because of its sheer majority per centage poll from the previous election but, until the results of the next election are known, it will be the only party entitled to public funding. Currently only three seats in Parliament belong to the opposition, decidedly a very weak position.

Moreover, the ruling ZANU(PF) has consistently remained to the left of Zimbabwe's political spectrum before and after independence. It has skillfully articulated populist policies on land, employment, indigenization of the economy, and anything and everything, particularly on the eve of each election year. Further, no other party has portrayed a more nationalist position than ZANU(PF), and it has a crafty, if articulate, spokesman in Robert Mugabe, whose rhetoric, more than that of any other leader, has thus far presumably remained closer to the psychology of the people.[18]

But more than anything else, ZANU(PF) rode a wave of terror consciously crafted during the liberation struggle to annihilate any form of opposition. Known as *gukurahundi,* it was a policy that swept ZANU(PF) into power; it was to be used after independence to crush PF-ZAPU, the party that could have offered a viable opposition, into submission, and result in the unity accord of 1987 when PF-ZAPU was "swallowed" by ZANU(PF).[19]

Future Prospects

The hitherto monolithic and mammoth party began to show cracks in the latter part of the 1980s. Its outspoken former secretary-general, Edgar Tekere, was the first leader to be expelled from the party in 1987 when he became increasingly vocal in his criticism of the party. He founded his Zimbabwe Unity Movement in 1989, the first party to be formed in nine years of independence and the first to pose a real challenge to ZANU(PF) after PF-ZAPU merged with it.

The decline in party "elite cohesion" continued to grow, as criticism and challenges to the party from within persisted. Margaret Dongo, ZANU(PF) central committee member and member of the 1990–1995 Parliament, defied the party after the politburo refused her candidacy for the 1995 parliamentary election. She ran as an independent candidate and lost, but cried foul. She won her petition to the courts against the results. A by-election had to be arranged, and she won the working-class Harare South constituency in the nation's capital by a 3 to 1 margin. Similarly, Lawrence Mudehwe defied the ZANU(PF) politburo, contested the executive mayoral race in the important eastern border city of Mutare, and won against the favored party candidate. Following these court victories, successful petitions were lodged through the courts for the nullification of city council and executive mayoral election results on grounds that there were "irregularities" in these elections in the important cities of Chitungwiza, Harare, and Masvingo.[20]

Perhaps the most interesting, if not most important, manifestation of a rupture in elite cohesion is that championed by the charismatic politburo member Dr Eddison Zvobgo of Masvingo, a province traditionally crucial to ZANU(PF) politics. In a widely read and debated speech delivered at an international conference in Harare in November 1995, Zvobgo called for the re-democratization of the Zimbabwe Constitution, particularly the aspects pertaining to the powers of the executive president, which, ironically, he drafted in 1987 when he was Minister for Legal and Parliamentary Affairs.[21]

In a contribution to Parliament in February 1998, another ZANU(PF) central committee member, Dzikamayi Mavhaire, commonly believed to be Zvobgo's surrogate, moved a motion to limit the presidential term of office with the words "The President must go." An irate President Mugabe demanded his supension from holding any office in the party for two years. Although he still remains in the party, Mavhaire has continued his call for a presidential term of not more that two five-year terms.

Cyril Ndebele is another case in point. As Speaker of Parliament, he defended Mavhaire's right to speak his mind in Parliament without recrimination, using the parliamentary immunity provision in the Constitution. Mugabe unsuccessfully demanded that Ndebele be disciplined. Ndebele was protected by his former PF-ZAPU colleagues in ZANU(PF), who threatened to withdraw from the unity accord of 1987. Fearing these consequences, Mugabe backed off.

The tendency has been to expel critics and opponents from the party: Tekere in 1987, Dongo in 1995, and Mudehwe in 1996. While Tekere formed his own party, ZUM, Dongo has not, at least not for now. But she is emerging as the rallying point for the "second independence movement," a sort of "liberation" from the ruling party. Whether Zvobgo and Mavhaire will fall victim to the same fate that befell Tekere and Dongo – being expelled from the party – remains to be seen. But some suggest he might miss his Machiavellian moment the longer he waits; others believe he has missed it already. Whether it is around Dongo, Zvobgo, or someone else, or a combination or permutation of the issues surrounding these individuals, it is likely that the ZANU(PF) electoral hegemony will be broken from within. The independent candidates phenomenon is but an early manifestation of this scenario.

Finally, the greatest asset ZANU(PF) has had thus far has been its leader, Mugabe himself. He is disciplined, articulate, learned, lucky, and inordinately Machiavellian. But he is 75, and of late has shown his vulnerability. Therefore, the choice of his successor and the manner in which he is replaced is likely to determine whether or how the independents and the weak opposition, as noted above, could be galvanized into a mammoth party. In this scenario, viable opposition might come from a splinter group from the ruling ZANU(PF) itself, an occurrence that would not be unlike the major ZAPU/ZANU split of 1963. Thus, Zimbabwe would have come full circle. It is hoped that its people will emerge wiser from the mistakes and experiences of the past.

However, a scenario in which a new leader could emerge from civil society supported by labour and grassroots organisations is not unlikely. A coalition of the trade unionist Morgan Tsvangirayi's Zimbabwe Congress of Trade Unions, independent MP Margaret Dongo's Movement for Independent Electoral Candidates, and University of Zimbabwe mathematics professor Heniri Dzinotyiwei's Zimbabwe Integrated Program,[22] which has been reported to have a political agenda, could galvanize other civil society formations and the weak opposition, as well as alienated ZANU(PF) members, into a credible opposition party as we move towards Election 2000 and beyond. Such a party could combine popular appeal with the serious intellectual capacity and skills required to solve Zimbabwe's daunting political and socioeconomic problems.

To that end, civil society formations have coalesced into the National Constitutional Assembly (NCA) demanding a new constitution for Zimbabwe. At the top of NCA's agenda is the rehauling of Zimbabwe's Electoral Act. The demands are that there be a permanent Independent Electoral Commission to oversee and administer the conduct of all elections – local, parliamentary, presidential, and the by-elections that may arise. Under mounting pressure, the ruling party and government have begun a separate initiative to reform the country's Constitution and have agreed to the idea of a referendum on a new constitution before Election 2000. A referendum on a new constitution is a cardinal demand of the NCA.

Thus, on the surface, Zimbabwe might seem to be moving in the opposite direction from the rest of the southern African countries, but there are underlying forces at play that are moving it in the democratic direction as that of the rest of southern Africa, despite the personal attitudes of her leaders. Civil society, which is growing from strength to strength by the day, is that force. Therefore, Zimbabwe might conduct its next general and presidential elections on an even playing field; not only that, it may even have a viable new political party.

Notes

1. For instance, Sir Godfrey Huggins (later Lord Malvern) ruled Southern Rhodesia for 20 years before taking on federal politics as prime minister of the Federation of Rhodesia and Nyasaland in 1953. Ian Smith and his Rhodesia Front party ruled Rhodesia for 16 years until the eve of majority rule in 1979. Robert Mugabe and his ZANU(PF) party have ruled Zimbabwe since the 1980 independence election.

2. Zimbabwe has been a plural society since its inception in 1890 as Southern Rhodesia. White politicians conveniently came to this realization only ninety years later! See also note 3.

3. Every other party seemed to gang up against the "militant" ZANU(PF). Some, especially local white parties and foreign governments, even speculated on a factional arithmetic designed to deprive ZANU(PF) of victory. See Martin Gregory, "Zimbabwe 1980 Election: Politicization through Armed Struggle and Electoral Mobilization," *Journal of Commonwealth and Comparative Politics* 29, no. 1 (March 1981): 68.

4. One participant in the Lancaster House negotiations said, "Most of us didn't bitch about this one because we knew we were going to change it the moment we got into power. Moreover, we were in a hurry to get that power. We didn't want to lose momentum through the long process of drawing up constituencies, counting the number of adults, and registering them."

5. Donald Horowitz, "Democracy in Divided Societies," *Journal of Democracy* 4, no. 4 (October 1993): 18–38; Arend Lijphart, "Electoral Systems, Party Systems and Conflict Management in Segmented Societies," in R.A. Schrine, ed., *Critical Choices for South Africa* (Cape Town: Oxford University Press, 1990), 2–13; and Dieter Nohlen, *Elections and Electoral Systems* (Delhi: Macmillan India Ltd., 1996), 103–121.

6. Jonathan Moyo accepts the argument that proportional representation might incapacitate decision making through hung parliaments. He argues, however, that this "does not apply to countries which are in transition to democracy and which are generally characterized by a weak civil society." Moyo, *Voting for Democracy: Electoral Politics in Zimbabwe* (Harare: University of Zimbabwe Publications, 1992), 61. Moreover, experience has shown that developed countries (United States and Britain) are not immune to hung parliaments, notwithstanding the single member district electoral system.

7. Masipula Sithole, "The General Elections: 1979–1985," in Ibbo Mandaza, ed., *Zimbabwe: The Political Economy of Transition 1980–1986* (Dakar: CODESRIA, 1986), 76–81;Sithole, "Le governement et la vie politique au Zimbabwe depuis l'independance," in Jean-Louis Balans and Michel Lafon, eds, *Le Zimbabwe Contemporain* (Paris: Karthala, 1995), 114–116; and Sithole, "The Zimbabwean Experience of Constitution-Making: Lessons for South Africa?" in Konrad-Adenauer-Stiftung, *Aspects of the Debate on the Draft of the South African Constitution* (Johannesburg: Konrad-Adenauer-Stiftung, 1996), 19–21.

8. In the 1980 election under proportional representation, PF-ZAPU got four seats in the Midlands and one in adjacent Mashonaland West. In the 1985 election, many areas known to have large concentrations of Ndebele were split to include them in largely Shona concentrated areas.

9. In 1984, Sithole went into voluntary exile after an attempt on his life by what were believed to be ZANU(PF) operatives. Goodson Sithole was the surrogate candidate in the 1985 election.

10. See Moyo, *Voting for Democracy,* 156–163.

11. In a study of the 1990 elections, John Makumbe argued that while Zimbabwe's political development during the 1980s was marked by "politicization" and "participation," the 1990s and beyond would be marked by "de-politicization" and "de-participation." Makumbe, "The 1990 Zimbabwe Elections: Implications for Democracy," in Ibbo Mandaza and Llyod Sachikonye, eds, *The One-Party State and Democracy: The Zimbabwe Debate* (Harare: SAPES Books, 1991), 179–188.

12. The reliability of figures for the 1995 parliamentary and 1996 presidential elections is questionable since the voters rolls were reported to be in "shambles." This was suggested even by the Electoral Supervisory Commission. See *The Herald,* 14 March 1995, and *Report of Electoral Supervisory Commission on the 1995 General Elections.*

13. Ethnicity is salient in six subethnic groups in Zimbabwe politics: the Karanga (22 per cent), Zezuru (18 per cent), Manyika (13 per cent), Korekore (12 per cent), Rozwi (9 per cent, and Ndau (3 per cent). The Ndebele are 19 per cent. For an analysis of the Zimbabwe ethnic milieu and politics, see Masipula Sithole, "Ethnicity and Democratization in Zimbabwe: From Ethnic Conflict to Accommodation," in Harvey Glickman, ed., *Ethnicity and Democratization in Africa* (Atlanta: ASA Press, 1995), 122–160.

14. For an analysis of this and related elections, see Masipula Sithole "The Recent Elections in Zimbabwe: Implications for Democracy," *AAPS Newsletter* 1, no. 20 (January–April 1996): 2–6.

15. For example, the executive mayoral election in the city of Mutare was won by an independent against the ruling party's candidate, and in a Council by-election in Mbare in the city of Harare another independent candidate defeated the ruling party's candidate.

16. For instance, reports from reliable sources stated that on several spoilt ballots were written: "This is not an election"; "The election is already rigged"; "The results are already known"; "There is no democracy in Zimbabwe", and so on.

17. The Electoral Act requires that a candidate must lodge a notice of an intention to withdraw at least 21 days before the election. Muzorewa and Sithole announced their withdrawal only a few days before the election was to be held.

18. For instance, the nationalist position, defined as "struggle against domination by whites and foreigners," still motivates African people politically. Mugabe has periodically taunted whites and foreigners, particularly on the land issue and indigenization of the economy as a whole.

19. See also Masipula Sithole, "Is Zimbabwe Poised for a Liberal Democracy? The State of the Opposition Parties," *Issues: A Journal of Opinion* 1, no. 7 (1993): 26–34, and "Zimbabwe's Eroding Authoritarianism," *Journal of Democracy* 8, no. 1 (January 1997): 127–41. On the difficulties and dynamics of transforming ZANU(PF) from a liberation movement to a custodian of democracy, see John Makumbe, "From Freedom Fighters to the Seats of Power," in Curry Marias, Peter Katjavivi, and Arnold Wehmhorner, eds, *Southern Africa After Flections: Towards a Culture of Democracy* (Windhoek: Gamsberg MacMillan, 1996), 33–42.

20. The phenomenon of using the courts in the fight for democracy in Zimbabwe has solicited a new political concept, "democratization by litigation."

21. Eddison J.M. Zvobgo, "An Agenda for Democracy, Peace and Sustainable Development in the SADC Region," address delivered to parliamentarians at the CPA/IPU Joint Dinner, Miekles Hotel, Harare, 14 November 1995.

22. A lesser known personality in political circles, Professor Dzinotyiwei might be the opposition's dark horse. He is, however, well regarded in intellectual, professional, and business circles.

Bibliography

Gregory, Martin. "Zimbabwe 1980 Election: Politicization through Armed Struggle and Electoral Mobilization." *Journal of Commonwealth and Comparative Politics* 29, no. 1 (March 1981): 63–91.

Horowitz, Donald. "Democracy in Divided Societies." *Journal of Democracy* 4, no. 4 (October 1993): 18–38.

———. "Comparing Democratic Systems." In Larry Diamond and Marc F. Plattner. *The Global Resurgence of Democracy.* Baltimore: Johns Hopkins University Press, 1993, 127–133.

Lijphart, Arend. "Electoral Systems, Party Systems and Conflict Management in Segmented Societies." In R.A. Schrine, ed. *Critical Choices for South Africa.* Cape Town: Oxford University Press, 1990, 2–13.

———. "Constitutional Choices for New Democracies." In Larry Diamond and Marc F. Plattner. *The Global Resurgence of Democracy.* Baltimore: Johns Hopkins University Press, 1993, 146–158.

Makumbe, John. "The 1990 Zimbabwe Elections: Implications for Democracy." In *The One-Party State and Democracy: The Zimbabwe Debate,* edited by Ibbo Mandaza and Lloyd M. Sachikonye. Harare: SAPES Books, 1991, 179–188.

———. "From Freedom Fighters to the Seats of Power." In *Southern Africa After Elections: Towards a Culture of Democracy,* edited by Carrie Marias, Peter H. Katjavivi, and Arnold Wehmhorner. Windhoek: Gamsberg MacMillan, 1996, 33–42.

———. *Zimbabwe Democracy and Governance, Vol. 1: Margaret Dongo's Struggle for Harare South.* Harare: ZimRights Publications. Forthcoming.

Moyo, Jonathan. *Voting for Democracy: Electoral Politics in Zimbabwe.* Harare: University of Zimbabwe Publications, 1992, 156–163.

Nohlen, Dieter. *Elections and Electoral Systems.* Delhi: Macmillan India Ltd., 1996.

Sithole, Masipula. "The General Elections: 1979-1985." In *Zimbabwe: The Political Economy of Transition 1980–1986,* edited by Ibbo Mandaza. Dakar: CODESRIA, 1986, 75–98.

———. "Is Zimbabwe Poised for a Liberal Democracy? The State of the Opposition Parties." *Issues: A Journal of Opinion* 1, no. 7 (1993): 26–34.

———. "Le gouvernement et la vie politique au Zimbabwe depuis l'independance." In Jean-Louis Balans and Michel Lafon, eds. *Le Zimbabwe Contemporain.* Paris: Karthala, 1995, 109–144.

———. "Ethnicity and Democratization in Zimbabwe: From Ethnic Conflict to Accommodation." In *Ethnic Conflict and Democratization in Africa,* edited by Harvey Glickman. Atlanta: African Studies Association Press, 1995, 122–160.

———. "The Zimbabwean Experience of Constitution-Making: Lessons for South Africa? In Konrad-Adenauer-Stiftung. *Aspects of the Debate on the Draft of the South African Constitution.* Johannesburg: Konrad-Adenauer-Stiftung, 1996.

———. "The Recent Elections in Zimbabwe: Implications for Democracy." *AAPS Newsletter* 1, no. 20 (January–April 1996): 2–6.

———. "Zimbabwe's Eroding Authoritarianism." *Journal of Democracy* 8, no. 1 (January 1997): 127–141.

Sithole, Masipula, and John Makumbe. "Elections in Zimbabwe: The ZANU(PF) Hegemony and the Incipient Decline." *African Journal of Political Science* 2, no. 1 (1998).

Zimbabwe. "Report of the Electoral Supervisory Commission on the 1995 General Election."
———. "Report of the Electoral Supervisory Commission on the 1996 Presidential Election."
Zvobgo, Eddison J.M. "An Agenda for Democracy, Peace, and Sustainable Development in the SMD Region." Address delivered to parliamentarians at the CPA/IPU Joint Dinner, Miekles Hotel, Harare, 14 November 1995.

Appendix A

DESCRIPTION OF REGIONAL SURVEY RESEARCH: SOUTHERN AFRICA..1992– 1998								
Country	1992	1993	1994	1995	1996	1997	1998
Angola						July/August FG Title: Voices of Reconciliation Occasional Paper Series ."Angolans Speak on Peace and Democracy"	
Botswana							
Lesotho						July FG Title: "The 1998 Elections - Voter Mobilization, Voter Education & Political Change	
Malawi			**March/April** FG Title: "The Nation is the People", to gauge awareness of rural populations of political parties & symbols, extent of knowledge about elections & voting, hopes & expectations of multi-party demo-cracy **September** FG Title: "One Head does not Carry a Roof", to assess Malawians' perceptions of the democratic process, changes since elections/role of political parties & civic organisations	**April** FG Title: "Traditional Authority & Democratic Governance in Malawi", a research preparation for the National Constitutional Conference **September** FG Title: "It' s the People who make a Leader a Leader", to assess the attitudes of Malawians toward the political transformation in the wake of national elections **October - June 96** Quantitative & Qualitative Baseline Survey of Democracy & Governance NGOs in Malawi, to gain understanding of institutional development needs & how international funding agencies can best assist in capacity & effectiveness	**February** FG Title: "Alternate Ballot Procedures", to gather data concerning the feasibility of changing the balloting process **August/ September** FG Title: "Can you call yourself a Farmer if you don' t go in the Garden", a further in the civic participation & voter education series. To gain the level of delivery in terms of expectations met	**October** FG Title: "An Axe is best appreciated before cutting a Tree", investigating Malawian attitudes to post - election democracy and how it has affected their lives, levels of deliverance of politicians	**October** FG Title: "If We Elect You, Will You Listen to Us?"

Country	1992	1993	1994	1995	1996	1997	1998
Mozambique		**June** FG Title: "Project Vote", a research component of a larger Voter Education Program - to provide guidance on fears & obstacles to participation in elections	**April** FG Title: "Project Vote" in conjunction with the National Election Commission (CNE), to determine public attitudes about democratic process leading to elections - component of larger Civic Education Program **September** FG Title: "Project Vote", to investigate what Mozambicans really expect from 1st elections, democratic principles & voter turnout		**February** FG Title: "On the Road to Local Elections", gathering views of multi-party democracy & existing level of understanding of municipal elections, motivations for voting & perception of local authority	**July** FG Title: "Perceptions of the Democratic Process", to gain qualitative measurements of the effectiveness of NDI's Civic Education Program & to gather perceptions of Mozambican society regarding democratic transition	**January (cont'd) August 1997** FG Title: "Civic Education: A Report on Focus Group Research in Mozambique." (CLAIM)
Namibia					**March/April** FG Title: "Popular Perceptions of Political Institutions", to provide research to NDI, Parliamentarians & stakeholders regarding legislative institutions & democracy	**May** FG Title: "Popular Perceptions and Opinions of Namibian Students: Survey Findings of Students".	**August** FG Title: "What is yours is yours", prepared by Centre for Applied Social Sciences
South Africa	**September** FG Title: "Vote Education Project", conducted in five communities with purpose of informing & encouraging back participation ir National Elections	**August** Quantitative Survey Joint Collaboration of NDI/IRI/ Joint Center Pre-Election Survey, Opinion Poll of Attitudes of South Africans towards their 1st Democratic Elections	**December** FG Title: "Project Vote", to gauge the populace's understanding & attitudes towards the 2nd phase of elective democratic representation - Local Government Elections	**May** Quantitative Survey with focus on Voting, Local Government Elections, conducted in Gauteng, W. Cape & KZN. Voting period reopened as a result	**February** Quantitative Survey with focus on Voting - Local Government Elections, conducted only in KZN. Voting period extended as a result **October - November** FG Title: "Constitutional Multi-party Democracy & the Political Transformation in SA", 22 key informant interviews - Public Assessment Baseline Assessment **November/December** FG Title: "Making Democracy Work", conducted in all 9 provinces with themes of the Constitution, Government & Political Parties/Public Funding	**February** FG Title: "Making Democracy Work" Part II - conducted in the rural Eastern Cape with theme of the role of traditional authorities in government **December** FG Title: "Bringing the Constitution Home", the role of the New Constitution & the Rights it protects	**April** FG Title: "Development & Transformation of Policy Matters on Traditional Leadership - KZN. Traditional Leadership in Transition, in Search of a New Middle Ground"

Appendix B

REGIONAL DEMOGRAPHICS BY COUNTRY

Country	Head of State	Area (km²)	Population	GDP per Capita	Imports	Exports	Literacy	Urbanisation	Natural Resources
Angola	Jose Edurado dos Santos	1,247,000	11.2 million	US$427	US$1.6 billion	US$3.0 billion	40%	26%	Diamonds, Oil, Oil Products, Fish, Gas, Wildlife, Agricultural Products
Botswana	Mr. F. L. Mogae	582,000	1.5 million	US$3.303	US$1.7 billion	US$2.5 billion	66%	46%	Diamonds, Copper, Nickel, Cattle, Wildlife
Dem. Rep. of Congo	Laurent Desire Kabila	2,345,410	49 million	US$400	US$1.1 billion	US$1.9 billion	77.3%	42.5%	Cobalt, Copper, Cadium, Petroleum, Industrial & Gem Diamonds, Gold, Zinc, Silver
Lesotho	King Letsie III Prime Minister: Dr. Ntsu Mokhehle	30,355	2.1 million	US$439	US$0.897 billion	US$0.142 billion	60%	46%	Diamonds, Wildlife, Mohair, Wool, Water
Malawi	Bakili Muluzi	118,080	10.7 million	US$206	US$0.425 billion	US$0.311 billion	40%	13%	Tobacco, Tea, Sugar, Fish, Wildlife
Mauritius	President: Cassam Uteem Prime Minister: Dr. Navinchandra Ramgoolam	1,968	1.13 million	US$3.304	US$2.0 billion	US$1.6 billion	81%	43.5%	Textiles, Sugar, Wildlife

Country	Head of State	Area (km²)	Population	GDP per Capita	Imports	Exports	Literacy	Urbanisation	Natural Resources
Mozambique	Joacquim Chissano	802,000	18.0 million	US$94	US$0.989 billion	US$0.132 billion	44%	11%	Prawns, Fish, Coconut, Coal, Semi-Precious Stones, Wildlife
Namibia	Sam Nujoma	824,268	1.7 million	US$2046	US$1.9 billion	US$1.6 billion	76%	28%	Diamonds, Uranium, Cattle, Fish, Wildlife
South Africa	Nelson Mandela	1,221,000	42.3 million	US$3331	US$22.4 billion	US$28.7 billion	61.4%	56%	Gold, Coal, Platinum, Iron Ore, Copper, Timber, Sugar, Fish, Wildlife
Seychelles	France Albert Rene	455	78,641 thousand	US$7304	US$236 million	US$56.1 million	58%	64%	Fish, Copra, Cinnamon Trees
Swaziland	King Mswati III	17,364	0.94 million	US$1409	US$1.032 billion	US$0.705 billion	70%	23%	Sugar, Food Products, Wood Pulp, Wildlife
Tanzania	Benjcmin Mkapa	945,200	32.0 million	US$218	US$1.3 billion	US$0.763 billion	84%	30%	Cotton, Coffee, Cloves, Sisal, Cashew Nuts, Tea, Tobacco, Minerals, Wildlife
Zambia	Frederick Chiluba	753,000	9.8 million	US$344	US$1.1 billion	US$1.2 billion	75%	50%	Copper, Zinc, Cobalt, Electricity, Lead, Wildlife, Agricultural Products
Zimbabwe	Robert Mugabe	391,109	11.9 million	US$624	US$1.5 billion	US$1.1 billion	82%	27%	Asbestos, Gold, Copper, Nickel, Tobacco, Agricultural Products, Wildlife